Economic Analysis for Ecosystem-Based Management

Applications to Marine and Coastal Environments

**Daniel S. Holland, James N. Sanchirico,
Robert J. Johnston,
and Deepak Joglekar**

RFF PRESS
RESOURCES FOR THE FUTURE

Washington, DC • London

First published in 2010 by RFF Press, an imprint of Earthscan

Earthscan LLC, 1616 P Street, NW, Washington, DC 20036, USA
Earthscan Ltd, Dunstan House, 14a St Cross Street, London EC1N 8XA, UK
Earthscan publishes in association with the International Institute for Environment and Development

For more information on RFF Press and Earthscan publications, see www.rffpress.org and www.earthscan.co.uk or write to earthinfo@earthscan.co.uk

ISBN: 978-1-93115-76-4 (hardback)
ISBN: 978-1-93115-74-0 (paperback)

Copyedited by Kristin Hunter
Typeset by Andrea Reider
Cover design by Ellen A. Davey

Library of Congress Cataloging-in-Publication Data
Economic analysis for ecosystem based management : applications to marine and coastal environments / Daniel S. Holland ... [et al.].
    p. cm.
  Includes bibliographical references.
  ISBN 978-1-933115-76-4 -- ISBN 978-1-933115-74-0 1. Ecosystem management--Economic aspects. 2. Environmental policy--Economic aspects. 3. Environmental economics. I. Holland, Daniel S.
  QH75.E283 2009
  333.91'7--dc22   2009043140

A catalogue record for this book is available from the British Library.

The paper in this book meets the guidelines for permanence and durability of the Committee on Production Guidelines for Book Longevity of the Council on Library Resources.

At Earthscan we strive to minimize our environmental impacts and carbon footprint through reducing waste, recycling and offsetting our CO2 emissions, including those created through publication of this book. For more details of our environmental policy, see www.earthscan.co.uk.

Printed and bound in the USA by Edwards Brothers Inc.

The paper used is FSC certified.

Mixed Sources
Product group from well-managed forests and other controlled sources
www.fsc.org Cert no. SGS-COC-004946
© 1996 Forest Stewardship Council

About Resources for the Future *and* RFF Press

Resources for the Future (RFF) improves environmental and natural resource policymaking worldwide through independent social science research of the highest caliber. Founded in 1952, RFF pioneered the application of economics as a tool for developing more effective policy about the use and conservation of natural resources. Its scholars continue to employ social science methods to analyze critical issues concerning pollution control, energy policy, land and water use, hazardous waste, climate change, biodiversity, and the environmental challenges of developing countries.

RFF Press supports the mission of RFF by publishing book-length works that present a broad range of approaches to the study of natural resources and the environment. Its authors and editors include RFF staff, researchers from the larger academic and policy communities, and journalists. Audiences for publications by RFF Press include all of the participants in the policymaking process—scholars, the media, advocacy groups, NGOs, professionals in business and government, and the public.

Resources for the Future

Contents

Foreword: Economic Models and Complex Ecosystems

Ecosystem-based management has become the preferred approach to managing natural resources and the environment both domestically and internationally. Most current management institutions, however, are still organized around specific uses such as fisheries or mineral exploitation, resulting in separate management and regulatory regimes for each use. This traditional single-sector/single-species approach has resulted in negative spillover effects and conflicts among user groups, and has proven inadequate for sustaining the levels of goods and services provided by ecosystems. An important example of negative spillover effects are the fertilizers used in agriculture production that run off the land and end up in marine water bodies such as the Gulf of Mexico, the Baltic and the Black seas, causing oxygen depletion and dead zones devoid of fisheries and other marine life. Ecosystem-based management aims to correct these spillovers by taking a systems-wide view in setting management and regulatory policies.

Unlike earlier management paradigms, ecosystem-based management explicitly recognizes that human communities are interdependent and interact with the plant and animal communities within an ecosystem. As ecosystem-based management is applied to coastal and marine ecosystems, we expect managers and stakeholders to demand information for decision making produced by spatially and temporally dynamic models of human activities that account for linkages with biological, chemical, and physical components of those ecosystems. Models and analyses must integrate land use and other human activities in coastal watersheds and account for the value of all types of ecosystem services. Building such economic models presents significant challenges to marine resource economists.

A related challenge is to convince managers and stakeholders that these complex economic models and economic analyses are of sufficient value to warrant the funding necessary for their development. They will require data that usually are not readily available and economic research on a scale not heretofore funded. In other words, economists need to persuasively explain what economics has to offer in terms of ecosystem-based management. As one who labored for almost two decades trying to explain and convince the policy and natural science communities of the importance of including economic analysis in ecosystem-based management research programs, I know first-hand the difficulty of this challenge.

This book, written by three of the best and brightest marine resource economists, succeeds in meeting this challenge. The book explains, in terms accessible to non-economists, the role that economic analysis can play in science-based decision making for implementing ecosystem-based management. It explains how economic models can be used to explain and forecast human uses of marine resources and estimate the benefits produced by marine ecosystems; and provides advice on which economic tools to use to inform analysis of marine policy issues.

I hope that the contents of this book will help educate those concerned about the health of marine ecosystems about how economic analysis can contribute to superior policy making, and that it will inspire economists and other social scientists to improve and develop new tools to support the implementation of ecosystem-based management in our marine ecosystems.

Jon G. Sutinen
Professor Emeritus
Environmental & Natural Resource Economics
University of Rhode Island

Foreword: The Role of Economics in Ecosystem-Based Management

Traditionally, federal, state, and local agencies manage ocean resources sector-by-sector, with little consideration for connections between and within ecological and human systems. Overall, this approach has been unsuccessful. Recognizing the need for more effective ocean management, efforts to implement ecosystem-based management (EBM) are on the rise. A core element of EBM is a focus on ecosystem services—the myriad benefits that people obtain from the ocean. Implementation of EBM requires an understanding of how the ocean provides ecosystem services; how human activities affect these services; and how to assess the value of and weigh tradeoffs among options for managing human activities in a particular geographic area.

The field of economics offers a conceptual framework for thinking about interactions between humans and other components of the ecosystem. Many decisions regarding natural resource management hinge on the question of how people value resources and how those valuations can inform tradeoffs. Using economic methods, it is possible to examine values associated with disparate ocean resources and services, such as seabird nesting areas, seafloor mineral deposits, public beaches, eelgrass beds, piers, whales, fishing grounds, coastal hazard protection, and many others. Economic tools relevant to EBM include cost-benefit analysis, cost-effectiveness analysis, economic-impact analysis, and models that use various types of market and non-market data to quantify values and predict human behaviors.

Economic assessments and their derived values for ocean ecosystem services will undoubtedly play a pivotal role in the planning, implementation, and evolution of the Massachusetts Ocean Plan. Due to be initiated in January 2010, this first-in-the-nation endeavor to manage a state's ocean waters in a comprehensive, adaptive manner is an extraordinary opportunity to test and prove the worth of economic models in support of EBM. Practitioners (policy-makers, resource managers, and planners) can benefit from this book's discussion of the economic tools able to handle the multifaceted analyses needed for the complex marine environment—in fact, Massachusetts' ocean planners will soon be well positioned to report back on the lessons they learn, replete with laudable pitfalls and enviable successes.

Stephanie Moura
Executive Director, Massachusetts Ocean
Partnership

Acknowledgments

We are grateful for the financial, logistical, and intellectual support from Massachusetts Ocean Partnership (or MOP www.massoceanpartnership.org), especially Stephanie Moura and Nick Napoli. MOP is an independent public-private partnership created to advance ecosystem-based integrated multi-use management in the coastal ocean waters of Massachusetts. Its recognition of the importance of economics in developing and implementing effective management of coastal resources and activities led to our involvement with the organization and ultimately to the writing of this book. Several individuals (listed here in alphabetical order) provided critical and insightful comments that have improved the book immensely: Priscilla Brooks, Barry Gold, Andy Rosenberg, Andy Solow, Michael Springborn, and David Terkla. We also want to acknowledge the important feedback and advice from the RFF Press team, including Don Reisman, Ellen Davey, Andrea Titus, and three other anonymous reviewers. Finally, we would like to thank our families for their support.

About the Authors

Daniel S. Holland is a research scientist at the Gulf of Maine Research Institute. Dr. Holland's research is focused on the design and evaluation of fishery management tools and strategies that will lead to profitable and sustainable fisheries and healthy marine ecosystems with particular emphasis on spatial management tools. He has been actively involved in the development and evaluation of fishery management policies in New England, Alaska, and New Zealand. He is also an associate editor of *Marine Resource Economics*.

Deepak Joglekar is a doctoral student in the Department of Agricultural and Resource Economics at the University of Connecticut, Storrs. His research explores the challenges faced by developing countries as they try to balance economic growth with environmental considerations. The tools for his work include non-market valuation and computable general equilibrium modeling.

Robert J. Johnston is the director of the George Perkins Marsh Institute and professor of economics at Clark University. Among other appointments, he is president-elect of the Northeastern Agricultural and Resource Economics Association (NAREA); on the Program Committee for the Charles Darwin Foundation and the Science Advisory Board for the Communication Partnership for Science and the Sea (COMPASS); and the vice president of the Marine Resource Economics Foundation. Professor Johnston's work on valuation and benefit transfer has contributed to national, state, and local policy analysis in the U.S., Canada, and elsewhere.

James N. Sanchirico is a professor in the Department of Environmental Science and Policy at the University of California at Davis and a nonresident fellow at Resources for the Future. He has published extensively on the economic and ecological effects of marine and coastal policies such as catch shares, ocean zoning, and marine reserves. He currently serves on the NOAA Science Advisory Board and his past service includes an appointment with the U.S. National Academy of Science committee. In July of 2008, he testified on the economic benefits of fishing cooperatives and individual transferable quotas to a subcommittee of the Commerce, Transportation, and Safety Committee of the U.S. Senate.

Abbreviations and Acronyms

ACRE	Applied Coastal Research and Engineering
BBN	Bayesian belief network
CBA	cost-benefit analysis
CEA	cost-effectiveness analysis
CHC	Coastal Hazards Commission
CMR	Code of Massachusetts Regulations
DCR	Massachusetts Department of Conservation and Recreation
DMF	Massachusetts Department of Marine Fisheries
EBM	ecosystem-based management
EFH	essential fish habitat
EIA	economic impact analysis
EIA	(in references only) Energy Information Administration
EIS	environmental impact statement
EOEA	Massachusetts Executive Office of Environmental Affairs
GAO	Government Accounting Office
kWh	kilowatt hour
LNG	liquid natural gas
MAUT	multi-attribute utility theory
MMS	Minerals Management Service
MOS	margin of safety
NARW	North Atlantic right whale
NEP	Buzzards Bay National Estuary Program
NGO	nongovernmental organization
NIMBY	"not in my back yard"
NMFS	National Marine Fisheries Service
NOAA	National Oceanic and Atmospheric Administration
NOMES	New England Offshore Mining Environmental Study
NPV	net present value
NRC	National Research Council
PES	Peconic Estuary system
RPS	renewable portfolio standard
RUM	random utility model
TDML	total daily maximum load
U.S. EPA	U.S. Environmental Protection Agency
VMS	electronic vessel monitoring system
WTP	willingness to pay

CHAPTER 1

Economics and Ecosystem-Based Management

As human effects on ocean and coastal ecosystems intensify, successful management increasingly requires that policymakers reconsider traditional issue-based management in favor of approaches that recognize the often complex relationships between natural and human systems.[1] Two respected expert commissions that reviewed U.S. ocean management have recently highlighted the need to shift ocean management to a more integrated and holistic approach.[2] Marine and coastal ecosystem-based management (EBM) is one such framework, in which the goal is to protect ecosystem structure, function, and key processes, using policies that are specific to place and designed to account explicitly for the ecological, social, and economic interconnections within marine and coastal ecosystems.[3]

The need for integrated multi-use ocean management, or EBM, is arguably growing, as new uses for coastal waters compete with traditional ones. For example, ocean management regimes that focus primarily on the independent management of fishing, recreation, and shipping now increasingly face proposals for often conflicting but sometimes synergistic or commensal activities, such as sand and gravel mining, gas pipelines, harbor and port development, offshore wind and tidal energy facilities, liquefied natural gas (LNG) terminals, offshore aquaculture, and desalinization plants. The intensity of ocean and coastal uses and associated conflicts has increased the need for coordinated management regimes.

Around the world, many countries have already begun applying aspects of EBM to marine ecosystems, including Australia, China, New Zealand, the Netherlands, the United Kingdom, Ireland, Belgium, Canada, and the United States. One of the most significant and earliest implementations of EBM principles is the Great Barrier Reef Marine Park in Australia, where a vast and diverse marine area is zoned for conservation, while still allowing for a variety of recreational and commercial uses. The 1997 Canadian Oceans Act enables officials to work with fisheries, endangered species, and environmental-quality legislation to encourage the consideration of all activities on the ocean when designing management plans. Within the United States, there are a number of

EBM activities. The U.S. National Oceanic and Atmospheric Administration (NOAA) has designated ecosystem-based assessments and management as one of its key cross-cutting initiatives, and the California Marine Life Management Act promotes a more holistic approach to managing fisheries and other marine resource uses. Other EBM efforts include the Florida Keys Marine Sanctuary, Chesapeake Bay, Morro Bay, estuary reserves in the National Estuary program, and the Bay-Delta program in northern California. The objectives and management approaches associated with these efforts vary, but they all share a common intent to account for the interconnectedness of different ecosystem components and human activities in management.

In 2007, the Commonwealth of Massachusetts created the Massachusetts Ocean Partnership, a private-public enterprise, to pursue implementation of integrated multi-use ocean management "based on scientific principles of ecosystem-based management that incorporate human activities and reflect compatible spatial and temporal scales."[4] In 2008, Massachusetts passed the Oceans Act, which requires statewide comprehensive ocean-planning law and mandates the development of an integrated ocean management plan for state waters. The act requires balancing all uses, including offshore renewable energy development, fishing, maritime shipping, recreation, conservation, and others. In June 2009, the draft Massachusetts Ocean Management Plan was released, providing a blueprint for implementing these management goals. Economic evaluation of competing ocean uses in Massachusetts, as made explicit by the Oceans Act and Ocean Management Plan, provides the context for much of the discussion in this book.

Advocates and proponents of EBM agree that implementation is rarely straightforward. Various international agencies and numerous published articles have suggested principles and guidelines for successful EBM implementation,[5] but their ideas, while easily conceptualized, are not easily incorporated into current management institutions. Beyond challenges with the integration of management activities across disparate government agencies, an interdisciplinary scientific approach is required to advise the process because EBM considers many interconnected ecological, economic, and social issues simultaneously. Providing appropriate policy guidance within such interdisciplinary contexts requires that the integrity and validity of contributions from each natural or social science be maintained. With this in mind, our goal for this book is to clarify and explain the role that *economic* decision frameworks and analysis can play in a rigorous, science-based EBM decisionmaking process. This includes a discussion of the specific economic tools needed to inform, design, and implement well-thought-out EBM and associated policies.

Economic modeling tools, plus other tools that support decisionmaking, are well suited to the multifaceted decision and planning requirements of ocean policy. Among the tools available to economists are a number of approaches that quantify social benefits, costs, tradeoffs, and other impacts of management, together with methods to help predict the behavior of resource users. Most of these economic tools and methods can be further integrated with natural science models to provide insight that reflects the coordinated dynamics of both human and natural systems. Within this context, one of the advantages of economics is a strong theoretical foundation that enables the measurement of quantitative, logically consistent, and directly comparable measures of human benefits and costs. Hence, economics is well positioned to quantify the types of tradeoffs implicit in EBM. Economic theory also provides formal structures within which one may predict responses to incentives faced by individuals and groups and implications for policy design. These and other advantages place economics in a unique position to inform policy, particularly when economic insight is coordinated with input from other disciplines. Economic tools, however, can also be subject to misuse, misinterpretation, and misapplication, stemming from a common lack of familiarity with economic analysis by policymakers. Seemingly subtle differences between appropriate and inappropriate uses of economic tools can sometimes have substantial implications for results and policy implications.

We have conceived this book as a primer in the use of economics and its tools for EBM and integrated multi-use ocean management. Its chapters highlight ways in which economics can contribute to EBM, and the methods through which economics can help ensure that policy has desired long-term effects. Among other issues, chapters explain how various economic decision frameworks and methods can evaluate tradeoffs between competing uses of ecosystem resources and discuss methods of quantifying the costs and benefits associated with different actions or policies.

We also illustrate how economic models can be used to understand and predict human decisions in response to regulations, how economic incentives affect marine ecosystems, and how these impacts in turn affect the benefits humans derive from marine ecosystems. We pay special attention to approaches that are particularly salient for analysis of multi-use ocean policies. Chapters cover ways to account for uncertainty in evaluating policies and projects, approaches to regulating resource use, and spatially explicit management of marine resource use, for example. Our overall goal is a text that explains the economic methods and analysis most relevant for EBM to students interested in conservation and environmental studies, policymakers and their staffs, and stakeholders involved in and learning about ocean and coastal policy. The book is also designed for economists interested in the application of economic models and tools to the specific policy contexts of EBM and integrated multi-use ocean management.

The Scope and Purpose of Economic Analyses

Many local, state, and federal agencies share jurisdiction over the interrelated activities that occur on or affect marine and coastal waters—and they all have different mandates and different processes for involving stakeholders. These disparate agencies generally do not have an institutional structure to coordinate decisionmaking, especially when this coordination involves stakeholders and other agencies. Comprehensive planning with stakeholder involvement may offer at least a partial solution to this typical coordination failure.

Integrated multi-use ocean management has the *potential* to increase overall benefits to society from marine ecosystems and ocean resources. It offers the opportunity to substitute higher-value uses for lower-value uses, segregate conflicting uses, and eliminate or minimize activities that harm ecosystems without higher or commensurate benefit. Comprehensive planning and coordination alone, however, will not necessarily increase the sustainable public benefits derived from ocean resources or lead to desired or anticipated policy outcomes. To realize such benefits, planning and management must recognize the myriad ways in which management actions influence net economic benefits and consider the resulting changes in the spatial (where) and temporal (when) distribution and intensity of various human activities.

Economic tools can enhance policy analysis by evaluating incremental changes (e.g., in behavior, resource uses, net benefits, etc.) associated with alternative policy options. Economic intuition can also help reveal the incentives and predict behavioral responses of different groups under proposed or existing policy. As in other natural or social sciences, the accuracy of these and other economic predictions is generally highest for small (often called marginal) or localized changes. As one moves farther from the current condition, expected accuracy declines.

The potential role of economics in EBM, however, reaches beyond the outcomes of individual policies or ocean uses. Economic analysis can also characterize ways in which these outcomes might affect (or be affected by) other coastal and marine activities. Economists, for example, may be able to point out linkages, tradeoffs, or conflicts between different uses and users. They can call attention to ways that coordination between institutions and user groups may effect policy changes and create solutions that favor all. In many cases, the change in benefits associated with a particular policy will also be affected by, or spur, other policy decisions. For example, the value of improving a specific beach may be dependent on changes to other beaches in the region, as well as other recreational resources that can substitute for beaches.[6] Policies may also have economic consequences that reach well beyond intended objectives. For example, excluding fishermen[7] from one area may result in increased fishing pressure in other areas or on different types of fish. Although broader analyses that consider interconnections between different activities can be most informative in policy contexts such as EBM, they can also be highly complex; this complexity increases with the number of different uses and users considered.

Analytical complexity can also increase with the heterogeneity of users or other affected population groups. Although economic models often focus on aggregate or average outcomes (e.g., benefits and costs) realized over broad and often heterogeneous populations, the *distribution* of outcomes can also be highly relevant for policy development. Information on benefit distribution, for example, may be relevant both for broader equity concerns and as a means of promoting support for policies among different groups. For this reason, it may be useful to consider how winners might compensate losers or consider solutions advantageous to all or where "losers" receive some other form of acceptable or commensurate compensation. This compensation could be pecuniary (such as compensation for damages from placing the offshore LNG terminal in Massachusetts Bay) or some other form, such as formal or informal agreements to segregate conflicting activities in space or time.

Without such policy components, user groups disadvantaged by particular policies may seek to block these policies either by influencing policymakers or through legal actions. In such cases, economic analysis can be instrumental in identifying appropriate compensation or other mechanisms to offset inequities resulting from policy implementation. Economic insights can also help identify instances in which agreements between private individuals or groups might be able to achieve desired outcomes in the absence of government action (e.g., when property rights are well defined, groups are small and homogeneous, and transaction costs are low).

In summary, the development and implementation of EBM present enormous challenges. While the use of economics within decisionmaking and policy design cannot ameliorate all these challenges, there are a number of ways in which economic models and insights can encourage progress along the evolutionary path to EBM. This book discusses the use of economics to inform EBM policy development, emphasizing applications to coastal marine areas in developed countries, such as the United States. While it is not possible to foresee or address all potential applications of economics to ocean policy development and evaluation, chapters in this book cover common methods applicable to most ocean-policy contexts.

Outline and Topics Covered

A variety of frameworks is available to integrate economic information into management choices and policies that affect coastal and marine ecosystems. Among these are tools that can quantify and compare economic benefits, costs, and impacts. Chapter 2 discusses these approaches and provides specific examples drawn from coastal marine ecosystems and current situations. *Cost-benefit analysis* (CBA), for example, is one common means of providing economic insight and involves either comprehensive or partial assessments of long-term economic benefits and costs of projects or policies. CBA can help identify management outcomes that offer the greatest net economic benefit to society. Another approach, *cost-effectiveness analysis* (CEA), can reveal the tradeoffs required in cases where desired outcomes have already been determined but where there are alternative means of achieving those outcomes. It can help determine the most efficient means of achieving specified management goals when these goals are predetermined by legislation, prior consensus, or other means. CEA can also provide insight into the costs of various management outcomes where the information necessary to determine the benefits of these outcomes is unavailable.

Still another economic approach sometimes used to inform management is regional economic modeling, or *economic impact analysis* (EIA). Unlike CBA or CEA, economic impact analysis measures changes in *economic activity* or *indicators* (e.g., regional income, gross value of fish landings,[8] workers employed, gross expenditures) related to monetary flows between economic sectors. These flows quantify the level of economic activity within a given region but do not quantify economic benefits or costs. This distinction is particularly important; ignorance of this distinction commonly leads to misuse and misinterpretation of economic impact analyses, which in turn leads to pervasive misperceptions regarding the appropriate use and interpretation of such methods by policymakers.

Chapter 3 presents economic approaches used to forecast human behavior and resource use. These include models for understanding, quantifying, and predicting how humans use (or will use) goods and services provided by coastal and marine ecosystems. These models can also predict the benefits from goods and services traded in formal monetized markets (e.g., electricity and seafood), as well as those that do not involve monetary transactions (e.g., visits to a public beach or use of an estuary for recreational fishing). This chapter explains why certain types of models are appropriate for different uses and discusses the strengths and limitations of various modeling approaches. Chapter 3 also discusses how models of ecological, physical, and chemical processes in the coastal and marine ecosystem are used to understand better the benefits that people derive from ecosystem services and how human actions will affect those benefits. This discussion highlights important linkages between behavior (what people do) and the net benefits they receive.

The behaviors relevant to economic analysis are not always observed in market settings. Much of what people value in the coastal and marine systems—for example, the quality of natural amenities, such as open space, attractive views, good beaches, water quality, and recreational fishing—is not bought and sold in markets. Consequently, market analyses do not capture the full value of these services. In the absence of nonmarket valuation, the public's value of environmental and natural resource goods and services may be underappreciated, ignored, or assumed to be zero.[9] In many cases, this omission tends to inappropriately favor activities that promote development or market activity yet degrade or consume natural resources—because economic values associated with (often less tangible) ecosystem services are ignored. Chapter 4 summarizes the nonmarket valuation techniques that are most applicable to the types of policies encountered as part of EBM, the types of values estimated by these techniques, and the data that are required. It also discusses the basics of benefit transfer—or using value estimates measured in one study to approximate values in a different, unstudied area or policy context—as well as tradeoffs associated with the choice between benefit transfer and original studies. The methods detailed in chapter 4 are often used to quantify the nonmarket benefits and costs that represent an important component of CBA in many EBM policy contexts.

In most cases, there is uncertainty associated with estimates or predictions of physical, ecological, and human outcomes (such as how many intense storms will hit a beach when considering whether to add more sand to it). This uncertainty must be addressed in order to evaluate the expected costs and benefits of projects or policies, and can involve either economic or ecological aspects of management interventions. For example, uncertainty often arises when considering policy impacts on ecosystem services, defined as outputs of natural systems that promote human well-being or provide economic benefits. The provisioning and flows of these services are influenced not only by ecosystems but also by associated human systems, both of which are subject to considerable uncertainty. It is often not clear if the services in question will be available in the future, what the future demand will be for these services, what the demand might be for new services not yet realized, and whether the removal of a particular suite of services might result in the loss of other services. Chapter 5 reviews important economic concepts for decisionmaking under uncertainty and looks at how uncertainty can alter the efficient policy relative to a case in which policy impacts are certain. Related concepts discussed in chapter 5 include the precautionary approach, safe minimum standards, and adaptive management.

Even when detailed empirical analysis (e.g., of benefits and costs) is not possible, economic approaches can nonetheless help characterize the potential advantages of alternative policy approaches that might be used to promote a given set of outcomes, for example, contrasting regulations versus incentives or property rights in ocean management. Chapter 6 illustrates ways in which economic intuition may be used to characterize the pros and cons of alternative regulatory approaches. The most prevalent regulatory approach to management prescribes which activities are allowed, who can participate, and potentially when, where, and how specified activities are undertaken. This is sometimes described as "input-oriented" management or a command-and-control approach. The primary alternative is to regulate outputs or environmental impacts directly, either by setting and monitoring limits on outputs or impacts by individuals or groups, by taxing impacts, or by imposing liability for adverse outcomes.

Both input- and output- (or outcome-) oriented approaches to managing resource use and environmental impacts have advantages and disadvantages. Neither approach is superior in all cases, but different situations are better suited to one approach or the other. As outlined in chapter 6, the relative benefits of each approach depend on a number of factors, including the information held by the regulators and those being regulated, monitoring of costs, desire to keep the costs of reducing impacts the same for all users as much as possible, and economic and technical characteristics of the activity or environmental effect. Chapter 6 also discusses market-based regulatory approaches that create incentives to encourage users to engage in desired actions, without the necessity of command-and-control regulations.

In addition to decisions regarding the type of policy mechanism, there are often questions regarding the temporal and spatial scale over which to apply certain policies. Because the marine environment has such varied, innate spatial characteristics, each of which affects the value of ecosystem services, there are opportunities to increase the benefits humans derive from ecosystem services by managing where uses take place (restricting, permitting, encouraging, or discouraging activity in explicit areas). Chapter 7 explains the conceptual framework that economists use to analyze how to manage conflicting or complementary activities in the same or adjacent space. It discusses a number of examples in which society benefits from the use of explicit spatial management and the pros, cons, and constraints of doing so.

We conclude in chapter 8 with guidance in choosing the right economics tools to inform specific aspects of ocean and coastal management and in identifying appropriate policy questions. We use a set of three case studies to ground these discussions. Each case study relates to current issues in the implementation of EBM in Massachusetts, but the issues and discussions apply generally. Presented case studies involve wind energy, beach nourishment, and area-based policies for fishery management. We end with a plea to economists and other scientists to provide information to policymakers in integrative and user-friendly formats. Conducting research is only a necessary condition for elevating policy discussions; to have an impact on outcomes, research findings must be made understandable and accessible to policymakers and managers.

The appendices of the book provide additional detail on three case studies discussed in chapter 8 plus an additional case study on nutrient pollution. These appendices review relevant literature and consider the appropriate economic analysis of presented management issues. The purpose is neither to make policy recommendations nor to criticize the economic analysis already conducted. Rather, these case studies illustrate the potential use and interpretation of economics for policy guidance in specific instances, and are concrete illustrations of the type of policy insight that can come from different approaches to economic policy analysis.

Books such as this cannot address all possible ocean policy issues to which economics might be applied or detail all potentially applicable economic theories and methods. Moreover, to be more accessible, the book promotes broad concepts and comprehension over exhaustive technical detail. Readers considering direct applications of presented methods may want to consult other, more methodologically focused texts. Through the purposeful balancing of simple concepts with operational details, we hope that this book can provide a useful and broadly applicable introduction to the appropriate use and interpretation of economics to inform ocean and coastal management.

Endnotes

1. Lamont (2006, 7).
2. Pew Oceans Commission (2003) and U.S. Commission on Ocean Policy (2004).
3. McLeod et al. (2005).
4. Massachusetts Ocean Partnership Web site, www.massoceanpartnership.org./ whoweare.html.
5. For example, see World Resources Institute (2003), Lamont (2006), and Grumbine (1994).
6. For example, improving one beach may have ripple effects along the coast. Among other effects, such improvements could reduce funding available to other beaches for maintenance; attract users from other beaches, resulting in the overuse of the improved beach and underuse elsewhere; and may create political pressure for other beaches to be improved.
7. Throughout this book, "fishermen" refers to commercial fishers and "anglers" is used for recreational fishers. Fishermen is the term preferred by fishers of both genders worldwide.
8. Landings are the fish caught and actually brought back to shore for sale; they may not include the entire catch. Some fish and bycatch (marine species caught accidentally, which are not targeted by the fishermen) are thrown back.
9. Johnston et al. (2002b).

CHAPTER 2

Frameworks for Economic Evaluation

Policy decisions, such as those involved in EBM can have a wide range of economic outcomes, including changes in observable market activities, as well as in economic costs and benefits. To evaluate different types of economic policy outcomes, economists have developed various frameworks that measure and interpret well-defined economic benefits and costs, while others characterize indicators of economic activity. In some cases, however, methods purported to quantify "economic" outcomes have little or no relationship to economics at all! These include evaluation methods grounded in thermodynamic principles or energy transfers that have no quantifiable relationship to human values, preferences, or welfare.[1] Given the myriad potential uses and misuses of economic information, policymakers are sometimes confused as to the meaning and correct application of economic approaches for policy guidance—or, here, EBM policy.

Consider the example of a coastal wind farm, such as the Cape Wind project proposed (and progressing through federal permitting) for the Horseshoe Shoals area near Nantucket, Massachusetts, in 2009. Such projects can have many different effects, including benefits and costs realized by different groups. These include potential benefits related to renewable energy provision and a reduction in pollution associated with alternative energy sources. Such projects, however, may also cause marine habitat loss due to construction and maintenance activities, as well as damage to birds from turbine rotors. People who prefer an unrestricted view of the ocean may be negatively affected by impacts to the seascape, and there may be potential impacts on fisheries and boating. Economics provides a set of consistent and standardized frameworks through which such divergent effects on different population groups, may be balanced and compared. In contrast, sole reliance on commonly reported economic indicators, such as employment and income, as a means to evaluate projects will provide at best incomplete—and often grossly misleading—perspectives on economic benefits and costs.

This chapter reviews principal economic frameworks that provide information on economic outcomes of marine resource management and uses of marine resources, with an emphasis on an integrated management perspective, or EBM. Perhaps the most common framework for providing economic insight, *cost-benefit analysis* (CBA) entails either comprehensive or partial assessments of long-term economic costs and benefits of specific projects, policies, or management approaches. CBA is often used to compare the net economic benefits of different policy options that lead to different outcomes. Another of these frameworks, *cost-effectiveness analysis* (CEA), clarifies the tradeoffs made in cases where desired outcomes have already been determined. It helps identify the most efficient means of achieving a specified management goal when a goal has been predetermined by legislation, prior consensus, or other means. Still another economic framework sometimes used is regional economic modeling, or *economic impact analysis* (EIA). Unlike CBA or CEA, EIA measures changes in economic activity or its indicators (e.g., regional income, gross market revenues or expenditures, workers employed, etc.) as determined by monetary flows between economic sectors. These measures are only weakly related to net economic benefits, but they can hold interest for policymakers who are concerned with economic development or regional employment.

Among available evaluation frameworks, CBA is the only approach designed to estimate the full range of economic costs and benefits associated with management (or policy) actions. As such, it receives greater emphasis in this chapter. However, this chapter also presents alternative approaches, with an emphasis on cost-effectiveness analysis and economic impact analysis, that offer other relevant economic information to the policy process. Finally, the chapter highlights distinctions between economic analyses and analyses that are not based on economic theory and/or do not measure value or net benefits, as defined by economists. These include approaches that calculate values based on embodied energy, thermodynamics (the energy involved in the production of a product or service), or replacement costs, and other approaches that estimate values of local resources and scale them up to assess total values for entire ecosystems.[2] There is also a brief discussion of multi-attribute utility theory (MAUT), a cousin of CBA, that weights policy attributes using expert opinions or preferences rather than economic value. Different evaluation methods that answer different economic questions regarding ocean and coastal management and choosing the right economic tools to help ensure that policy evaluations provide the most useful and relevant information are among the central themes of this chapter.

Why Measure Economic Outcomes?

More and more, policymakers are asked to provide information on the economic implications of environmental policies, such as those that affect human uses of aquatic ecosystems. Behind the growing demand for economic information is recognition of the value of *ecosystem services,* defined as the outputs of natural systems that influence human well-being. Benefits of ecosystem services may be realized in or out of organized markets. In many, or perhaps even in most cases, analysis of market data alone will not provide complete measures of ecosystem service values. Moreover, policies that encourage greater market activity or economic growth at the expense of reducing ecosystem services or depleting natural resources may not necessarily enhance long-term public benefit. Public welfare encompasses an often complex interplay between natural and human systems. Economics, when appropriately applied and interpreted, offers a number of consistent and reliable analytical frameworks that can help policymakers understand how such interactions influence economic outcomes, both in and out of markets, and how these economic outcomes relate to human well-being.

Economic tools can predict the effects of policy options on individuals, groups, or society as a whole. They are particularly well suited to quantifying tradeoffs, for example, balancing the gains and losses experienced by different groups. Predictions of different economic outcomes using these tools can be particularly useful to policymakers when benefits (or costs) are not obvious or are realized outside of organized markets. Benefits conveyed by goods and services not exchanged in markets are called nonmarket benefits. An example would be the benefit received by an individual, or the increase in that individual's well-being, that might result from visiting a public beach or viewing a scenic coastal vista. Although the individual might be *willing* to pay for such sources of enjoyment, the fact that they are available outside of markets means that no payments are typically observed. As a result, alternative economic methods are required to measure these nonmarket benefits. Chapter 4 provides more details.

Like any tool, economic tools can be used incorrectly. Many economists—the authors included—have noted a disturbing trend toward incorrect or oversimplified uses of economics to support often predetermined policy goals. These faulty uses of economics can lead to inaccurate understandings of how natural and human systems interact and may promote actions that are not in the best interest of the public (actions that reduce long-term social welfare). Poorly applied economics can also lead to public outcry if policy outcomes adversely affect either public welfare or natural resources—or both. Hence, when considering various economic frameworks for policy evaluation, it is important to understand the type of information required by each framework and how each framework can guide policy.

Defining and Measuring Economic Values

Methods used to quantify relevant economic outcomes can sometimes be surprising to non-economists. For example, policymakers and the media often consider increases in employment (more jobs) to be an economic benefit. If modeled within an economic framework, however, employment increases are rarely considered an *economic* benefit of a project or policy. The reason is that if one consistently tracks both the benefits and costs associated with additional employment—and if the value of goods or services produced by newly employed individuals is measured appropriately elsewhere—then the benefits and costs of new employment wash out, leaving no additional net benefit of the created jobs. As a simple illustration, consider that the wages received by an employee (a benefit to the employee) are exactly offset by the wages paid by the employer (a cost to the employer). Although in reality the situation is somewhat more complex than this simple illustration, the common misperception that jobs are benefits illustrates that appropriate economic modeling does not always comport with common public understanding of what comprises an "economic" benefit or cost.[3]

Similarly, policymakers will often request information—for example, the "total" value of a very large ecosystem, such as the Chesapeake Bay—that is effectively meaningless from an economic perspective. Continuing the Chesapeake example, the nonsensical nature of "total" benefit measures relates to the lack of a consistent and meaningful baseline from which benefits or costs could be compared. Without a clear and detailed description of what it would mean to be "without" the bay in its entirety—something impossible to envision or characterize with any validity—measures of total value remain devoid of meaning. This lack of meaning has not prevented the publication of myriad reports that attempt to quantify exactly these types of values. The guidelines that determine the appropriate quantification of economic outcomes—be they economic impacts, benefits, costs, or other measures—are designed to promote consistent, comparable, and meaningful measures across policies and projects.

To illustrate the different ways that economists measure the effects of policy on public well-being, consider the relationship between economic values, economic impacts, and policy, as described by Bockstael et al. (2000):

> In economics, valuation concepts relate to human welfare. So, the *economic* value of an ecosystem function or service relates only to the contribution it makes to human welfare, where human welfare is measured in terms of each individual's own assessment of his or her well-being. Of course, this is not the only possible concept of value, nor is it always the most relevant. But for purposes of benefit-cost analysis in assessing policy options and for purposes of determining liability when natural resources have been harmed, this concept has considerable precedence as well as legal standing.[4]

Economic values or benefits are assessed only in comparative terms, relative to a well-defined baseline. They reflect the well-being of one or more individuals, such that "economic value of a policy change is defined by the amount (either positive or negative) of compensation that individuals would need in order to be as well off (by their own reckoning of well-being) as they would have been without the policy-induced change."[5]

Individuals or firms can realize economic benefits and costs. For individuals, benefits are generally measured as the maximum amount of other goods or services that the individual is willing to forgo in order to obtain the outcomes resulting from the policy in question. This reflects the individual's *willingness to pay* (WTP) for the policy change. Although WTP is often denominated in money units, it can be expressed in any unit of exchange. (For example, in some nations, cattle historically represent a common unit of exchange, and WTP could be denominated accordingly.) An individual's economic costs reflect the value of goods or services forgone as a result of the policy-induced change.

For producers or firms (e.g., shipping companies, commercial fishing vessels), the net benefits realized from production activity reflect the difference between earned revenues and production costs, over all units of a produced good or service. Revenues can be measured as a product of price and quantity sold. Production costs are often measured as the money spent to obtain production inputs, although more complex quantification methods can be required in a variety of circumstances, such as when inputs are unpriced (e.g., the labor of a company owner or the use of natural capital, such as timber, that is already owned by the firm). These and similar measures are well defined by economic theory and provide a systematic means of measuring the benefits and costs that come from a given policy.

Any activity (policy, recreation, manufacturing, etc.) that influences the quality or quantity of coastal or marine ecosystem services will likely generate benefits or costs to various groups. Hence, even the absence of EBM results in real and ongoing benefits and costs. Conversely, any set of guidelines, regulations, or incentive structures aimed at mitigating ecosystem impacts or restoring ecosystems will imply its own set of economic benefits and costs. Appropriate analysis of economic benefits and costs compares net social benefits in the *absence* of a specified policy to net social benefits in the *presence* of that policy. The difference represents the net social benefits (or costs) of the policy, as measured by CBA. When calculating this difference, it is also critical to isolate the changes in benefits or costs that are due only to the project in question, in addition to any changes that might occur in the absence of the policy. In contrast, CEA focuses on the cost side of the equation only, quantifying appropriately measured economic costs (or value given up) associated with various approaches to predetermined management goals.

When conducting or interpreting economic analysis, it is important to recognize the distinction between efficiency and equity (or benefit distribution). Efficiency relates to total or aggregated net benefits (benefits minus costs) realized by all affected groups. More efficient policies generate greater total benefits for all affected parties combined, compared to all available alternatives.

Efficiency does not imply that all groups are better off, only that the combined benefits over all groups outweigh the combined costs. As typically implemented, CBA measures aggregate net benefits with the goal of promoting efficient policy, or policy that maximizes total net benefits aggregated over all groups. Policymakers may also consider impacts on equity, or the distribution of net benefits across different user groups. Although this is not a usual focus of CBA, the framework and methods can be easily adapted to answer questions related to the distribution of benefits and costs across different affected groups. Recognizing that different stakeholder groups are likely to derive different types of benefits, for example, CBA can be used to quantify tradeoffs among the net economic benefits received by different groups. This aspect can be particularly relevant when assessing EBM policies because these policies typically affect many different groups.

It is also important to recognize that economic benefits and costs are not necessarily related to compensation in dollars or other money flows. Increases in economic activity or payments do not always lead to economic benefits and may create hidden economic costs. Conversely, individuals can experience a change in real economic benefits or costs without any change in market-based economic activity or money payments. For example, the opportunity to view marine mammals such as whales can provide significant benefit to individuals, even if no money changes hands (e.g., if whales are viewed from shore or private boats). Recreational fishing or trips to the beach can provide similar nonmarket benefits. In these and many other instances, proper assessments of economic benefits and costs do not rely solely on measurements of pecuniary flows or market activities.

As an example of how measuring market activity alone can generate misleading inferences, consider a situation where a reduction in nutrients improves the water quality at recreational beaches and shellfish beds. These improvements might lead to negligible changes in market activities or money flows, but nonetheless could bring substantial benefits to local beach users. Conversely, disasters such as Hurricane Katrina (which caused extensive damage to the southern coast of the United States in 2005) can generate substantial economic activity (e.g., rebuilding damaged buildings and infrastructure), yet leave society much worse off.[6] Common economic measures of regional income, employment, and production—while seemingly simple to understand—cannot by themselves identify public policies that are in the long-term best interests of society.

In contrast, comprehensive assessments of the net benefits from EBM are generally complex and multidisciplinary, combining ecological and other natural science models with models of human behavior and welfare. The net benefits from any given policy depend not only on ecological and other parameters characterizing responses of natural systems (i.e., how the natural world responds to human activities) but also on the short- and long-term behaviors of various user groups. Complicating the analysis is the fact that EBM policies often have different effects on different groups—while many groups will gain from EBM policies, some may lose. An appropriate economic analysis recognizes these divergent effects.

EBM rarely incorporates all-or-nothing policies. (See chapters 6 and 7 for discussions of policy mechanisms.) Instead, it often involves relatively small changes in the activities or incentives facing various user groups. Economists refer to small changes as "marginal" changes; for example, the marginal benefit of catching a fish reflects the benefit of catching one additional fish on top of those already caught. Decisionmakers must consider whether a marginal policy change, such as closing an extra fishing area or constructing one more offshore wind turbine, will increase or decrease total net benefits to all groups combined. Because the marginal value of each additional EBM activity will differ, depending on management measures that are already in place, regulators must consider the net economic effects of successive small policy changes. Managers must balance, at the margin, the losses by sectors (or groups or individuals) whose activities are restricted (or whose resources are degraded) with the net benefits gained by all the others. As one moves farther from the margin, the accuracy of economic forecasts often declines (as do those of virtually any natural or social science model).

It is also important to understand the distinction between indicators of market or nonmarket activity and well-defined measures of benefit or cost. While economic values are often related to human activities, simple indicators viewed in isolation (e.g., number of beach visits) can sometimes provide misleading perspectives. For example, simple activity indicators ignore values realized by nonusers or benefits related to unmeasured activities (i.e., activities not captured by the indicator in question). Because of these and other limitations, indicators of economic activity sometimes increase due to negative changes in the environment. Suppose that closing local beach A due to pollution causes more people to visit neighboring unpolluted beach B. An analyst looking solely at visitor numbers for beach B might incorrectly conclude that this represents a positive change at beach B, when in fact more visitors to beach B simply reflects the closure of beach A (a substitute beach). Using the appropriate economic frameworks for analysis can prevent such misleading conclusions. Simple behavioral (and other) indicators can sometimes provide a cost-effective means to help guide policy—but they can also contribute to incorrect conclusions if not paired with more comprehensive economic analysis.

Subsequent sections of this chapter summarize various economic evaluation frameworks—CBA, CEA, and EIA, plus alternative non-economic analyses, such as EMERGY and embodied energy analysis—that can be used to inform EBM. Because this chapter focuses on frameworks for economic policy evaluation, there is greater coverage of CBA and CEA, techniques that are grounded in economic theory and can be used to prioritize management options based on social welfare.

Cost-Benefit Analysis

Cost-benefit analysis is a subdiscipline of economics that is devoted to measuring social well-being. It measures net economic benefits received or lost by society or by various groups; its primary practical purpose is to assist decision-making by providing information on the gain or loss of net economic benefits. As described by Lipton and Wellman (1995), CBA is "a methodology that compares the present value of all social benefits with the present value of opportunity costs" associated with specified activities, policies, or resource uses. Here, opportunity costs reflect the value of the highest valued alternative given up in order to follow any given course of action—it is what we give up in order to obtain something else. The U.S. Environmental Protection Agency (2000) provided a similar description of CBA: "benefit-cost analysis evaluates the favorable effects of policy actions and the associated opportunity costs of those actions. The favorable effects are defined as benefits and the opportunities forgone define economic costs." In simple terms, CBA is designed to help resource managers make decisions that increase the net social productivity or benefits of society's resources. Under the general umbrella of CBA is a set of methods that measure economic benefits in a variety of conditions and for a variety of groups. CBA is also characterized by rules and guidelines for using different measurement methods and aggregating results from various methodologies.[7]

Conducting CBA involves careful development and application of studies, using one or more market and nonmarket valuation methods. (See examples of valuation methods in chapter 4.) The specific method used to estimate economic benefits depends upon the resource, good, or service of interest. For example, estimation of net benefits associated with the commercial harvest of red snapper (or any other fish) requires methods that quantify net benefits realized by producers and consumers in organized markets (i.e., related to the production and consumption of fish that are bought and sold). In contrast, estimation of recreational values associated with the same species typically requires nonmarket valuation methods that use data on recreational behavior to estimate anglers' willingness to pay, along with market valuation methods to estimate net benefits realized by commercial purveyors of recreational charter services. (Chapters 3 and 4 discuss these methods.) Although CBA methods were historically market based, the increasing recognition of nonmarket benefits and their relevance for policy has led to a large body of research on nonmarket valuation methods. As noted in chapter 4, much of what people value in ocean and coastal systems—including open space, attractive views, good beaches, clean water, and recreational uses of aquatic wildlife (e.g., fish, shellfish, marine mammals)—is not bought and sold in markets. Market analysis does not capture the value of these goods and services. Nonmarket valuation methods can therefore be critical components of CBA in coastal and ocean policy contexts and frequently are the only economic means available to assess certain costs and benefits of management actions.

A full-scale CBA is often costly and time-intensive. Where time or budget constraints prohibit full-scale analysis, significant insight can still be gained through select analysis of specific areas of benefits or costs that are likely to be substantial or particularly relevant to the policy issue at hand. Most CBAs conducted by government agencies follow such a strategy, quantifying only a portion of the many benefits and costs associated with a policy change. To prevent major omissions in such cases, one must make particular effort to identify and quantify the primary areas of benefit or cost, leaving the smaller or more trivial effects unquantified or given only verbal characterization. One may also use more costly (and usually accurate) primary studies to estimate areas of benefit or cost expected to be the largest, and use benefit transfer to estimate others. As discussed in chapter 4, benefit transfer is the use of prior research conducted elsewhere (the study site) to approximate benefits or costs for a site at which policies will be implemented (the policy site).

The net economic benefits realized by various groups will also depend on the future state of the world—information that may be unavailable at the current time. Accordingly, a CBA will often assess the roles of risk and uncertainty in determining the net economic benefits—either in the aggregate or as realized by specific groups. In many cases, uncertainties mean greater potential economic consequences (gains or losses) to some groups than to others. (See chapter 5 for more discussion of decisionmaking under uncertainty and more formal definitions of risk and uncertainty.)

Although details vary across policy contexts, most applications of CBA share a set of common attributes. These include a foundation in established economic theory, the use of accepted methods for quantification of benefits and costs, incorporation of uncertainty, and discounting of future impacts. (Discounting allows meaningful intertemporal comparisons of benefits and costs. See the subsection "Discounting and the Time Value of Money," below.) CBAs also follow similar steps, regardless of application. Table 2.1 summarizes the steps of a full-scale CBA as two recent works define it: they categorize CBA components differently but include the same activities.

Within the context of EBM, large-scale policy changes are likely to generate benefits and costs for a wide range of user (and nonuser) groups. Each affected group may realize various types of market and nonmarket benefits and costs that should be counted in CBA. It is important, however, to be aware of cases where apparent benefits or costs must be *omitted* to avoid double counting and other biases. (See the subsection "Secondary Effects in CBA.")

Methods for Market and Nonmarket Valuation

Total economic value is generally composed of a number of different types of market and nonmarket values, associated with different aspects of natural resource goods and services. As mentioned above, benefits and costs may be realized both through activity in organized markets (market benefits and costs) and through changes that do not occur in markets (nonmarket benefits and costs). The primary difference between market and nonmarket benefits (or costs) in CBA is the methods available to measure them. Methods that assess net economic benefits differ depending on the source of the net benefit and the group receiving the benefit. These include established methods based on analysis of consumer and producer behavior in markets (market valuation), and methods designed to estimate values that are not reflected in organized markets (nonmarket valuation).

To understand the difference between a market and nonmarket benefit in conceptual terms, ask whether the benefit—or the commodity (good or service)—that directly provides the human benefit can be purchased in an organized market. Fish for human consumption is a market good; one obtains benefits by purchasing this good directly in a market. The fish provides the benefit and is also the commodity, which is purchased. Water quality at a beach used for recreation, in contrast, provides nonmarket benefits; in this case, benefits from water quality are realized through the allocation of time and other resources to beach recreation. These benefits cannot be directly purchased in a market, and hence market prices and quantities alone cannot be used to estimate them.

Both market and nonmarket valuation techniques are based on an internally consistent model of human welfare that allows resulting benefit and cost measures to be aggregated and/or compared. The theoretical basis of this model allows one to link estimated monetary values (e.g., benefits, costs, and willingness to pay) with the well-being of individuals, households, or groups. The linkage implies a utilitarian perspective to human behavior that, after considering the pros and cons of all options, humans choose behaviors that are expected to provide them with the greatest long-term satisfaction or utility. The related theory of human value and behavior—called neoclassical welfare economics—distinguishes economic analyses and measurements of social value from those of all other social sciences. It has also led, at least indirectly, to the important role that economic assessments of benefits and costs play in government policy decisions; when estimated appropriately, economic benefits and costs can always be interpreted and compared using the same consistent framework. Whenever one measures economic benefits or costs, one is relying at least implicitly on the same underlying theoretical structure.

Chapter 4 discusses nonmarket valuation in more detail. These valuations employ carefully designed methods that measure values where markets do not provide the price, quantity, and other data necessary to measure values. Market valuation, in contrast, uses often simple supply and demand patterns—easily observed in markets—to estimate values derived by both consumers and producers of valued products. Because time or budget constraints sometimes permit only a few market or nonmarket valuations for any particular policy question, the choices among competing approaches can have critical implications for the benefits and costs that are estimated. As a result, policy analysts must have sufficient understanding of the economic methods that may be employed for coastal policy issues, as well as the implications for specific type of values that are measured.

TABLE 2.1 STEPS IN A COST-BENEFIT ANALYSIS

CBA steps (from Lipton and Wellman 1995)	CBA steps (from Boardman et al. 2001)	Description
1. Specify the program.	1. Specify the set of alternative projects. 2. Decide whose benefits and costs count.	This component of CBA includes a characterization of the baseline or status quo conditions, as well as the various policy alternatives that are under consideration. This component also includes decisions regarding those groups that should have standing (or whose benefits should count) within the analysis. This component is often conducted with substantial input from policymakers and other non-economists.
2. Describe quantitatively the inputs and outputs of the program.	3. Catalog the impacts and select measurement indicators. 4. Predict impacts quantitatively over the life of the project.	This component of CBA includes describing and quantifying both the physical and behavioral impacts (inputs and outputs) of the various policy alternatives relative to the status quo (i.e., what would happen in the absence of policy). These may include both direct and indirect impacts, but only those that affect human well-being. This set of steps often requires substantial input from non-economists, including natural scientists, engineers, and others.
3. Estimate benefits and costs.	5. Monetize (attach dollar values to) all impacts. 6. Discount benefits and costs to obtain present values.	This component includes many of the primary economic elements of CBA, in which economic values are assigned to each quantified input and output identified in prior research steps. This may include various methods for market and nonmarket valuation, depending on the resources and uses affected. Monetized values are then discounted to account for the time value of impacts (or money).

Continued

TABLE 2.1   STEPS IN A COST-BENEFIT ANALYSIS *(Cont.)*

CBA steps *(from Lipton et al. 1995)*	CBA steps *(from Boardman et al. 2001)*	Description
4. Compare benefits and costs.	7. Compute the net present value (NPV) of each alternative. 8. Perform a sensitivity analysis. 9. Make a policy recommendation based on NPV and sensitivity analysis.	The final steps in a CBA combine aggregated, discounted benefits and costs to generate a final present value or net benefit (positive or negative) of the various project or policy alternatives. From an economic efficiency standpoint, alternatives with greater net benefits are preferred. This last stage may also include analysis of distributional impacts, or benefits and costs to different affected groups. Sensitivity analysis may be conducted at this stage to account for areas in which risk exists, to show the potential effects of different future possibilities on CBA results. One may also calculate expected values or option prices, where possible and appropriate, to address risk.

Demand and supply curves, such as those in figure 2.1, can be estimated using statistical analysis of historical price and quantity patterns, combined with additional market data (e.g., the income and demographics of consumers). Although the example of the softshell clams in figure 2.1 is an uncomplicated hypothetical case, analysis of more complex instances often includes straightforward extensions of the simple model illustrated here.[8]

Secondary Effects in CBA

Occasionally EBM policies that affect one market (e.g., softshell clams) may affect prices of other goods or species (such as scallops), solely due to market forces. For example, if clams become more scarce (and, hence, more expensive) due to a change in EBM policy, consumers may instead purchase different shellfish, such as scallops or oysters. This places upward pressure on the prices of these substitute products—in other words, it affects their prices and causes the prices to rise. In general, apparent benefits or costs related to these secondary price or quantity changes should *not* be counted in CBA. The rationale lies in the concept of double counting. *If one appropriately measures net benefits in primary markets, these measurements have already captured effects in secondary markets.*[10] Measuring effects in secondary markets most often double counts the same benefits or costs, which will bias the measure of benefits and can potentially misinform policy decisions. Although secondary effects may be important from an equity

FIGURE 2.1   MEASURING BENEFITS TO CONSUMERS AND PRODUCERS USING A MARKET MODEL: A HYPOTHETICAL EXAMPLE OF SOFTSHELL CLAMS (STEAMERS)

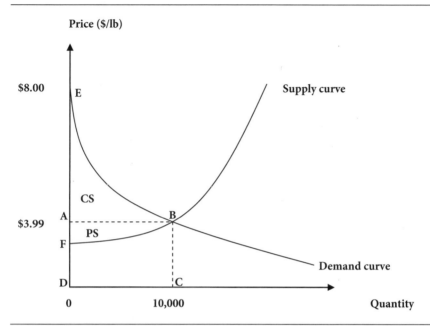

As a straightforward example of empirical techniques for measuring *market values*, figure 2.1 shows a simple market supply-and-demand model of a stylized market for softshell clams, or steamers. The *demand curve* shows the number of pounds of steamers that the hypothetical consumers will purchase, based on the current market price (in dollars per pound). The demand curve also shows the amount that consumers are *willing to pay* for each additional pound of steamers, based on the total quantity purchased. The area underneath the demand curve represents the total willingness to pay for all pounds consumed. The *supply curve* shows the quantity of steamers that the producers will provide, which is also determined by the current market price. The intersection of the supply and demand curves shows the market-clearing or *equilibrium price*, which is the price expected to occur in free markets.

The difference between the amount that a person or group is willing to pay to obtain a particular product and the amount that is actually paid is defined as *consumer surplus* (*CS*), and represents the net economic benefit obtained by the individual or group. Given the market price of $3.99 per pound in figure 2.1, consumers will purchase 10,000 pounds of steamers and will pay the same amount ($3.99) for each pound purchased. The total amount that consumers will spend is $3.99 × 10,000 pounds = $39,900. The rectangle *ABCD* shows this expenditure. However, the total amount that consumers would have been willing to pay for these clams is given by the entire area underneath the demand curve, between 0 and 10,000 pounds on the graph, in the roughly triangular area *EDCB*. Subtracting what the consumers actually pay (*ABCD*) from what they would be willing to pay (*EDCB*) for 10,000 steamers gives an estimate of the benefits gained by consumers. This area, *EBA*, is the consumer surplus. Think of it as a measure of "unpaid-for benefits," or the difference between costs and benefits for consumers.

Benefits to producers (here, the suppliers of softshell clams) are calculated as the *difference between total revenues and production costs*. In this simple case, the producers' revenues are the same as consumer expenditures—area *ABCD* ($3.99 × 10,000 pounds = $39,900). Economic theory states that the area underneath the supply curve also indicates the total (variable) cost of producing steamers. This total cost is equal to area *FBCD*. Hence, the difference between revenues and costs is equal to area *ABF*, which is the *producer surplus (PS)*. This is the economic measure of benefits received by producers and is conceptually similar to profits.[9]

perspective, they should—in general—not be counted in aggregate net social benefits. This is a very common mistake made by inappropriate economic analyses—they seek to count both primary and secondary effects, and consequently double count the same benefits (or costs).[11]

Likewise, secondary support industries may also see changes in economic activity due to price or quantity changes in the primary market. For example, in the market for softshell clams, there may be secondary effects on the firms that supply fuel, process the catch, repair boats, and offer other needed services to fishing vessels. When a beach is nourished,[12] there may be secondary effects on local restaurants and hotels as the number of beach visitors increases. Again, these secondary effects should generally not be counted in cost-benefit analysis. Similarly, changes in the revenues of fish markets or other firms in the supply chain are generally secondary effects; instances when such effects should be counted are rare. This assumes, of course, that all primary effects have been properly measured.

As discussed by Boardman et al. (2001), the theory explaining why secondary effects should not be included in CBA can sometimes be complex. However, the basic intuition is often quite simple. To help clarify this point, Johnston and Sutinen (1999) used an example of recreational fishing to explain why CBA should *not* include secondary effects on hotels, restaurants, and other businesses. Individuals often change from one form of recreation to another (substitution). For example, if they do not go charter fishing (say, for sea bass), they may spend their time hunting, camping, or hiking. Accordingly, if recreational sea bass fishing increases in one community, then anglers spend more money in that community's hotels, restaurants, and other establishments. Such an increase will almost always be offset by revenue losses (of hotels, restaurants, and establishments) in another community with different recreation opportunities. This is because the individual has substituted time spent in the recreational fishing community for time that would otherwise be spent in a community with hunting or trout fishing (different species), for example. The financial gain by one area's secondary businesses is generally offset by financial losses elsewhere. When one properly accounts for all secondary effects in both communities, the net economic benefit of this shift is, most times, very close to zero.[13] Given such patterns, which are ubiquitous throughout the economy, appropriately conducted CBA does not consider secondary effects. Indeed, if secondary effects were included, the result would be an upward bias, or overestimation, of changes in net economic benefits.

Although it is appropriate in economic terms to ignore secondary effects in CBA, regional policymakers often have a political economy motivation to assess these effects, especially if they affect aggregate *economic activity* in their jurisdiction. EIA can aid such analysis and may be an important consideration when policymakers value regional economic growth or activity. However, it is important to note that such measurements of secondary impact should not be interpreted as indicators of net economic benefit; rather, they are measures of aggregate economic activity. (These and other details of EIA are discussed later in this chapter.)

Benefits and Costs to Different User Groups: An Example from Essential Fish Habitat Regulation

This section and the following subsections highlight examples of the type of benefits and costs that should be measured by an appropriate CBA, as well as those that should be omitted. The issues are framed in a policy scenario influenced by EBM—the case of essential fish habitat (EFH) regulations in fisheries.

The examples come from Johnston et al. (2003) and illustrate the appropriate application of CBA to designate and minimize adverse effects on EFH under the 1996 Sustainable Fisheries Act (Public Law 104-297). Although policies designed to protect EFH represent only one component of EBM, they may nonetheless lead to nontrivial benefits and costs to a variety of groups. Related policies may also have impacts that, while commonly associated with economic benefits or costs, should not be incorporated within an appropriate CBA. Although these examples deal with EFH regulations, similar rules and patterns also apply to a wide range of potential policies falling under the general umbrella of EBM.

For simplicity, these examples present a static perspective on benefits and costs during a single time period. Clearly, appropriate renewable resource policy addresses dynamic aspects of resource use and renewal over time. A full-scale assessment of fisheries policy, for example, would combine the measurement of net benefits (outlined below) with suitable economic-ecological models. These models quantify the linkages between economic behavior and ecological systems, together with implications of these linkages for dynamic changes in economic net benefits over time. (See chapters 3 and 4 for discussions of economic-ecological models.)

Table 2.2 summarizes the calculation of net economic benefits realized by different groups in a hypothetical EFH policy scenario. The subsections below discuss ways in which each of these groups can be affected and how one measures associated benefits. Note that secondary effects on commercial fishermen, vessel owners, and fishery support industries are not included, and that certain indicators, such as the number of fishermen employed, are also missing. While the creation of jobs may be desirable from a variety of perspectives—and may represent an informative *economic indicator*—it does not usually represent an economic benefit that is counted in CBA. As a general rule, changes in employment alone are not—and do not result in—economic costs or benefits.[14]

Net Benefits to Commercial Fishermen

Long-term net economic benefits in the commercial fishery are measured as a change in fishing profits, which are equal to total ex-vessel revenues[15] (from

TABLE 2.2   GROUPS REALIZING NET ECONOMIC BENEFITS IN A HYPOTHETICAL EFH POLICY SCENARIO

Group affected by EFH policy	Measurement of net benefits
Commercial fishing vessels	Change in *economic profits* = change in *total revenues* minus *total costs*. Alternatively, the change in producer surplus = change in *total revenues* minus *total variable costs*.
Recreational (e.g., charter) vessels	Change in *economic profits* = change in *total revenues* minus *total costs*. Alternatively, the change in *producer surplus* = change in *total revenues* minus *total variable costs*.
Recreational anglers	Change in consumer surplus = change in *willingness to pay* minus *actual expenditures* for fishing.
Seafood consumers	Change in *consumer surplus* = change in *willingness to pay* minus *actual expenditures* for seafood products.
Land-based businesses	Change in *economic profits* = change in *total revenues* minus *total costs*. Alternatively, the change in *producer surplus* = change in *total revenues* minus *total variable costs*.
Other consumer and producer groups (e.g., divers, other marine/coastal users, and residents, etc.)	Benefits and costs may include changes in consumer surplus and/or nonuse values, where significant. Businesses that also *directly* benefit from improved habitat (e.g., dive operators) may realize additional producer surplus. Other businesses whose activities are constrained directly may lose producer surplus.

the sale of fish products) minus the total costs related to fishing activities. This measure of *net economic benefit reflects the difference between economic costs and economic benefits.* In general, it is *not* equivalent to other single economic indicators, such as vessel expenditures, fish landings, ex-vessel revenues, etc. In the case of EFH, there are generally two groups of commercial fishermen (they may overlap) impacted by policy changes: 1) fishermen who benefit from a fishing activity that inflicts damage on the EFH and 2) fishermen who harvest species that rely on the habitat protected by EFH policy.

Fishermen Who Benefit from Activities That Damage EFH: Certain fishermen benefit from behavior (e.g., using mobile fishing gear, such as dredges or bottom trawl nets, in vulnerable habitat) that damages fish habitat—usually in terms of higher profits or *producer surplus.* For these groups, EFH restrictions in most cases 1) reduce their harvest and resulting ex-vessel revenues, 2) increase their resource costs associated with fishing, or 3) both. As a result, the net benefits received by this group of fishermen will likely decline when the EFH designation is imposed. The actual change in net benefits depends on a variety of factors, including but not limited to the particular EFH restrictions imposed; the availability of alternative fishing methods, areas, or species; entry and exit in the fishery; reactions of the biomass to reduced fishing pressure; and changes in market prices related to reduced supply.[16]

Fishermen Who Harvest Species That Rely on Protected EFH: Some fishermen's livelihoods are harmed when fishing or nonfishing activities damage EFH upon which their target species depend. EFH policies are designed to reduce habitat damage and consequently improve the growth, recruitment (reproduction and maturation), or sustainable stock size of particular species. Hence, for this group of fishermen, EFH restrictions are designed to 1) increase potential harvest and resulting ex-vessel revenues, 2) decrease costs associated with fishing, or 3) both. As a result, with EFH restrictions, the net benefits received by this group increase, ex-vessel revenues will generally increase, and fishing costs will often decline. The ultimate change in net benefits depends on a variety of factors, including but not limited to the effectiveness of the EFH restrictions in improving habitat, entry and exit in the fishery, fishery management mechanisms in place, reactions of the biomass to improved habitat, and changes in market prices related to increased supply. However, if the habitat recovers slowly, there might be a significant delay before these fishermen realize benefits.

Net Benefits to Fish Consumers

Consumers of seafood products benefit when prices decline, when product quality improves, or when availability (supply) improves. Typically, because price, quality, and availability are related (changes in product quality or availability are expected to influence price, for example), any changes will occur simultaneously and will manifest as shifts in either or both the market supply or demand curve. Appropriate CBA will measure net benefits to the final consumers of fish (for whom price, availability, or quality are affected by EFH regulations)—as long as these changes represent a *primary effect* of the new EFH policy. Primary effects are related to direct changes in the cost or efficacy of fish harvesting, either positive or negative, and these effects carry through to the consumer market in terms of price changes. The resulting net benefits to seafood consumers are typically measured as changes in *consumer surplus*, or the difference between what consumers are willing to pay to obtain seafood products and what they actually pay in the market. (Note that net benefits to consumers are not equal to their total expenditure on seafood products.) EFH gear or area restrictions often increase the cost of harvesting or reduce harvest efficiency of the fishing activity that otherwise would damage habitat; this is a primary effect. Net benefits or costs (i.e., changes in consumer surplus) caused by resulting price changes in consumer markets should be counted in CBA. Presumably, the EFH regulations will benefit other species, resulting in decreased harvest cost or increased efficiency for other fisheries. This, again, is a primary effect, and resulting price changes at the consumer level will result in net benefits that should be measured using standard market analyses (i.e., of demand and consumer surplus).

Net Benefits to Recreational Vessel Operators (Charters or Party Boats)

Although recreational charter vessel operators and commercial fishermen work in different sectors and provide different products, their net economic benefits are measured the same way. Net economic benefits to charter vessels are equal to total revenues associated with providing recreational fishing opportunities (i.e., revenues received from anglers) minus the total resource costs of providing these fishing activities (e.g., fuel, labor, docking, and other costs). Just as with commercial fishermen, some recreational vessels may lose net benefits because of EFH restrictions, while others may gain. Given that EFH restrictions are typically placed on commercial activities that damage habitat, such as dredging and otter trawling, one might expect to see net economic gains in the recreational fishery.[17] Beneficiaries of such policies include vessels that directly harvest species that rely on EFH, including recreational vessels. However, note that recreational charter vessels only realize net economic benefits if the EFH protections result in either increased revenues or decreased costs. Changes in harvest rates alone are not sufficient to alter net benefits to charter vessels because charter vessels' profits are not directly related to harvest but rather to the number of anglers served. Also, note that changes in economic benefits in the charter sector are not equal to changes in revenues alone.

Net Benefits to Recreational Private-Boat Anglers

Economic value received by recreational anglers is subjective; it is equal to the amount that an individual would be *willing to pay* to obtain a recreational fishing experience minus what the angler *actually pays*. This difference represents the net benefit that the recreational angler realizes. For example, if an angler is willing to pay $500 for a fishing trip and the actual cost of the fishing trip is $200, then the angler realizes a net economic gain of $300.

Why is total expenditure not equal to economic value? In the same way that the price of a good does not represent consumer surplus, the actual expense of a fishing trip (price of the trip) does not represent the net benefits of the trip. If EFH policy changes either the amount that an angler is willing to pay for a fishing trip or the amount that the angler actually pays, then the net benefits received by anglers will change. This change in net economic benefits should be counted in an appropriate CBA.

Net Benefits to Land-Based Firms

When land-based firms are restricted by EFH policy, the change in economic benefits to these firms should be incorporated in an appropriate CBA. For example, if a power plant has to restrict the intake or outflow of water it uses for cooling to protect fish habitat, then it is appropriate to measure and count the net costs that are imposed on both the power plant owner and its customers. As above, the net benefits to land-based firms are equal to total revenues minus total costs. Changes in net benefits to consumers are measured as changes in consumer surplus, as above. It is important to note that only *primary or direct effects* on land-based firms should be addressed, such as when EFH or other habitat regulations directly affect the activities of a firm. Secondary effects, like those for the commercial fishermen, should not be included in an appropriate CBA.

Other Benefits and Costs from EFH Policies

EFH policies may have direct economic effects on those not involved in fishing. Because appropriate economic analysis accounts for all social benefits and costs within the predefined region of interest, these nonfishery net benefits should, at least in theory, be measured. Whether they are measured in practice often depends on their size relative to net benefits (positive or negative) realized in the fishery and data availability.

For example, actions to preserve EFH may increase the food supply for local birds (i.e., juvenile fish) that are in turn valued for hunting or viewing. Similarly, EFH policies that prevent trawling or dredging on the seafloor may—in limited cases—benefit certain user groups, such as recreational divers. In such cases, economic benefits may be realized by hunters, bird-watchers, or divers in the form of increased consumer surplus, and measured as the difference between what these groups are willing to pay to hunt, bird-watch, or dive minus what they actually pay. Other individuals may also realize *nonuse* or *passive-use benefits*, defined as a change in well-being that is unrelated to any active use of a resource or observable behavior.[18] For example, some individuals may benefit from simply knowing that healthy fish stocks are being passed on to future generations, aside from any actual or planned use of these resources. Depending on the policy context, nonuse values may be either smaller or larger than other types of economic value, and are no less legitimate from an economic perspective.

Similarly, policies that establish marine protected areas for the purpose of habitat protection may have wide-ranging impacts on a variety of user and nonuser groups, including recreational divers, boaters, etc. While these groups may not participate in local fisheries, changes in their net economic benefits— where significant—should be addressed by appropriate economic analysis.

Discounting and the Time Value of Money

In most cases, the benefits and costs of projects occur over many years. To account for the time value of money in aggregating multiyear benefits and costs, CBA applies an approach known as *discounting*.[19] This is similar to methods used to assess the market value of a business that provides a flow of revenues every year. Just as a bank recognizes the time value of money by charging borrowers interest, a CBA must recognize the time value of benefits or costs by discounting those received in the future. For example, the (present) value of a business is the sum of all the expected cash flows generated by that business—in essence, someone who purchases the business is paying now for the opportunity to make income in the future. However, people usually will not pay a whole dollar today for the opportunity to obtain a dollar in the future. Future cash flows, then, are worth less than present cash flows, which reflects the time value of money. As a result, future cash flows (or benefits and costs) must be *discounted* in order to make them comparable to cash flows today.

Assuming that time is counted in discrete units and discounting is calculated accordingly, a simple formula for the present value (PV) of a future payment of $X—what that future payment is worth today—is given by

$$PV = \frac{\$X}{(1+r)^t},$$

where r is the discount rate per time period in decimal notation (i.e., 6% = 0.06) and t is the number of periods into the future when the payment will be received. Using this formula, a discount rate of 6% means that a dollar to be received next year is worth 94.3 cents today, a dollar to be received two years from now is worth 88.9 cents, and a dollar to be received 20 years in the future is worth only 31.2 cents today. Adding up all the (discounted) future benefits and costs associated with a project, over all time periods, results in the *net present value* (NPV) of the project. An NPV greater than zero implies that the discounted benefits exceed the costs (a good investment), and an NPV less than zero implies that the discounted costs exceed the benefits (a bad investment).

Although discounting is the most appropriate means of aggregating benefits and costs over time, it can lead to unintended consequences when assessing projects with very long time horizons. For example, if one uses common discount rates between 4% and 10%, then benefits or costs in the distant future (e.g., 50 to 100+ years) often have little impact on NPV. At a discount rate of 6%, a 1-dollar benefit to be received in 100 years is worth less than 1 cent. For this reason, researchers have proposed a number of alternative discounting approaches for project with long-duration effects. One approach is *sensitivity analysis*, where one assesses the NPV of a project under a variety of different discount rates to evaluate the impact of different discount rates on CBA results. Other options may include a time-declining rate of discount, which might begin at a standard 4%–10% value and then decline slowly over time. For most projects, however, standard discounting procedures will generate the most accurate reflections of true economic benefits and costs.

Limitations of CBA

As discussed above, CBA is the appropriate means to assess net economic benefits from EBM policies. However, actual quantification of these net economic benefits may sometimes pose empirical (and some conceptual) challenges. As with all forms of empirical research, the quality of the results depends on the quality of the data and analysis methods. CBA is also reductionist, in that it collapses often complex and multidimensional policy changes into a small set of (often monetized) results. Moreover, the use of CBA implies a set of testable and untestable assumptions—many are associated with utilitarian theories of value and an ability to link willingness to pay to social welfare—that may not apply in all circumstances. For example, CBA presumes that individuals engage in well-informed behaviors that maximize their well-being, so that observations of behavior (e.g., alternatives that are chosen or not chosen) provide insight into human value and welfare.

The following sections discuss other important characteristics and limitations of CBA and identify attributes that may be used to identify unreliable or invalid analysis. This section is not meant to provide a comprehensive list of all potential limitations of CBA in all circumstances, but rather to highlight some of the primary limitations of which those using CBA methods should be aware.

Distribution and Equity Implications of CBA

CBA analysis can assess net benefits and costs for different groups affected by policy decisions, as well as the distribution of benefits and costs within an affected group. However, in practice, CBAs typically report the average benefit received by a representative group member, even if the representative member is part of a heterogeneous population. For example, a typical CBA might report the gain in average producer surplus or loss of an average commercial fisherman, without considering the differences in impact between a fisherman from a small rural community and one operating out of an urban center. However, given the uneven distribution of policy benefits among fisheries and fishermen, such aggregate net benefit measures might provide an inadequate representation of policy effects. Alternatively, a CBA might estimate the average impact of an offshore wind energy facility on the well-being of coastal property owners, without explicitly recognizing that its impacts will differ across individual owners. Policymakers often wish to consider both the total benefits of a policy and the distribution of benefits across regions and population groups. This requires information concerning who receives the benefits from a particular policy and where those individuals are located.

Often because of data limitations or concerns that equity issues are outside the scope of the analysis, some CBAs obscure ways in which benefits of natural resource policies are distributed. Despite this tendency, available CBA tools do allow economists to assess the distribution of benefits across relevant population groups and subgroups—given such information, resource managers may consider these distinct sets of net benefits when making policy choices. The advantage of such an approach to CBA is that it can show how benefits are explicitly distributed among affected groups. Such approaches, however, often add to the complexity and cost of the analysis and may require data that are not readily available.

Another potential complication associated with the use of CBA to address benefit distribution is that it raises often difficult questions that resource managers must address. For example, policymakers must decide whether benefits to different groups will be given equal distributional weight in the analysis. For example, some policymakers might argue that greater weight should be given to the net benefits received by commercial fishermen (whose livelihoods depend on fishing), compared to recreational anglers (whose benefits are related to recreational activities). Economists generally resist such arguments, and give equal weight to net benefits received by all concerned groups. Policymakers, however, may wish to emphasize benefits received by specific groups (e.g., those with less income); such choices will affect the outcome of a CBA.

Measurement Issues in CBA

Like measurements in any empirical science, economic measurements may be subject to inconsistencies or errors. Simple errors in CBA arise for many reasons. One common source of error is inaccurate data, such as errors in the observation, recording, or interpretation of events. Clearly, any such measurement errors will carry over into CBA results, leading to potential bias. Another set of potential errors may occur in forecasting future events or trends. For example, assessments of producer and consumer surplus for various products depend on an accurate estimate of prices as they will exist at the time of the policy change. Accordingly, if future prices shift unexpectedly, earlier surplus estimates will not produce accurate estimates of net economic benefits. Not surprisingly, economists cannot predict the future conditions with certainty, and ex ante CBA results are generally conditional on at least some assumptions made about the future. Inappropriate behavioral or model assumptions by researchers can also generate potential errors.

Additional potential measurement errors can come from specific market and nonmarket valuation methods, including a variety of revealed and stated preference methods, discussed in chapter 4. Each valuation method has a large and growing literature supporting it. Although discussion of the potential errors associated with each of the existing methodologies is beyond the scope of this chapter, resource managers must be aware that improperly conducted market or nonmarket valuation assessments can result in biased benefit estimates. Accordingly, valuation research must be conducted according to stringent quality standards and guidelines. (Chapter 4 provides additional information.)

In summary, CBA is capable of generating valid, accurate, and reliable benefit estimates and/or approximations, but it is also subject to possible measurement errors and other biases. The validity and accuracy of CBA results depend on the quality of the underlying analyses and the data used by those analyses.

Intrinsic and Other "Non-economic" Values

Assessment of net economic benefits provides an anthropocentric, or human-based, view of value. When valuation estimates the monetary value of natural resource damages, for example, one assumes that the resources only have value insofar as they provide services that people directly (or indirectly) value. Some individuals may find such assessments incomplete or misleading because they fail to consider "intrinsic" values, or values apart from those held by people. For example, some ecologists argue that nature has a "value" unto itself—apart from any human perception or sense of its worth. The potential legitimacy of such arguments aside, CBA only measures anthropocentric benefits or costs—those realized by humans. Anyone seeking to incorporate "intrinsic" or other concepts of value into policy deliberations must look to other, non-economic frameworks for guidance.

CBA tools are also poorly equipped to deal with moral, religious, and cultural issues. For example, it may be empirically difficult (although perhaps not theoretically impossible) to measure the net economic benefit associated with the culture of a fishing community or the religious, sacred, or cultural value that some cultures place on natural resources (e.g., the value that some native American tribes place on salmon runs in the western United States). In addition, legitimate economic effects may cause social impacts that are difficult to assess using CBA. For example, the collapse of a commercial fishery in a rural village and the accompanying large-scale unemployment might lead to increased local rates of alcoholism or other social problems. Where such concerns arise, CBA may provide an incomplete assessment of all factors relevant to management, but remains the tool of choice for measuring net economic benefits. In such cases, however, policymakers might also wish to consider the large variety of non-economic tools that can be applied to such issues.[20]

Cost-Effectiveness Analysis

Sometimes it may be unnecessary or impractical to estimate benefits associated with EBM alternatives. At times, for example, policymakers may conclude that the need to establish an ecologically safe minimum standard trumps the need to optimize net social benefits—particularly where long-term human effects on ecological systems are uncertain.[21] In these and other cases, CEA may be more appropriate, useful, and practical than CBA. Moreover, many of the most difficult challenges in CBA concern the measurement of benefits associated with difficult-to-observe or quantify changes in nonmarket goods, services, or resources. The use of CEA eliminates the need to measure these benefits.

CEA estimates the costs associated with various options for achieving stated and given goals, and identifies those that are most cost-effective (that cost the least to implement). CEA "compares (mutually exclusive) alternatives on the basis of the ratio of their costs and a single quantified but not monetized effectiveness measure."[22] This is an important distinction from CBA, which compares benefits and costs as a means of determining which goals are most socially beneficial. With CEA, the goals have already been identified—and the sole purpose is to find the most cost-effective means of realizing those goals. For example, one might estimate the least-cost means of ensuring the future survival of the North Atlantic right whale with a certain ecological degree of certainty, or the least-cost means of maintaining a certain area of beach for recreational use.

CEA is frequently applied in cases where policy goals are not based on economic grounds. For example, in evaluations of competing pharmaceutical products, a primary consideration is often cost per life saved—the goal of saving lives is a given. Similarly, in cases where irreversible ecological consequences are possible (such as extinction of a species), policymakers may desire information on the least-cost means of achieving a given preservation goal (preventing extinction). Still other examples involve specific objectives established by statute.

Aside from these primary distinctions, CEA shares many of the same methods as CBA. Both CBA and CEA are based on neoclassical welfare economics to validate methods and estimates; both assess impacts on humans, and the same guidelines for appropriate cost estimation apply to both. Although CEA is often more straightforward than CBA (because benefits need not be monetized), there are different types of CEA and associated choices that confront analysts. One of the primary choices involves whether the CEA will be sensitive to scale. This, in turn, relates to the definition of the established policy goal(s). In some instances, policy goals are highly specific; this includes specificity with regard to scale. For example, the policy goal may be to restore 50 acres of beach for recreation on a given site. Here, the scale is specified (50 acres of beach), and the sole question is which management approach will meet this goal with the least cost. This is the simplest form of CEA.

However, the policy might also stipulate goals without precise details as to scale. What if the goal is to restore a beach or wetland and does not specify the number of acres? In such cases, CEA might calculate the average cost per unit of effectiveness, or the average cost per acre of beach maintained. Projects can then be judged according to their cost-effectiveness per acre of beach restoration, on average. (This approach, however, faces difficulties when projects have different scales.) Consider the three mutually exclusive options for beach restoration illustrated in table 2.3.

The simple example in table 2.3 shows how issues of project scale can be critical to proper interpretation and use of CEA results. Analysts who use such methods must decide whether they want the most cost-effective approach, regardless of policy scale (e.g., cost per acre), whether they wish to set a minimum possible scale for the project (cost for a project of at least 50 acres), or whether they want to set a limit on the project budget (the most cost-effective project that costs less than $250,000).

The steps of a CEA are relatively similar to those of a CBA, but notice that table 2.4 omits information regarding policy benefits. This is because CEA takes the policy goal as given. However, it is important to note that, in some cases, the *costs* assessed within a CEA may be *benefits lost* by a user group because of a policy change. These are opportunity costs. When nonbudgetary or nonfinancial opportunity costs (costs that do not affect the money cost of a project) are significant, CEA does not eliminate all difficulties associated with these hard-to-measure benefits or costs. A common and potentially misleading solution with many CEAs is to ignore nonbudgetary costs. When nonbudgetary costs are small, ignoring them may still provide an acceptable approximation of true project cost-effectiveness, but it can result in substantial biases if these costs are large.

Note, too, that CEA in many cases incorporates similar mechanisms as CBA to address issues, such as the time value of costs and uncertainty in final project outcomes. For example, CEA discounts future costs, just as CBA discounts future costs and benefits. Similarly, CBA and CEA can apply identical methods to account for risky or uncertain project outcomes, particularly

TABLE 2.3   COST-EFFECTIVENESS OF HYPOTHETICAL BEACH RESTORATION OPTIONS

	Beach restoration Option 1	Beach restoration Option 2	Beach restoration Option 3
Acres restored	50	50	20
Total cost ($)	$500,000	$600,000	$100,000
Cost per acre (cost-effectiveness)	$10,000	$12,000	$5,000
Cost per 50 acres	$500,000	$600,000	N/A*

* Assumes that projects may not be duplicated; hence option 3 can restore a maximum of 20 acres.

As shown by the table, the most cost-effective policy depends on what scale one uses to measure cost-effectiveness. On a cost-per-acre basis (cost-effectiveness), option 3 is preferred, with a cost per acre of $5,000. If the policy goal is to restore beach acres using the most cost-effective means, choose this option. However, if the goal is 50 acres of restoration, the most cost-effective approach becomes option 1. Option 1 is not the most cost-effective per acre, but it is the most cost-effective way to restore 50 acres. This is because option 3 can only be implemented once and therefore can restore a maximum of only 20 acres.

TABLE 2.4   STEPS IN A COST-EFFECTIVENESS ANALYSIS

CEA steps	Description
1. Specify the set of policy goals and alternative projects.	Identify established policy goals and the alternative policy options under consideration.
2. Decide whether nonbudgetary costs should be assessed, and whose costs should count.	Determine those groups that should have standing (or whose costs should count) within the analysis, and whether the analysis should include non-budgetary costs.
3. Quantify the impact of each policy option on the policy outcome of interest.	Where scale is relevant, quantify the scale of impact resulting from each policy option (e.g., how many lives saved, how many acres restored?).
4. Monetize costs for each policy option.	Quantify all significant budgetary and (where appropriate) nonbudgetary costs associated with each identified policy option.
5. Discount costs to obtain present values.	Where costs are incurred over different time periods, use discounting to account for the time value of money.
6. Compute the cost-effectiveness of each alternative.	Combine aggregated, discounted costs and divide by a measure of project outcomes to generate a final cost-effectiveness ratio for the various project or policy alternatives. This last stage may also include analysis of distributional impacts, or costs to different affected groups.
7. Perform a sensitivity analysis.	Sensitivity analysis may be conducted at this stage to account for areas in which risk exists, to show the potential effects of different future possibilities on results. One may also calculate expected values or use other mechanisms (e.g., option prices) to account for risk.
8. Make a policy recommendation based on CEA results and sensitivity analysis.	Recommend the option with the greatest cost-effectiveness for the predetermined policy outcome.

where a variety of contingencies are possible (see discussion in chapter 5). CEA and CBA are also subject to many of the same caveats and guidelines for possible measurement errors, omission of secondary effects, and the treatment of cost distributions over heterogeneous populations.

Considering the issues just noted, CEA is most often useful in cases where 1) policy goals have already been established, 2) benefits are difficult to measure, and 3) nonbudgetary costs either are easily measurable or are trivial. Where these conditions apply, an appropriately conducted CEA can provide significant insight into the optimal means of achieving stated goals. Moreover, this insight is often less expensive than a full-scale CBA.

Economic Impact Analysis

When many people think of economic analysis, they envision forecasts of outcomes, such as regional employment and income. These forecasts, which come from *economic impact analysis*, or EIA, are commonly reported by the media and often used to justify public projects. EIA provides a snapshot of the financial linkages among sectors in a regional economy. In simple terms, it tracks monetary payments as they move through a regional economy—measuring the transfer of money from one sector to another. It estimates changes in gross output, income, and/or employment that result from exogenous policy changes.[23]

EIA provides familiar measures of economic impacts resulting from environmental policy, including those influencing coastal and marine resources. EIA is an appropriate tool for regional planning and regional industries and governments often use it to assess the impact of policy changes or development proposals on the distribution of income and employment. However, despite its common use in assessing aggregate *economic impacts* of policy decisions, *EIA is not a substitute for either CBA or CEA*, and does not provide an estimate of the net economic benefits of policy changes.[24] EIA can be used in conjunction with a properly performed CBA to provide additional information about income distribution among industry sectors. However, it cannot be used alone to determine the most socially beneficial (or productive) use of any coastal resource or policy decision within an EBM framework. Moreover, the distribution of income among industry sectors (as forecast by EIA) does not have any systematic relationship to the distribution of net economic benefits or costs; there is no relationship (even in direction) between changes in net economic benefits and changes in economic impacts such as regional income or employment. A project that generates larger economic impacts will *not* necessarily generate larger net social benefits.

These distinctions can be a source of confusion to non-economists. EIA is not designed to identify those policies or situations that generate the greatest possible social benefits—rather, it identifies only those options that may increase observable economic (market) activity. Nonetheless, it is used frequently to inform policy and can be influential in policy debates. Put simply, EIA is not designed to find optimal solutions.[25] EIA cannot determine which of a set of EBM policies is best for society—only which policy will generate the greatest gross economic activity. Despite these limitations, if the level of market activity in a region is a primary concern of policymakers, EIA can be a useful tool for policy analysis.

Use, Elements, and Assumptions of EIA Models

Although the models required for many types of impact analysis can be mathematically complex, software packages (such as IMPLAN or REMI) that allow non-experts to estimate such models are increasingly available. The resulting explosion of EIA has provided sought-after information to policymakers, but has also caused many to question the validity of its many applications and to point out the many critical issues upon which appropriate EIA depends. EIA can be an important element in the policymaker's toolbox, but it is subject to considerable risk of misuse and misinterpretation. For example, small (often unnoticed) changes in model assumptions can lead to large changes in estimated economic impacts.[26] Moreover, many of the outputs of EIA have no relationship to net policy benefits realized by the public or by any stakeholder group.

EIA is based on a "parsimonious accounting of financial links among industries, households, export markets, and, often, the public sector."[27] Primary financial links between sectors are defined as input links (which capture payments for resources or inputs that are part of the production of a final good or service purchased by consumers) or output links (which represent financial payments for final products, generally from consumers to industries). Other types of linkages capture taxes and other transfers (e.g., transfers of funds between government agencies, government subsidy payments, etc.) involving the public sector. Industries within a given region are divided into relatively homogeneous sectors, where each sector has similar inputs and outputs. Based on surveys or other data, links can be specified among industry sectors and among consumers and industries. EIA draws distinctions between households in a given region and those outside the region, between payments for imported inputs and outputs, and between payments to inputs and outputs produced within the region.[28]

Results of EIA are based on the patterns of predicted monetary payments as they move through a regional economy. They are based on a snapshot of past monetary flows between identical sectors during prior time periods and on the assumption that future flows will match past patterns.[29] For example, production of a good or service by an industry sector (e.g., "production" of recreational fishing trips by charter boat operators) requires monetary payments to other (secondary) sectors to purchase inputs (such as bait, tackle, boat fuel). These secondary sectors then use these funds to hire labor, pay the owners of productive assets, purchase inputs from still other industries, etc. In this way, money is "recycled," producing income for various sectors as it travels through the economy. A *transactions flow table* records these linkages and tracks financial transfers. This table, along with associated multipliers, may be used to forecast the income changes for any industrial sector that will be generated by policy-induced changes to any other sector. (A multiplier is calculated within the EIA model and indicates the projected effect of a change in one industry sector on broader measures of economic activity, such as regional income.) Note, however, that EIA results are determined solely by the flow of money. If an economic change does not result in money changing hands, it is not reflected in an EIA.

Leakage from the regional economy occurs when money is spent on imports (or paid to a sector that removes it from the local economy) or is saved by households. All else being equal, the more times that a dollar earned by an industry sector is "recycled" before "leaking" from the regional economy, the greater is the income generation attributed to that dollar. Accordingly, EIA may also be interpreted as a measure of the self-sufficiency of a regional economy. In a highly self-sufficient economy (such as one with few imports), every additional dollar earned by an industry sector will likely have a relatively large impact on regional income because the dollar will change hands many times within the economy before being spent on imports and leaving the economy. Estimated economic impact also depends on the definition of the region. If the local economy is defined on a small scale (say, a rural community), then the estimated economic impact of any policy change will likely be small because nearly all industrial and consumption inputs are imported from outside the local economy. However, if the defined local economy is a state (a larger scale), for example, then the estimated economic impacts of the same policy change will be much larger because more industrial and consumption inputs will be purchased from local sources.

Within an EIA, the effects of an exogenous EBM policy change on income and production are typically described in terms of three levels of effect: 1) direct effects, 2) indirect effects, and 3) induced effects. The direct effects of an increase in production of one sector (i.e., as might result from a policy change) reflect the direct purchase of inputs from other industry sectors within the economy. This initial increase in demand generates indirect effects as these secondary industries re-spend the resulting dollars for inputs into their production processes over several rounds of economic activity, effectively recycling the same dollars. Induced effects capture the secondary labor-consumption effects as new income earned by labor and as payments to the owners of capital and natural resources are spent on new products—again creating a feedback loop through which money is recycled within the economy. Table 2.5 illustrates the type of economic impact estimates generated by an EIA.

Once the spending and re-spending of dollars, resulting from a policy change, is complete, the total income from all rounds of spending may be expressed by different types of output or income multipliers. Various types of multipliers exist with different interpretations. For example, some multipliers are expressed in terms of regional incomes, while others are expressed in terms of regional employment. However, each is based on the fundamental idea of the "recycling" of dollars within a regional economy plus a financial accounting of the resulting transfers. The standard output multiplier reflects the "overall, or total effect of a change in final expenditures on regional production, divided by the initial, direct effect" on a single industrial sector.[30]

Contrasting EIA and CBA for Policy Guidance

The principal reason that EIA is not an appropriate normative tool for policy decisions (i.e., a tool that indicates what policies ought to be pursued, based

TABLE 2.5 SUMMARY OF TOTAL ECONOMIC IMPACTS FROM PARTY AND CHARTER FISHING IN MAINE

Category	Total angler expenditures	Direct impact	Indirect impact	Induced impact	Total impact
			Sales		
Nonresident	$1,117,336	$646,318	$227,280	$163,891	$1,037,489
Resident	$275,750	$143,860	$50,880	$29,819	$224,559
Total	$1,393,086	$790,178	$278,160	$193,710	$1,262,048
			Income		
Nonresident	$1,117,336	$194,516	$105,912	$92,713	$393,141
Resident	$275,750	$41,106	$22,948	$17,451	$81,505
Total	$1,393,086	$235,622	$128,860	$110,164	$474,646
			Jobs		
Nonresident	$1,117,336	31.1	3.8	3.7	38.6
Resident	$275,750	8.3	0.8	0.8	9.9
Total	$1,393,086	39.4	4.6	4.5	48.5

Sources: Steinback (1999) and Johnston and Sutinen (1999).

Interpreting the results in table 2.5, a total of $1.39 million in total expenditures for party and residential fishing in Maine generated total regional sales of $1.26 million, total regional income of $474,646, and 48.5 "new" jobs. These results are also broken down into the impacts of expenditures by residents and nonresidents, and into direct, indirect, and induced effects. If one accepts the assumptions of the underlying EIA (created in IMPLAN), these estimates indicate the aggregate economic activity that is generated by party and charter fishing in Maine (Steinback 1999), after all the spending and re-spending of money by various sectors is complete.

on social welfare) is that it does not measure economic benefits. Although this limitation is well known by EIA practitioners, it is sometimes ignored by interested parties who may wish to use associated results to argue for specific policy alternatives. It bears repeating that economic benefits are comprised of benefits to consumers (consumer surplus) and benefits to producers (producer surplus). Total economic performance increases when the sum of surpluses increases. EIA models do not measure benefits to consumers at all and do not accurately measure benefits to producers. EIA analysis simply measures economic transfers—the shift of money from one group to another. CBA estimates the economic net benefits to society of a policy or activity. This determines whether resources are being best used; activities or policies with higher net benefits have a greater net positive effect on aggregate or average social well-being. In contrast, EIA measures changes in economic activity and associated financial gains and losses within various sectors of the economy. These financial gains and losses are not measures of net benefit, do not provide insight into social well-being, and cannot be used to determine which policies are in the best economic interests of society.

TABLE 2.6　COMPARISON OF EIA AND CBA

	EIA	CBA
What it measures?	Includes indicators of regional economic activity, such as changes in total income, jobs, and expenditures.	Includes changes in net economic value (benefits minus costs), such as value to producers and consumers of both market and nonmarket goods and services.
Scope of analysis?	Can be conducted for specific regions or nationwide.	Often measures net social benefits on a national scale, but can be implemented at any desired scale.
Accounts for the value of alternative uses of resources?	No. Opportunity costs are ignored.	Yes. Opportunity costs are incorporated.
Measures net economic benefits to consumers?	No. Benefits to consumers are not considered. Consumers enter analysis only as a source of expenditures.	Yes. Estimates consumer surplus.
Measures net economic benefits to producers?	Not directly, but results may be used to provide an approximation of profits or producer surplus.	Yes. Estimates producer surplus.
Assesses changes in social well-being resulting from EBM policies?	No	Yes
Accounts for changes in labor and input use patterns?	No. Is based on a static snapshot of labor and input-use patterns.	Yes. Can account for predicted changes in labor and input uses.
Accounts for indirect and induced effects?	Yes. These effects are critical to EIA, even though they may be offset by counter-effects in other regions.	No. These effects are assumed to be negligible, given likely offsetting effects.
Accounts for offsetting impacts?	No	Yes
Assesses the net economic return generated through ecological services?	No	Yes
Considers distribution of revenues and expenditures?	Yes. Considers distribution of impacts on income and employment.	Often no, but can be used to assess benefits and costs to different groups.

Continued

TABLE 2.6   COMPARISON OF EIA AND CBA *(Cont.)*

Useful for estimating effects on regional economic development and employment?	Yes. This is one of the primary purposes of EIA.	Partially. CBA incorporates forecasts of producer and consumer activities within a regional economy, but is not explicitly designed to forecast regional economic development or employment.
Can be used to identify policy options which are best for society from an economic perspective?	No	Yes

Accordingly, the limitations mentioned here apply to all EIA, even those conducted with the most stringent quality standards. However, additional problems will occur if EIA is not performed properly, if the data are poor quality, or if the results are misinterpreted. (These same caveats apply to all economic frameworks.) This does not suggest that EIA does not have legitimate uses. For example, if the stated goal of a policy change is to increase regional employment (regardless of whether this will provide economic benefits), then an EIA can help identify policies that will most effectively promote this goal. The same applies to regional income. However, the measurement of economic benefits, efficiency, or social well-being is not one of the legitimate uses of an EIA.

Put another way, EBM policies that generate the greatest income, revenue, or employment are *not necessarily* preferred from an economic standpoint. The common myth that income, revenues, or jobs are equivalent to economic benefits is propagated by general confusion over what constitutes economic value. The economic value of revenue, income, or new jobs cannot be ascertained without information about the opportunity costs, or alternative uses, of productive assets. Recall that revenue to one group is simply an expense to another group—the simple transfer of money does not create economic value. The 1989 Exxon Valdez oil spill illustrates the difficulty with this argument. This disaster brought hundreds of millions of dollars of revenue to those involved in cleaning up the oil, as well as additional revenue to area hotels, restaurants, etc., but it did not create economic value and left the local community (and society) much worse off. Similarly, sole reliance on EIA to guide EBM policies can also reduce the long-term well-being of society, if it is not placed within an appropriate context.

Hence, while EIA results may be attractive to policymakers whose primary interest is maximizing economic development or economic activity, they cannot substitute for or even reasonably approximate the results of CBA or

CEA. Measures of net economic benefits and measures of economic activity are not necessarily correlated, even in terms of algebraic sign (positive or negative). Economic activity does not approximate economic benefit, although it may provide relevant information in its own right.

Alternatives to Economic Analysis

As noted above, economic analysis—whether CBA or CEA—is based on neoclassical economic theory, which assesses value based on the well-being of humans. Economic value is subjective and is based on people's individual needs and wants. It is also subject to the current state of information: as the amount of available information about different goods and services changes, so may individuals' willingness to pay. For example, new information about mercury contamination of certain fish products may change individuals' demand for similar or substituted products and, hence, affect or change the measurable market value. It is also important to note that the use of CBA to guide policy does not guarantee that any specific ecological resource or service will be sustained. Appropriate use of CBA can help ensure that policies will encourage maximum sustainable benefits to society, but this may involve improvements in some ecological resources or systems and declines in others. In addition, appropriate economic analysis can be costly, intricate, and data-intensive. It is also "rare in the [CBA] literature [to find] examples of wide-scale changes, very small changes, or the consequences of long-term ecological and economic change."[31]

For these and other reasons, some non-economists have expressed dissatisfaction with economic approaches to inform policy. For example, some ecologists, voicing concerns about value systems based on subjective human values, have proposed alternatives based entirely on the functioning of natural systems. These non-economic approaches are often founded on thermodynamic principles and include embodied energy valuation and EMERGY.[32] These and similar non-economic valuation methodologies quantify values based on the energy required or the "work" previously done to make a product or service. According to energy theories of value, people's values and preferences play no significant role in assessing the benefits, costs, or values of resource policies.

Energy-based theories of value are internally consistent and provide results that policymakers might wish to consider when weighing alternative policy options, *but they bear no relationship to economics or social welfare,* nor do public values and well-being play any role in the calculation of values within these theories. As a result, energy-based theories of value have been widely criticized by economists.[33] Much as EIA tracks the flow of money through economic systems, embodied energy models track the flow of energy through ecological systems, based on average patterns observed in model systems. Neither approach, however, shows the impact of these flows on human welfare.

Moreover, while proponents of thermodynamic approaches often criticize the assumptions implicit in CBA, these approaches require their own set of sometimes questionable assumptions. For example, EMERGY relies on the fundamental assumption the value of a resource or commodity is determined by the solar energy directly and indirectly required to produce that resource or commodity through ecological systems, regardless of effects on people.[34]

When contrasting energy-based theories of value with economic approaches, three differences are paramount. First, as noted above, policies guided solely by EMERGY or other thermodynamic value models will *not* necessarily improve the well-being of society, either in the short or long term. Thermodynamic models of value have no formal relationship to human values or well-being. For this reason, they are often referred to as *ecocentric* theories of value by practitioners.[35] An EBM policy that maximizes EMERGY or embodied energy will not necessarily maximize human welfare and may indeed diminish it.

Second, because these approaches sever the relationship between human welfare and assessed values (they are based solely on thermodynamic and ecological relationships), they avoid the perceived subjectivity of human values and sensitivity of these values to information. This property also allows EMERGY values to be calculated for resources even if the total contribution of those resources to human welfare is unknown. This independence from human subjectivity, knowledge, and information is one of the primary reasons that some ecologists and other natural scientists champion such methods.

Third, thermodynamic models of value are entirely "donor based." That is, they quantify values based on the ecological cost of producing goods or services (what is required to make them), rather than the benefit that is derived from these services. From an economics perspective, this confuses the concepts of benefits and costs, and can lead to counterintuitive results. For example, according to EMERGY and other such methods, the "value" of a gallon of whale oil is constant, even though the human or economic value of whale oil has changed dramatically over the past 200 years. Similarly, "two paintings with similar EMERGIES can have drastically different [human] values, especially if one of them is by a renowned painter."[36] The inability of EMERGY to account for such patterns can lead to difficulties when resulting values are applied to policy development. For example, EMERGY results can favor policies that appear to make humans unambiguously worse off.

Yet another set of approaches that is sometimes proposed for the valuation of ecological systems is based on the concepts of *replacement costs* and *defensive costs*. Replacement costs quantify the value of an ecological good or service based on the cost of either replacing that good or service using technological or other means. Defensive costs are costs incurred to offset the negative impacts caused by the loss of a good or service. For example, a replacement-cost approach might value the water filtering services of a wetland based on the cost of replacing those services with technology, such as a water treatment plant. Defensive cost methods, in contrast, might attempt to estimate or bound the value of drinking water quality using the costs that households are willing to incur to protect themselves when water quality declines, such as purchasing bottled water.

Like the thermodynamic approaches summarized above, valuations based on replacement costs do not generally provide appropriate measures of economic value or benefit to human welfare. This is because, again like thermodynamic theories of value, replacement-cost approaches do not distinguish between benefits and costs. The failure of replacement-cost approaches to provide well-defined measures of social benefits is well known. Per the U.S. Environmental Protection Agency, "alternative approaches that estimate the total value of ecosystems based on the replacement cost of the entire ecosystem or its embodied energy (e.g., Costanza et al. 1997; Ehrlich and Ehrlich 1997; Pearce 1998; Pimentel et al. 1997) have received considerable attention as of late. However, *the results of these studies should not be incorporated into benefit assessments.* The methods adopted in these studies are not well grounded in economic theory nor are they typically applicable to policy analysis."[37]

Under narrow circumstances, some types of replacement costs (mainly incurred defensive costs) may be used to estimate appropriate measures of economic benefit or cost.[38] The conditions under which this applies are restrictive and do not apply to most cases where replacement cost measures of value have been proposed: 1) the expenditures on defensive or replacement behavior must be *voluntary*, 2) the costs must *actually be paid* by the affected individual or group, and 3) there must be *no joint production*[39] or additional utility or disutility (i.e., benefit or harm) associated with the defensive or replacement behavior. The third condition implies that the replacement is an exact match—in terms of services provided and related benefits—to the original natural resource in question. Unfortunately, these conditions, and particularly the third, rarely hold. Hence, as a generalization, one should treat replacement or defensive cost measures of value with skepticism—at least if measuring social value is the aim.

For these and other reasons, most economists are highly critical of thermodynamic and replacement-cost theories of value largely because such theories cannot be relied upon to promote policies that are in the best short- or long-term interests of society (i.e., that encourage maximum sustainable human welfare). Defensive-cost methods have a somewhat greater role, particularly in some areas of economic analysis. The primary area in which these approaches have been applied appropriately is to estimate the value of environmental damage that causes direct human health effects; there have been fewer appropriate applications to coastal and ocean policy. Nonetheless, these methods offer a competing perspective to other economic approaches in the EBM policymaker's toolbox.

Multi-attribute Utility Theory

A final framework, discussed here briefly, is multi-attribute utility theory. MAUT is a cousin of CBA in that it allows assessment of policies, such as EBM, where multiple attributes (i.e., policy characteristics or outcomes) are affected. Like CBA, MAUT provides a method whereby one can evaluate alternative policies and attempt to choose the one that is, at least, arguably "best" for society. However, the ways in which MAUT evaluates policy are distinct from those of CBA, relying generally on the opinions of experts rather than on estimated values of affected individuals to evaluate policies.

Steps in a MAUT analysis vary, but generally include seven steps:[40]

Step 1   **Identify objectives and attributes**—Identify relevant policy attributes through literature reviews, background research, or expert interviews.

Step 2   **Quantify attributes**—Measure or estimate the magnitude of physical impacts on the attributes identified in step 1.

Step 3   **Verify the relevance of assumptions**—Explore various functional forms for the overall utility (or benefit) function and assess implications for behavioral expectations.

Step 4   **Examine the single attribute utility function**—Estimate functional forms that identify the "utility" or relative weight given to each single attribute in the overall utility function.

Step 5   **Determine the importance of attributes**—Ranking (or choice tasks) by experts are used to determine weights given to each attribute.

Step 6   **Construct the multi-attribute utility function**—Combine information from steps 1–5 to construct the final utility function used to rank policies.

Step 7   **Assess tradeoffs**—Use the final utility function to rank policies and assess policy tradeoffs.

Like CBA, MAUT attempts to estimate a single cardinal value that policymakers can use to prioritize policy options or choose the preferred policy from a set of alternatives. (One of the policy alternatives is often the status quo, or no policy change at all.) However, unlike CBA, the weights or relative importance given to each policy attribute are not determined by economic value or the willingness to pay of affected households or individuals. Indeed, one of the primary motivations for using MAUT is the discomfort that some analysts feel with the concept of monetization. Instead, within a MAUT analysis, generally decisionmakers, well-informed stakeholders, policy experts, or analysts define the weights. These weights may be directly assigned or estimated based on the results of ranking tasks designed to reveal the implicit weights given by experts to each policy attribute.[41]

For example, assume that policymakers have requested an evaluation of alternative beach nourishment programs. The relevant characteristics (attributes) of each program include the amount of sand required, the resulting width of the beach, the location from which the sand would be obtained, the frequency with which the sand would have to be replaced, the cost of the program, etc. A MAUT might ask experts to rank a large number of possible beach nourishment options from most to least preferred, where each option would be characterized by different levels for each of the attributes listed above. By analyzing experts' rankings using statistical procedures, one could then estimate the weights (or relative importance) that the average expert gave to each attribute, when deciding which options were preferred. These weights could then be used to calculate a utility score for any possible beach nourishment program, whereby that program could be compared to alternatives.

The distinction between ranking policies based on aggregate net benefits (as measured by aggregate willingness to pay) versus weighting and assessment of policy attributes using expert-determined attribute weights is one of the primary differences between MAUT and CBA. Although MAUT approaches have been applied to a number of policy decisions,[42] they neither measure nor attempt to measure economic value. Rather, they seek expert values, opinions, and preferences to determine the weights of the attributes that represent policy benefits. Put another way, CBA evaluates policy at least in part based on the subjective preferences and values of individuals and households; these preferences and values are a fundamental factor determining economic values and benefits. In contrast, MAUT is grounded in a belief that experts and well-informed stakeholders are best suited to identify the policy choices that are in the best interests of the public. Hence, using either MAUT or CBA is often decided by philosophical beliefs about whether individuals can identify choices and behaviors that are in their own best interest, and have sufficient information to do so.

A similar analytical tool—multigoal analysis—does not seek to reduce various impacts to a single score, but rather only quantifies impacts on different valued attributes. The ability of MAUT-influenced policy decisions to improve social well-being depends on the relationship between the values and the perceptions of the experts or stakeholders (who determine the weights of MAUT attributes) and the values of the public at large. MAUT also requires that one accept a variety of testable and nontestable assumptions in order to derive final policy rankings, and some of these do not correspond to common neoclassical economic perspectives. As a result, economists are often skeptical of MAUT results used in isolation to rank policies. However, as a complement to CBA or other economic approaches to policy evaluation, MAUT approaches can provide an alternative perspective that policymakers may wish to consider when choosing among EBM policies.

Conclusion

Policy analysis often involves numerous forms of natural and social science assessments. Quantification of the economic outcomes associated with EBM alternatives can provide important information regarding the effects of these policies on social welfare. Different approaches to evaluating outcomes—both economic and non-economic—exist. There are also various ways that one can integrate economic information into the policy process, each with unique interpretations and appropriate uses. While each of these methodologies can represent an important addition to the policymaker's toolbox, it is incumbent upon those using such tools to be aware of their appropriate uses, interpretations, and limitations.

EBM by its very nature addresses simultaneous impacts on multiple ecological resources and user groups. As a result, economic analysis that includes all affected resources and groups may be impractical. In such cases, policymakers must balance the need for information from economic analyses against the cost of the analyses, in addition to deciding which resources require detailed assessments. Where data are available at reasonable cost, appropriate CBA—either full or select components—will generally provide the most appropriate economic guidance for EBM policy decisions. (Few would argue, however, that CBA should be the *only* consideration informing policy.) CEA can provide similar information on costs when policy goals have been predetermined. EIA, in contrast, quantifies economic activity and money flows that are often interesting to those promoting regional economic development or employment. Any economic analysis should, of course, be conducted according to professional standards by experts familiar with the methods in question. Any presentation of results should make clear the limitations and assumptions associated with the data or analysis used, and sensitivity analysis is often necessary to illustrate the impact of uncertain parameters on key results.

In summary, policymakers must be aware that different analytical methods provide different, and often incomparable, results. Appropriate use and interpretation of the empirical results of economic analysis can help make certain that EBM encourages the most socially beneficial long-term use and preservation of coastal and marine resources.

Endnotes

1. See, for example, Odum (1988).
2. See, for example, Costanza et al. (1997).
3. For example, some net benefits can be generated if a project hires previously unemployed workers or causes a broader wage increase. See Boardman et al. (2001) for discussion of these and related issues.
4. Bockstael et al. (2000, *1386*).

5. Ibid.

6. See Lipton and Wellman (1995, *24–25*) for additional examples and straightforward discussion of such issues.

7. Quotes are from Lipton and Wellman (1995, *27*) and U.S. EPA (2000, *20*), respectively. Various sources provide discussions of CBA at different levels of technical difficulty. For example, see Lipton and Wellman (1995) for a discussion aimed at policy audiences, Boardman et al. (2001, 2006) for an intermediate-level text that presumes some familiarity with economics, and Just et al. (2004) for a technically more rigorous presentation suited to those with extensive economics background. Other works that highlight particular aspects of CBA, such as nonmarket valuation, are Freeman (2003), Champ et al. (2003), Kopp and Smith (1993), Sassone and Schaffer (1978), and Garrod and Willis (1999), for example. Government agencies also provide guidelines for the use of associated methods (e.g., U.S. EPA 2000, 2002a).

8. For additional discussion regarding the underlying theory at varying levels of technical rigor, see Boardman et al. (2001, 2006) or Just et al. (2004), for example.

9. The difference between profits and producer surplus lies in the treatment of fixed costs, or costs that do not vary with the quantity of production in the short run. For example, a mortgage payment for a factory or fishing vessel is a fixed cost because it must be paid regardless of the quantity produced in the short run. Such fixed costs are considered when calculating profits; they are not considered when calculating producer surplus.

10. See Boardman et al. (2001, 2006) and Just et al. (2004) for additional development of these issues.

11. Secondary *nonmarket* benefits or costs should often be counted, however. This is because these benefits and costs, unlike secondary *market* benefits and costs, are not generally captured elsewhere in the analysis. Continuing the softshell clam example from above, if the increased secondary effect on scallop consumption leads to increased ecological damage to the ocean floor from scallop dredges, and if this damage causes a loss of nonmarket benefits to recreational divers or anglers who use the same areas, then these nonmarket losses should be included in a comprehensive CBA. See Boardman et al. (2001, 2006) for additional discussion.

12. As beaches undergo erosion, beach nourishment is the process of replenishing the sand and spreading it across the beach to restore it to initial conditions.

13. Occasionally, proponents of certain policies will argue that secondary effects *should* be counted if one is *only* interested in benefits and costs realized in a specific region. For example, one might argue that residents of Alaska do not care if secondary benefits to local hotels and restaurants in Alaska are offset by secondary losses elsewhere. However, even in this case, it is generally inappropriate to count secondary effects—at least at their full value. The reason is that if one is truly interested only in regional benefits and costs, then one must subtract all nonregional effects. This includes all benefits realized by visitors, nonresident business owners, and consumers who live outside the region, for example. Considering these and other factors, a regional perspective rarely provides a legitimate argument for counting secondary effects that should otherwise be ignored (Boardman et al. 2001, 2006). At the very least, policy analysts should be consistent when add-

ing and subtracting benefits realized in different areas, so that double counting does not occur.

14. Economic impact analysis often presents estimates of the number of jobs that will be lost or gained in different industry sectors as a result of policy changes. A common assumption is that these employment changes represent an economic cost or benefit. In cases where 1) current residents (who are otherwise unemployed or underemployed) gain new jobs or 2) new jobs result in a sectorwide wage increase, a relatively small portion of new job income may be considered an economic benefit. The converse applies if jobs are lost. This implies that the creation of jobs may generate real economic benefits in communities where jobs are scarce (i.e., workers would otherwise be unemployed). In communities where jobs are plentiful, however, new jobs are typically taken by new workers, immigrants, or workers who are already employed in the region (i.e., those leaving one job to take another), resulting in negligible net benefits to the region.

15. In the short term, the benefits are defined by producer surplus, which differs from economic profits in that it does not consider fixed costs. In the long term, the concepts are identical because long-term fixed costs are always zero (i.e., all costs are variable in the long run). See additional comments in footnote 9 above.

   Ex-vessel revenue may be defined as the quantity of fish landed by commercial fishermen multiplied by the price they receive per unit of quantity.

16. "Entry" is when a new fishing vessel begins to operate in a fishery in which it had not operated previously. "Exit" is when a fishing vessel ceases fishing in a particular fishery. Fish biomass refers to the total mass of living fish matter within a given ecosystem, sometimes disaggregated by species or species group.

17. For measuring net economic benefits in different fisheries sectors, see Sutinen and Johnston (2001). For EFH restrictions on commercial activities and related economic effects, see Hicks et al. (2001, 2004). In dredging, the boat drags a steel box along a shallow sea bottom. At the same time, the boat pumps seawater through a large hose, forcing water into the sand, "temporarily fluidizing it," which permits the dredge to pass through the sand. Bars on the bottom of the dredge are specifically spaced to allow smaller clams and other species to fall through and hold in larger clams (or other sought-after species). In otter trawling, boats drag a large net along the sea bottom (or just above the bottom) to catch fish or shellfish. See www.fishingnj.org/techhd.htm.

18. Freeman (2003).

19. See Boardman et al. (2001, 2006) or Goulder and Stavins (2002) for a general nontechnical discussion of discounting.

20. Turner (1999b) provides a good discussion of issues related to economic and noneconomic perspectives on value.

21. Swallow (1996).

22. Boardman et al. (2001, 437).

23. The commercial software package IMPLAN, for example, can analyze changes in a broad range of sectors in regions across the United States.

24. See Edwards (1990) and Lipton and Welman (1995) for further discussion.

25. For more on EIA and policy dos and don'ts, see Crompton (1995), Tyrrell and Johnston (2006), Hushak (1987), and Edwards (1990, 1991).

26. Crompton (1995) provides good examples of this in his discussion of the use of EIA to assess sports facilities and events.
27. Edwards (1990, *10*).
28. This section draws from prior work of Johnston and Sutinen (1999), as well as from Edwards (1990).
29. As with any approach that tries to predict future scenarios, if future money-flow patterns do not match past patterns, bias will be introduced into the analysis.
30. Edwards (1990, *12*).
31. U.S. EPA (2000, *98*).
32. "EMERGY analysis . . . is a technique of quantitative analysis which determines the values of nonmonied and monied resources, services, and commodities in common units of the solar energy it took to make them." Embodied energy analysis, similarly, is "the process of determining the energy required directly and indirectly to allow a system (usually an economic system) to produce a specified good or service" (Brown and Herendeen 1996, *220*, both quotations). Odum (1988) pioneered this concept.
33. See discussion by Hau and Bakshi (2004). To illustrate the basis for these criticisms, consider the basic process of EMERGY valuation. "The EMERGY of renewable energies, nonrenewable resources, goods, services, and even information are determined by the energy required to make them. When values are expressed in these terms, we call the new measure EMERGY and define it as the amount of one type of energy that it takes to make another . . . To derive solar EMERGY of a resource or commodity, it is necessary to trace back through all the resources and energy that are used to produce it and express them in the amount of solar energy that went into their production. This has been done for a wide variety of resources and commodities and the renewable energies driving the biogeochemical process of the earth. When expressed as a ratio of the total EMERGY used to the energy produced, a transformity results . . . As its name implies, the transformity can be used to 'transform' a given energy into EMERGY, by multiplying the energy by the transformity. For convenience, in order not to have to calculate the EMERGY in resources and commodities every time a process is evaluated, we use transformities that have been previously calculated" (Brown and Herendeen 1996, *221*). Notice that this process has no basis in human preferences, welfare, or behavior.
34. Hau and Bakshi (2004) and Brown and Herendeen (1996) discuss many of the assumptions implicit in EMERGY analysis.
35. Hau and Bakshi (2004).
36. Ibid., *219*.
37. U.S. EPA (2000, *98*, emphasis added).
38. See detailed discussions in Freeman (2003) and Champ et al. (2003), for example.
39. Joint production refers to a case in which the same process produces multiple valued outcomes. An example would be when a defensive behavior in question (e.g., purchasing bottled water to avoid waterborne illness) provides other benefits as well (e.g., bottled water tastes better than tap water).
40. Kim et al. (1998).
41. See Gregory et al. (1993) and Kim et al. (1998) for more detail.
42. Some argue strongly for their use over CBA, such as Gregory et al. (1993).

CHAPTER 3

Modeling Human Behavior

To understand and quantify the ecological and economic impacts of policies or projects that affect coastal and marine ecosystem resources and
services, one must understand how they affect the decisions of people who
use and value these resources and services. For instance, people and firms are
likely to respond to improvements in the quality or availability of ecosystem
services or resources (e.g., better water quality at a beach or higher catch rates
at a recreational fishing site) by increasing their use of them. On the other
hand, they can also be expected to take action(s) to reduce any harm they
suffer from policies, projects, or events. For example, a reduction in water
quality at a beach may induce some users to go to a different (substitute) beach
or a lake. These individuals reduced their economic harm from the poor water
quality at the beach because they found close substitutes offering a similar level
of enjoyment at a similar cost (including the opportunity cost of time). Similarly, improved water quality that allows a closed beach to reopen will translate
into a greater net economic gain to the extent that it provides a superior or less
costly alternative to the individuals who are attracted to that beach.

Thus, the feedbacks between individuals' responses, both contempora-
neously and in the future, to changes in the quality or availability of ecosystem goods are critical factors to include in any economic assessment of those
changes—because these feedbacks will affect the net benefits associated with
them. These responses may also have ecological or socioeconomic spillover
effects if they directly impact the ecosystem or affect other users of ecosystem
resources. By predicting changes in use patterns, policymakers may be able to
increase the benefits or reduce the harm associated with changes in use. Conversely, inability to predict (or ignorance of) behavioral reactions may lead to
unforeseen policy implications: "surprises" or unintended consequences are
often the result of not explicitly considering human behavior and responses.

This chapter discusses a variety of models that can be used to understand, quantify, and predict the human use of, and impact on, coastal and
marine ecosystems. It includes models that apply to goods and services that
are traded in formal monetized markets (such as electricity and seafood), as
well as those that may not involve monetary transactions (e.g., visits to a public beach or recreational fishing in an estuary). While the chapter points out
when different types of models are appropriate and discusses their strengths

and limitations, it is not a comprehensive review of all modeling approaches or previous studies.

"Models," in the context of this chapter, are mathematical or graphical representations that illustrate or quantify the choices that individuals, firms, or groups of people make when allocating resources (e.g., time and money) between alternative uses. The focus here is on representations of decisions to use particular coastal or marine ecosystem goods or services. The basis for these behavioral models is an assumption that individuals attempt to allocate resources in ways that maximize their personal well-being (utility).[1] Similarly, models assume that firms will make decisions that maximize their profits. These assumptions are basic to most economic behavioral models, although the models may allow for behavior that deviates from maximizing utility or profit as a result of incomplete information, uncertainty, and regulatory constraints. Models of utility can be quite flexible, factoring in that people value things that do not provide them with any direct use (e.g., existence of right whales). The models can also allow for values and interests that differ substantially across individuals and population segments.

While it is useful to consider and model the decisions that individuals make in direct response to a policy, project, or event, it is also necessary to understand the ripple effects of these decisions, both in the short and long run. For example, an improvement in the habitat quality of an estuary that leads to increased fish stock and higher catches may attract new recreational fishermen. The increased number of anglers at this site may affect (change) the quality of the fishing experience for all anglers in the area (congestion effects), offsetting some of benefits associated with the increased catches. In the longer term, if the anglers catch more fish, they may reduce the fish stock, thereby lowering catch rates and potentially reducing the productivity of the resource toward the original level. Understanding how people react to changes in productivity can help policymakers avoid or mitigate negative impacts from increased use—and thus avoid dissipating some of the original gains.[2]

The example above illustrates the need to consider (and perhaps model) behavior at different time periods and to account for how human behavior changes the ecosystem. For example, a model might characterize the extent to which existing fishermen will benefit from bigger catches and quantify how the bigger catches will affect demand for fishing in this location in the short term (e.g., more or longer trips by current users and attraction of new users). To understand how such increased use will impact the fishery resource in the longer term, however, the analyst may need to pair this model with a biological model of the resource. Such a combined economic-ecological model can better predict the dynamic feedbacks between the resource and its users as they unfold over time.

There is significant overlap between the basic concepts discussed in this chapter and the techniques in chapter 4 on nonmarket valuation. This is intentional and unavoidable because, in many cases, appropriate calculation of nonmarket values requires that one appropriately predict the activities or behaviors that generate those values. For instance, the random utility model discussed here is used by economists both to determine the value of goods and services and to determine how that value is affected by the characteristics of the goods and services. The focus in this chapter, however, goes beyond the calculation of values and discusses the importance of understanding and modeling behavior and outcomes in terms of levels of use. (Chapter 4, in contrast, discusses in more depth how measures of value are derived from these models and details other modeling techniques, such as contingent valuation, that are useful for valuation but less relevant for predicting behavior.)

Traditional Market Models Based on Aggregate Data

Much of economics is concerned with the behavior of individuals and firms in formal markets for goods and services, and the outcomes of that behavior as measured by the quantity and price of the goods and services traded. The quantities and prices are determined by the intersection of a demand curve and a supply curve, where demand curves represent the quantities consumers would be willing to buy at various prices and supply curves represent the quantities firms would be willing to produce and sell at different prices. The intersection defines the market equilibrium and indicates the quantity and price one would expect to observe in an actual market (see figure 3.1 below).

The theoretical foundation for demand and supply curves is a combination of utility (use) maximization by individual consumers and profit maximization by individual firms. Because individual-level data are often not available, an aggregate perspective can be very useful and more practical than modeling individual choices. For example, companies, industrial associations, nongovernmental organizations (NGOs), and government agencies routinely collect data on sales or use of particular goods or services over time. When coupled with information on prevailing prices of those goods and services, this aggregated information can form the basis of an aggregate demand and supply model for a particular good or service.

Box 3.1 Importance of Including Supply and Demand Responses of Land Markets When Preserving
Biodiversity via Land Purchases

Armsworth et al. (2006) illustrated how naive biodiversity planners, who do not consider how their actions will impact the supply and demand of land, can actually do more harm than good. For example, if they purchase land for protection, the increased demand for land and the resulting higher prices will entice landowners to sell. This can potentially result in a situation where the species richness of the area decreases if this land is developed and becomes unsuitable for species that live there. This is just one unintended consequence that is possible when behavior and economic feedbacks are not considered in environmental planning.

Market analysis can help predict how the aggregate level of production and consumption and the prices of goods and services will change in response to changes in exogenous factors, such as changes in prices of substitutes, inputs to production, or changes in income. The models can also help reveal how the net benefits to consumers (consumer surplus) and profits for producers (producer surplus) will be affected.

In addition to modeling the use of manufactured goods and services produced by humans, these models of standard markets can also help one understand the economic consequences of a variety of policies, projects, and events that affect the use of ecosystem resources and services. These may include markets for inputs or outputs of businesses that utilize the marine ecosystem, such as commercial fisheries (inputs = fuel, nets, etc.; outputs = fish caught). If data are available on actual market activity, either in the particular location or in comparable markets, traditional models may be useful for modeling the demand for variations of market goods (local sustainably caught fish or renewable electrical energy from wind or tidal power) different from the standard products (fish or electricity from uncertain origins) and due to special qualities related to the local marine ecosystems.

Box 3.2   Market for Green Electricity from Wind Power

There is increasing demand for electricity produced from renewable resources, but a standard demand analysis may not capture the full value of electricity produced from wind power, for example. Borchers et al. (2007) used an experimental approach designed to estimate consumer preferences and willingness to pay (WTP) to participate in a voluntary "green energy" electricity program. Their model estimated WTP for a generic (no choice) green energy source and compared it to WTP for green energy from specific sources, including wind, solar, farm methane, and biomass. Their results showed that there exists a positive WTP for green energy electricity, but they found that consumers have a preference for solar over a generic green source and wind. Biomass and farm methane were found to be the least preferred sources.

For a standard good or service (see figure 3.1), the demand curve slopes down, indicating that as the price decreases the quantity that people will purchase increases. The supply curve of the good or service generally slopes up, indicating that the quantity that firms are willing to produce and sell increases as the price they can get for the good rises. The slope and shape of a demand function typically reflect how the purchase and use decisions of multiple potential consumers will shift as the price of the good changes. As prices rise, some individuals reduce their use (or purchase) or drop out of the market completely. Similarly, the slope and shape of the supply curve may represent production decisions by multiple firms. As prices decrease, some firms reduce or stop production. As prices rise, existing firms increase production and new firms may enter the market. The intersection of these curves indicates the market-clearing equilibrium price and quantity levels. Thus, the quantity traded is the result of many individual decisions, but this model (in figure 3.1) contains only the aggregate result of those decisions in terms of prices and quantities traded.

Demand and supply curves are mathematical functions whose shapes can be estimated statistically. Estimation, not surprisingly, requires the inclusion of various factors (variables) that are expected to influence demand and supply. The availability and prices of substitute goods, population size, and income are typical variables of the demand function. For example, one might model the demand for electricity (quantity) as a function of the price of electricity, as well as a function of the price of substitutes, such as natural gas or oil. The availability of close substitutes tends to flatten out the demand curve, such that a small change in price will result in a large change in quantity demanded. (This is elastic demand.)[3] If close substitutes are not available, the demand curve will be steeper, indicating that the quantity demanded is unresponsive to price change (i.e., inelastic demand). Other factors may affect the quantity demanded at all price levels. For example, an increase in population or average income is likely to increase demand for electricity independent of a price change. These factors act to shift the demand curve outwards (increased demand) or inwards (decreased demand), as well as change its curvature.

On the supply side, prices of inputs to production or other factors that affect production capacity or costs may be included in the estimation of the supply function. The change in the price of an input (e.g., coal for producing electricity) may shift the supply curve inwards (less supply) or outwards (increased supply)

FIGURE 3.1   DEMAND AND SUPPLY FOR A MARKET GOOD

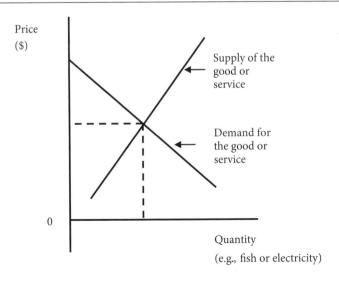

at all price levels. The steepness of the supply curve reflects increases in production costs at higher production levels. These production costs, which include the opportunity costs of diverting these resources away from other sectors of the economy, may reflect the need to procure inputs from more expensive sources, pay overtime, develop new production facilities in less optimal sites, etc.

In some cases, one may need to model only the demand side of a market and not the supply side. For example, if the supply of a good is fixed or is in the direct control of a policymaker (e.g., the total allowable catch from a fishery), one may simply want to model how demand would change in response to a change in price or what price would not leave excess or insufficient demand for a given quantity of output. Other times, developing interdependent models of both supply and demand is needed, so that together they determine price and quantity levels (e.g., where the regulatory limit on fish catch is not binding and the amount landed increases with the market price). These models must capture a fluid, reciprocal process in which prices affect quantities and quantities affect prices. Economists have statistical techniques to account for this interrelationship by estimating supply and demand functions simultaneously.[4] The details of these models are not discussed here, but one should be careful about modeling demand by itself, in isolation, if the quantity of the good supplied to the market is responsive to the price.

In order to determine the shape of the supply and demand curves and how they shift in response to various factors, it is necessary to observe variation in quantities and prices that corresponds to different market conditions. This requires either a series of observations of market activity over time (time series) or simultaneous observations of comparable markets (cross sections). In either case, it is necessary to observe variations in prices and quantities sold as various market conditions change, in order to trace the shapes of the demand and supply curves and how they shift. The use of time-series data versus cross-sectional data has important ramifications for interpreting the results of the model.[5] Models based on cross-sectional data usually operate under the assumption that the market is in a long-term equilibrium, and thus price elasticities calculated from the models are interpreted as long-term elasticities.[6] Models based on time-series data provide estimates of short-run elasticity, corresponding to the time unit of the data. (For example, monthly sales data reflect price elasticity on approximately a monthly time scale.) In general, one expects short-run price elasticities to be smaller in absolute magnitude (i.e., result in a smaller quantity change for a given price change) than long-term elasticities because people generally are better able to adjust to price changes in the long run by substituting other goods, thereby resulting in a larger change in consumption or production for a given price change.

Models Based on Individual Behavior

In contrast to market models derived using aggregate data, natural resource and environmental economists often model behavior using data on individual choices. These choices may be observed directly by the researcher, elicited by a survey, or drawn from a secondary data source, such as logbooks filled out by fishermen. An individual-level decision model looks at observations of choices or responses to questions by a representative sample of a larger population. The models can then be used to extrapolate predicted behavior to the larger population and are often used to reveal the net benefits to users or consumers (consumer surplus) from specific activities or goods.

Individual-level data provide "a close congruence between data and theory,"[7] but collecting this data can be expensive and extrapolating predictions from these models to the broader population can sometimes be problematic and controversial (as discussed later in this chapter). Nevertheless, individual-level modeling is often necessitated because there are no market data (e.g., when the good or service in question is not bought and sold in a formal market) or because many of the goods in question are available without charge (either provided by the government or by nature) or for a nominal fee that does not reflect a market-clearing price. In these cases, there are no readily available data that will reveal the value people place on the good or service or how their decisions to use it may be affected by changes in its quality. This often occurs in the use of coastal recreation amenities, such as beaches and recreational boating or fishing. So, if one is unable to get the data needed to evaluate how total demand for these goods changes as their price changes, one uses observations of individual decisions to infer the value put on use of the good (revealed preference models) and how their level of use is affected by factors that influence the quality of the good or the implicit cost to the individual of using it (e.g., travel time to the beach). Alternatively, one has to rely on approaches that survey individuals (stated preference models) to determine how decisions to use an ecosystem service would be affected by changes in its quality or the cost of accessing it.

Individual-level models have some advantages over aggregate data models that, in some cases, make them preferable, even for goods traded in formal markets where aggregate data are readily available and inexpensive. For example, individual choice modeling can be useful to differentiate the behavior of different population segments and to understand what factors or attributes of goods and services determine the value people place on them and their decisions to purchase or use the goods. An individual-level approach based on stated choices or actual choice experiments may also be necessary when considering a new product or product variation for which there are no available market data.

There are several types of economic models that utilize individual-level data to model behavior and estimate the value of various goods and services. Models such as the travel-cost model, contingent valuation, or hedonic pricing (see chapter 4) are designed specifically to determine the value people place on something but generally are not used for modeling behavior, in the sense of predicting active choices made by people in how they allocate their time and resources to use an ecosystem good or service. This chapter focuses on economic behavioral models that are generally referred to as random utility models and are more useful for modeling participation and use decisions. The emphasis here is on the rationale for using these models, their applications, and how they can be used to predict participation and use of ecosystem goods and services. (Chapter 4 discusses in more detail how these and other models can be used for valuation.)

The Random Utility Model

Random utility models (RUMs) are used to model people's choices among discrete alternatives, as a function of the characteristics of those alternatives and the attributes of individual decisionmakers. Models of individual choice may be estimated statistically (i.e., the parameters of the model are determined by finding those that provide predictions that best fit the data), by actually observing behavior (revealed preference models), or by using surveys that ask respondents to choose among alternative choices, or rank or rate them (stated preference models). RUMs have been used to model choices for a wide variety of things, including recreational choices, such as which beach to visit; location choices of both commercial fishermen and anglers; transportation choices, such as train versus plane; and policy choices, such as where to site a landfill or whether and where to preserve open space.[8] How the choice is modeled can be binomial (e.g., yes or no) or a choice among several alternatives. Figure 3.2 illustrates a more complicated decision tree that considers whether or not to recreate, then what type of recreation, and finally where to recreate.

If the model is designed correctly and is restricted to observations of choices by a sample of individuals who are representative of a larger population, then the model can be used to predict how choices of that population will be affected by changes in the attributes of the alternatives. RUMs are often used to determine how specific attributes of the good and changes in its attributes affect its value to people. If certain conditions are met,[9] one can approximate the net benefits that the population derives from its use of the good and how those benefits would be affected by changes in the attributes of the good or by elimination of access to it (e.g., reduction in water quality at a beach or closure of the beach). One can also understand how individuals trade off attributes against each other (e.g., distance from home versus congestion at a beach) without monetizing the value of the attributes.

FIGURE 3.2 EXAMPLE OF A DECISION STRUCTURE FOR A RANDOM UTILITY MODEL THAT CONSIDERS DECISIONS ON MULTIPLE TYPES OF RECREATION

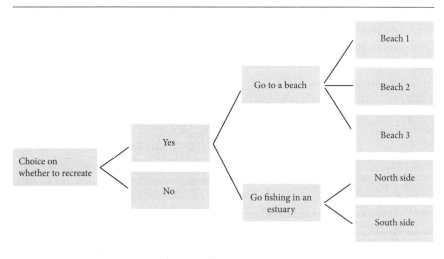

Box 3.3 A Random Utility Model of Fishing Location Choice Response to Determine Costs and Effort

Redistribution

Restrictions on fishing location choices or practices can initially be expected to reduce the profitability of fishermen, but the net losses will depend on the value of the alternative choices still available. Net losses can be estimated by comparing the revenues or, preferably, the profits that the displaced fishermen can expect to make from their next most valuable option relative to the restricted option. Curtis and Hicks (2000) and Hicks, Kirkley, and Strand (2004) used location-choice models to estimate welfare losses associated with area closures. Specifically, they calculated the amount of money necessary after the closure of some sites to hold utility at a level as if the closures never happened (equivalent variation).

To estimate a RUM, the analyst compiles data on people's choices from a set of discrete alternatives available to them (e.g., beaches A, B, and C) or their choices to select or not select alternatives. Information about the characteristics of the alternatives they are choosing between is also needed, such as how large the beach is, how crowded, how clear the water is, etc. The analyst may also have information specific to the individuals that affects the utility of the alternatives they face, for example, the distance of beaches A, B, and C from the individual's house. The analyst proposes a utility function with parameters that allow utility to increase or decrease as a function of the attributes of the activity chosen. The analyst observes the individual's choices and assumes that the alternative chosen generates the highest expected utility or benefit for that individual. The parameters of the model are fitted (adjusted) to maximize the correspondence between the choices the model predicts provide the highest utility and the actual observed or stated choices.

Utility is a function of characteristics of the alternative and of the individual—that is, one can allow for the model to predict different choices based on combinations of the characteristics of the choices, in conjunction with the characteristics of the individual making the choice. These character- istics may be described by a combination of variables, including continuous numbers (e.g., miles from the individual's home to the beach), categorical variables (e.g., whether the water at the beach is clear, partially transparent, or opaque), or presence (absence) of a characteristic (e.g., whether there are lifeguards at a beach). The model estimates the probability of individuals choosing various choices and how that probability changes if the attributes of the choices are changed.

RUMs can be estimated either with data on actual choices or with data from a survey. For example, when modeling location choices in a commercial fishery, it may be possible to rely on data routinely collected by regulators, such as logbooks that tell when and where fishermen fished and what they caught. These data are then combined with information that describes the relative quality of the fishing locations, such as average catch rates; variability of catch rates; and other information specific to the fishermen that may also af- fect their location choices, such as their home port and the size of their vessel. If existing data that document individual choices are not available, they can be collected via a survey that presents people with hypothetical choices between alternatives. As with the models based on observations of actual choice, in- formation on the individuals surveyed is also typically collected to determine how the characteristics of the individual, together with those of the alterna- tives, influence choice.

Issues with Defining and Describing Alternatives and Choice Sets

Two important, and not always obvious decisions that the analyst must make are 1) how to determine the set of the discrete alternatives and 2) what char- acteristics should be used to model the utility functions associated with them. These choices must meet the needs of the end user of the model's informa- tion, and the model structure (and the information it is based on) should cor- respond to how the population being modeled perceives and compares the choice alternatives. For example, a policymaker might be interested only in predicting aggregate annual visits to a set of large parks. It may be necessary, however, to collect data on individual visits and the specific activities chosen by the individuals in order to understand what drives individuals' park choic- es. One can aggregate (or extrapolate) from a set of microdata to determine aggregate use of the overall parks. A model with more detailed choices permits the analyst to predict the change in number of visits when some activity is no longer available in a particular park at a certain time of year. A model based only on the number of visits each person made to a park per year and the overall characteristics of the parks will likely not provide such information.

There are, however, costs to adding more choices and more specificity to the model. Generally, more data are required and it is more costly to collect and to compile the extra data. An additional disadvantage stems from the difficulty in explaining complex models to stakeholders. Achieving a balance among realism, complexity, and transparency requires close interaction between the analyst and the users of the analysis.

Ideally, how alternatives are depicted will correspond closely to the way people perceive the choices. Thus, it is important to carefully identify the populations whose behavior the analyst wants to model. For models based on survey data, the modeler can control the definitions and descriptions of the alternatives. When designing a survey, it makes sense to describe alternatives and their characteristics in terms similar to the way that people think and talk about them. For example, a survey would not use technical terms for water quality, but might describe the water as clear, safe to swim in, safe to eat fish caught from it, etc.[10] It is standard procedure to conduct interviews or focus groups to elicit how choices are perceived (and described) by the respondent individuals and to design the survey to be consistent with these perceptions and commonly used language. This interaction can also determine what characteristics of alternatives affect choices and should be included in descriptions of the alternatives.

In some cases, the alternatives facing individuals are not unambiguous, discrete units, so the analyst may be forced to invent somewhat artificial choice alternatives to match data availability. For example, a fisherman may choose to set his gear for short periods in several specific locations, but the analyst may have data only on how much time a fisherman spent in a few large areas on a monthly basis. Even when data limitations constrain how alternatives are defined and what variables are used to characterize them, interviews or focus groups are useful to determine which variables should be included in the model. They may also be critical when interpreting the results of the analysis.

RUMs have often been used to quantify ways in which attributes of an alternative affect the value of that alternative, relative to other choices. For example, suppose one is primarily concerned with how catch rates affect the relative desirability and value of fishing locations. In this case, it may be sufficient to model the choice among a set of fishing locations. However, if the model needs to predict overall fishing effort by location or the overall net benefits of improvement in catch rates in one or more locations, then the model should include a decision to fish versus doing something else. If the overall level of fishing effort can be predicted independently—perhaps because it is tightly constrained by regulations—it may be sufficient to model only the probabilities of alternative location choices and multiply these by total effort.[11] However, if total effort is determined by the quality of the fishing alternatives available relative to nonfishing alternatives, then the model may need to include the participation decision, as well as the location choice.[12] Effectively, this widens the choice set, but it also simply aggregates all the nonfishing alternatives. A potential problem is that the model is unlikely to represent the value of an aggregate alternative well, since it is actually comprised of many different alternatives that differ for each person. Modeling the nonfishing alternatives explicitly may provide superior predictions but will also add model complexity and increase data needs. As a result of these and other issues, RUM models usually require an analyst experienced in both theory and empirical methods.

Issues with Aggregation from Individual Models

To apply models of individual choice to determine outcomes that may be based on the choices of a large number of people, one must aggregate the predictions of the models in a way that is consistent with the population of individual decisionmakers being modeled and accounts for the potential interconnectedness of their decisions. In general, the model will (or should) have attempted to use a sample of observations of choice decisions that is representative of the population being modeled. If one has no need to differentiate the choice behavior of different population segments, the model may simply utilize a random sample of observations or people to survey. In this case, calculating an aggregate response to a choice scenario may be as simple as taking the average choice predictions from the model and multiplying them by the population size. For example, if a model based on data from a survey of a random sample of all Massachusetts residents predicts that 10% of residents would pay a 5% premium for electricity from a renewable source like wind power, and 5% of the population would pay a 15% premium, it is a simple calculation to determine the number of Massachusetts residents who would opt to switch to renewable electricity at different price premiums.

In some cases, however, one may also want to predict the behavior of particular market segments. If the data used to estimate the model include individual characteristics, such as demographics, and these prove to be statistically significant predictors of choices, then the model can be used to predict choice probabilities that are representative of different population segments. These results are multiplied by the number of people in each segment to obtain aggregate results. This can be useful for understanding the distribution of benefits across groups, since various policies or events may have quite unequal impacts on different groups and perhaps create winners as well as losers. Understanding these distributional impacts may also be useful for predicting whether a policy will be accepted (particularly if it is subject to a referendum) and may help policymakers craft policies with more desirable distributional effects.

If people's decisions are interconnected, this can cause additional difficulties in making predictions about aggregate decisions. An important example of this is a case in which the number of people making a choice tends to reduce the benefits for those making that choice—commonly called congestion externalities. For example, if more people use a road, it creates congestion and increases the time, fuel costs, and annoyance for those driving on it. Similarly, more people visiting a remote beach will reduce the quality of the experience for visitors who were attracted to the beach because of the lack of congestion. If this problem can be foreseen, it may be possible to incorporate it in the model structure and adjust the survey instrument or data collection accordingly. For example, the attribute of crowdedness can be included in a survey instrument designed to predict beach visits to different sites.

Aggregation over time can also present difficulties, particularly when modeling repeated choice decisions of individuals over time. Choices at one point in time are likely to be affected by earlier choices and possibly by expectations of future choices. When considering consumption of a product or visits to a recreation site, one might expect the marginal value of consumption to decline with additional visits. However, visits to a particular site may also increase the person's knowledge of, or attachment to, the site, causing them to prefer it in future. Several studies of commercial fishermen have found a strong tendency by fishermen to return to locations (or use the same fishing strategies) where they had fished previously.[13]

Incorporating Behavioral Models into Biophysical-Economic Models

Combined models of ecological, physical, and chemical processes in the coastal marine ecosystem are often needed to understand the benefits people derive from ecosystem services and how those benefits are affected by human actions. For example, analysts might use an ecological model coupled with a model of hydrology to predict how conversion (or restoration) of a wetland or salt marsh will reduce (improve) water quality and shellfish production in an adjacent estuary. Figure 3.3 displays such a framework for a situation where a policymaker is interested in understanding the potential costs and benefits from conversion of a portion of a salt marsh. The arrows symbolize how the effects of reducing the acreage of the salt marsh would flow to various ecological and biophysical aspects of the system. In practice, there are many more characteristics and many of these relationships are interconnected in a nonlinear manner. Here, for simplicity, figure 3.3 encompasses only a few of the characteristics and relationships.

Researchers can quantify the economic costs of the physical and biological changes that result from reducing the salt marsh, using a combination of market and nonmarket valuation methods. In figure 3.3, the costs are highlighted.

FIGURE 3.3   EXAMPLE OF LINKING BIOPHYSICAL, ECOLOGICAL, AND ECONOMIC ENDPOINTS

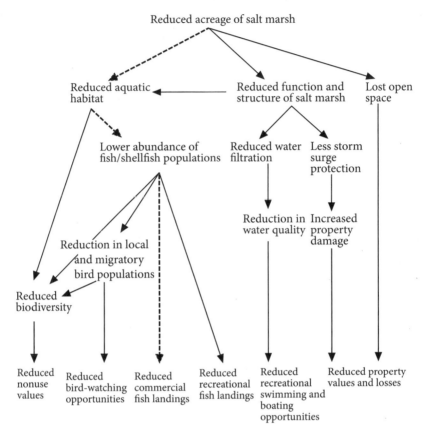

These costs can be compared to the benefits from converting the salt marsh to other uses in order to evaluate the desirability of undertaking the project.[14]

The costs and benefits of the salt marsh conversion project depend on the size and location of the project in the coupled human-natural systems. They also depend on the responses of the individuals to the changes—responses that may be influenced or constrained by policies and regulations, as well as by market conditions and the changing state of the ecosystem itself. Focusing on a small subset of the relationships in figure 3.3 demonstrates the potential conclusions that can be drawn and how this information can better inform decisionmaking for coastal land use. Note particularly how the dashed line traces the changes in the salt marsh to changes in the quality of aquatic habitat, then to changes in abundance of shellfish and fish populations, and finally to the resulting losses to commercial fishing operations from these changes.

Bioeconomic (production) analysis techniques can translate the linkages in figure 3.3 into quantitative effects that could be used in a cost-benefit or cost-effectiveness analysis. For example, as Barbier (2000) noted, "a coastal wetland that serves as breeding and nursery habitat for fisheries could be modeled as part of the growth function of the fish stock, and any welfare impacts of a change in this habitat-support function can be determined in terms of changes in the long-run equilibrium conditions of the fishery or in the harvesting path to this equilibrium."[15] Utilizing the bioeconomic methods discussed by Barbier (2000), figure 3.4 can be derived, which shows the profits for different numbers of vessels fishing for a particular species (or set of species), both with and without the coastal marsh present.

In figure 3.4, the presence of nursery areas provided by coastal wetlands and salt marshes can increase the profitability of the fishermen and potentially permit greater levels of employment (more fishing vessels) than would exist without the wetlands. The flip side of this result is also illustrated in figure 3.4, where one of the potential values of the wetland depends on how many fishing vessels are permitted to fish. If local fishery managers do not control the number of fishing vessels (or fishing effort), the fishery may not gain any value from the wetlands because overfishing offsets the gains from the wetlands. The important role of

FIGURE 3.4   MEASURING THE VALUE OF COASTAL WETLANDS AS THEY CONTRIBUTE TO COMMERCIAL FISHING

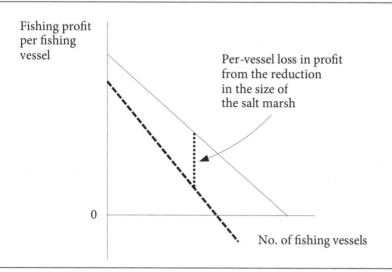

The differences between the lines in figure 3.4 illustrate the extent to which the fishery is more valuable because higher fish population levels are generated by the presence of proximate wetlands, all else equal. For any number of boats, the distance between the two curves represents the increased value of the fishery due to the nursery area of the fish stock. It is even possible that for some levels of fishing effort, the loss in the salt marsh could turn a profitable fishery into one experiencing a loss, seen in figure 3.4 where the curve, once the salt marsh is cleared, goes negative.

governance and institutions in determining the value of ecosystem services is a point often lost in the discussions on the provision of these services.[16]

In situations like that illustrated in figure 3.4, analysts may need to consider whether changes in use will occur as a result of improved or decreased quality of an ecosystem resource (here, a salt marsh) and how those changes will affect the resource. For example, if the changes increase productivity of the shellfish fishery, it may attract new fishermen to the area, leading to a short-term increase in harvests. In turn, this increased fishing pressure may lead to overfishing and reduce harvests in the longer run. By coupling a model that can predict fishing effort and harvesting to the biological model, the analyst may be able to predict the long-run changes with and without additional policies designed to constrain increased harvesting.

How may a coastal planner use the analysis presented in figure 3.4? In addition to the costs of converting the salt marsh, in terms of lost storm protection and lost nonuse values, etc., one can add the costs due to the reduced profits of fishing the species that depend on it. In other words, the larger the development project (in terms of the number of hectares of salt marsh converted), the greater the opportunity costs of converting each additional acre of marsh. The opportunity cost of "supplying" an additional acre of the salt marsh for development can be thought of as a supply curve. It slopes upward because, as each additional acre is lost, the value of the remaining acres, and thus the opportunity cost of losing them, increases. In contrast, the benefits of the development project decrease as the size of the project gets larger—in other words, the marginal value of development decreases so that the marginal benefit curve (the demand curve) slopes downward.

Putting supply and demand curves for salt marsh acres together in figure 3.5 below, the choice of the development project that maximizes the net benefits occurs at the intersection of these supply (marginal cost) and demand (marginal benefit) curves. If coastal land planners do not consider the value to the fishery and choose a development level at the intersection of the lower supply curve (without the value to fisheries included), they are likely to permit a larger development project than would otherwise be allowed. Although not depicted in figure 3.5, it could also be that the opportunity cost of clearing the first acre of the marsh is so high in this particular location that no development project of any size is initiated (costs outweigh the benefits).

The difference between the size of the project that only balances the benefits and costs, with and without considering the wetlands, depends on the same factors that lead to greater fishing profits in figure 3.4. That is, it depends in nontrivial ways on economics, ecology, governance, and the behavioral responses of the individuals within this context. All of these are interconnected, and a model that ignores these interconnections may provide quite misleading results.

Human responses to changes in ecosystem services may also affect benefits without directly impacting the ecosystem. Consider, for example, the results

Box 3.4 Example of Economic-Ecological Model for Valuing the Peconic Estuary System

A study of the Peconic Estuary system salt marsh productivity by Johnston et al. (2002a, 2002b) links ecological and economic models to assess the benefits of improved ecological productivity. The study estimates primary (plant) and bottom (amphipods, worms, etc.) production rates from ecological models and the fraction of the additional production passed up through the food web. It translates this into increases in commercial fish and shellfish production and landings, using average estuarine values and species-specific fishery information for landings from the Peconic Estuary system. The table summarizes their results with respect to the commercial and recreational fishing, where the asset value calculates the net present value of the annual returns over a 25-year period with a 7% discount rate.

NET PRESENT VALUE OF INCREASED FISH AND SHELLFISH PRODUCTION IN COASTAL WETLANDS

	Existing habitats		Created habitats		
Wetland type	*Annual value per acre*	*Asset value per acre*	*Years to become fully functional*	*Asset value per acre*	*Estimated number of acres in PES (millions)*
Eelgrass	$1,065	$12,412	10	$9,996	6.04
Salt marsh	$338	$4,291	15	$3,454	13.51
Intertidal mud flat	$67	$786	3	$626	14.05

Note: PES = Peconic Estuary system

of a beach nourishment program that stabilizes the shoreline position and provides increased protection from storm damage to houses. The expectation that this program will be maintained may encourage more development in the area since the risks to homeowners are reduced, as well as perhaps their insurance premiums. However, the increased development may actually increase the potential damage from storms or erosion that does occur. An assessment of costs and benefits of a long-range beach stabilization program would ideally include an assessment of how it would affect development in the area and how that would affect the overall costs and benefits of the program through time. With this information, policymakers may be able to counteract or mitigate unintended consequences, for example, by implementing policies to discourage development in these areas.

The models used by economists to understand integrated economic-ecological systems often assume that the system in question will tend toward equilibrium (as with the beach nourishment example) and stay there unless some important driver of the system changes (or is changed). By observing the system in a variety of states, it may be possible to statistically estimate the

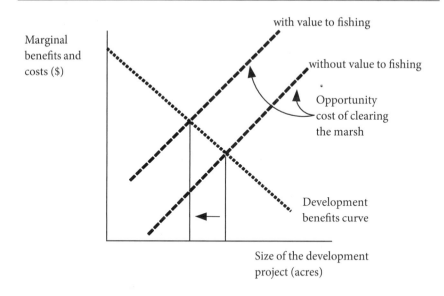

parameters of the model. The assumption underlying the estimation is that the
system was in equilibrium at each point it was observed (much like what is assumed when estimating a supply and demand system). By specifying a structural relationship between observed outcomes (catches, revenue, and effort)
and variables (such as output prices and input costs), the analyst can identify
the parameters of the bioeconomic system.

These bioeconomic models have commonly been used to analyze policies to manage fish catches or fishing effort. One of the most heavily used and
widely known of these models is the Gordon-Schaefer[17] model of a fishery.
This model characterizes the equilibrium outcome of open-access management[18] of a fishery and compares it to optimal outcomes. It can also help one
understand how changes in prices and costs (which could be influenced by
policies such as taxes on fish landings) affect biological and economic outcomes. The model typically assumes that fishermen, in aggregate, will behave
in a certain way—they will increase effort as long as they generate additional
profits by doing so—rather than using an empirically estimated model of fishing behavior. The model incorporates a logistic growth function[19] for the fish
stock that requires knowledge of the intrinsic growth rate of the fish stock
and the carrying capacity of the fishery (e.g., the maximum stock size that the
ecosystem can support with no fishing) to predict the sustainable yield for the
fishery at different effort levels.

The equilibrium models discussed above can be useful for understanding
bioeconomic systems, but they have important caveats that must be considered

---

Box 3.5   Example of Economic-Ecological Model Used to Value Mangrove Habitats

Barbier and Strand (1998) used a bioeconomic model to evaluate the role of mangroves in gross revenues from a shrimp fishery in Campeche, Mexico. They found that mangrove loss has a rather small effect on the fishery and that overexploitation was the main cause of welfare losses. Barbier, Strand, and Sathirathai (2002) used a similar approach to estimate the welfare losses to inshore artisanal fisheries in Thailand from conversion of mangrove swamps for shrimp farming. They estimated losses of consumer surplus of between $11,000 and $408,000 per acre. The range is due to varying assumptions of elasticity of demand about which they had no information. They ignored producer surplus, which was deemed to be zero, as it was a classic open-access fishery.

---

when trying to estimate the parameters of the model from real-world observation. First, the assumption that the system is in equilibrium may be incorrect. If a system is still "adjusting" (i.e., in between states of equilibrium) when it was observed, then the parameters calculated may be substantially biased. Second, these models typically require a simplified model of the system just to be able to generate hypotheses on system behavior. Even if these assumptions are unlikely to hold in a particular setting, which is true more often than not, there remains value in understanding the potential magnitude of these relationships from these simplified models.

An alternative to models that focus on equilibrium outcomes is to incorporate human behavioral responses into a dynamic process-oriented simulation model of the biological, ecological, or physical system. Such approaches often compile information from separate studies on components of the system (e.g., growth rates, migration rates, recruitment rates for different fish species in a multispecies fishery). Box 3.6 has an example of this approach, where simulation models of fish stocks are combined with a model of the fishing to explore the consequences of alternative area closures over time.

Another example of these dynamic simulation models is the work by Wilen et al. (2002) that investigated the effect on model predictions when the model does and does not incorporate behavioral reactions of fishermen. Their work stands in contrast to most of the ecology and fishery biology literature, which "assumes away" behavior, typically by presuming that fishermen do not react to changes in fishery productivity or harvest. Using data from the California red sea urchin fishery, Wilen et al. showed that assumptions of uniform distribution of fishing vessels (and constant fishing mortality) across the fishing grounds provide very different economic and ecological results, compared to a more realistic model in which fishermen are allowed to change the amount and location of their fishing effort (for red sea urchins) in order to maximize fishing benefits. For example, although the aggregate catch was identical, Wilen et al. found that the spatial pattern of harvest was considerably different when

---

Box 3.6   Using Spatial Bioeconomic Models to Analyze Year-Round Fishery Closures

Holland and Sutinen (2000a) combined a model of key fish stocks with an empirically estimated fleet dynamics model of the New England groundfish trawl fleet. Vessel location choices were modeled as a function of relative revenue per unit effort in alternative fishing areas and whether the vessel had fished there in the past. (Vessels in the study were more likely to fish in areas they had fished in the past.) This bioeconomic model was created to explore how permanent marine sanctuaries on Georges Bank might affect fishery catches and revenues and the spawning stock of principal groundfish species in New England. The simulations explored how the location of sanctuaries relative to major ports and their orientation relative to seasonal movement patterns of fish stocks had an impact on the effectiveness of the sanctuaries and the distribution of benefits across groups of fishermen from different ports. The simulation results also demonstrated that the impacts of sanctuaries can vary greatly across species, sometimes increasing yields for some while decreasing yields for others.

---

fishermen were modeled as moving across the system to find the patches with the greatest return. They went on to show that the spatial patterns of fishing altered the predictions of egg production and survival of the red sea urchins across the system. Such changes feed back into the likelihood that each patch's urchin population is sustainable. Hence, implications for system ecology and sustainability depend critically on whether one makes appropriate assumptions regarding human behavior

Dynamic process models also have some disadvantages. First, they may contain a large number of parameters for which accurate values are not available. A solution to this, proposed and analyzed by Johnston et al. (2002b), is to use expert opinion to derive the parameter estimates. Second, some parameters may change over time, even though analysts often assume that they remain constant for the time frame of the analysis. A rigorous analysis would investigate potential biases of these effects with a sensitivity analysis. Such an exercise, however, is difficult and can produce a sometimes too wide range of possible outcomes, if there are many parameters that are not accurately known. Care must also be taken in using parameters that are codependent but have been quantified through independent studies. For example, the growth rate of individual fish might be related to the overall size of the fish cohort, as seems to be true with the large year class of haddock (fish in the stock born in the same year) on Georges Bank.[20] A model that assumes a fixed growth rate from an independent study of haddock length at a certain age will tend to overestimate how the stock biomass will grow. In contrast, a model such as the Gordon-Schaefer model, based on aggregate harvests and biomass, would have implicitly incorporated this compensating effect.

Conclusion

Models that fail to account for human reactions to policy-induced changes can generate misleading results. This chapter has discussed a variety of techniques used by economists to model human behavior—the choices of people and firms in consuming and producing various goods and services. Standard economic models of demand and supply based on aggregate market data may be useful for evaluating use and value of goods and services that are bought and sold in competitive markets. However, for many ecosystem goods and services, market data are not available because often there is no market. In these cases, analysts can utilize models based on observations of the choices individuals make to forecast the underlying utility associated with these goods and services. The models may be based on observations of actual behavior or on choices elicited through surveys. These models can also be used to predict individuals' decisions to utilize ecosystem resources and how these decisions might be affected by policy changes. These same models can be used to predict aggregate outcomes and quantify the value of ecosystem goods and services and how these values may be affected by various projects or policies being considered.

Behavioral models can be used to translate the results from biological and physical models into economic terms and human impacts. In cases where human behavior will affect the future production or quality of the ecosystem good or service in question, it may be useful to construct models that integrate the natural and human systems and provide predictions that incorporate their interdependence. Models of complex, coupled human and natural systems may often provide inexact predictions due to uncertainty about the true structure of the system or unpredictable factors that affect the system. However, these models still provide useful qualitative insights and can provide probabilistic bounds on outcomes that can guide decisionmaking.

Endnotes

1. While the most common approach used by economists to model human decision-making under uncertainty is expected utility theory, cognitive psychologists and behavioral economists have shown that *individual* decisionmaking under uncertainty often diverges from normative behavioral models based on expected utility theory (Rabin 2000, Camerer 2000). Prospect theory (Kahneman and Tversky 1979) is an alternative approach to understanding human behavior under uncertainty. McFadden (1999) provides an excellent review of prospect theory and a variety of other theories and observations about human decisionmaking under uncertainty that conflict with expected utility theory.
2. See, for example, Wilen et al. (2002).

3. The price of goods that might be produced locally but have near perfect substitutes produced in competitive national or global markets (e.g., frozen seafood or produce), may be unresponsive to changes in local production. Prices may fluctuate in the short term in response to a temporary imbalance of supply and demand, but in general it is reasonable to assume that prices are determined by the national or global market.

4. See, for example, Judge et al. (1988, *ch. 15*) and Green (2000, *ch. 16*).

5. Boardman et al. (2001).

6. The term "elasticity" in this context refers to the relative responsiveness of quantity demanded or supplied to changes in price. Quantities that are more elastic are more responsive to price changes. Less elastic quantities are less responsive to price changes.

7. Boardman et al. (2001, *316*).

8. For recreational choices (which beach to visit), see Bockstael et al. (1987) and Haab and Hicks (1997). For location choices by commercial fishermen and anglers, see Adamowicz (1994), Bockstael et al. (1989), Feather et al. (1995), McConnell et al. (1995), Milon (1988), and Parsons and Needelman (1992), plus Johnston et al. (2006) for a meta-study. For transportation choices, see papers compiled in Brog et al. (1981), Hensher and Stopher (1979), and Stopher and Meyberg (1975). For policy choices on sites for a land fill, see Swallow et al. (1992), and for whether and where to preserve open space, see McGonagle and Swallow (2005).

9. See discussion in Freeman (2003, *470*).

10. Johnston et al. (1995).

11. See, for example, Holland and Sutinen (1999).

12. See, for example, Smith and Wilen (2003).

13. See, for example, Eales and Wilen (1986), Smith and Wilen (2003), and Holland and Sutinen (2000).

14. See, for example, Boyd et al. (2004) for a further discussion of bioeconomic models and other techniques for the assessment of habitat benefits.

15. Barbier (2000, *49*).

16. Barbier (2000), Boyd et al. (2004), and Sanchirico (2007).

17. See, for example, Gordon (1954).

18. In open-access fisheries, there is no rule on who can fish and no limits on how many can fish for the resource. It is often used synonymously with unmanaged fishery.

19. The logistic growth function specifies growth of the fish stock X as a function of intrinsic growth r, and carrying capacity K. If harvest H equals growth, then the fishery is in equilibrium and the harvest could, in theory, be taken indefinitely while maintaining the fish stock at the same level, $\dfrac{dX}{dt} = rX(1 - \dfrac{X}{K}) - H\cdot$

   Harvest in the common Gordon-Schaefer model is assumed to be a function of effort E, a catchability coefficient q, and the fish stock $H = qEX$.

20. See Brodziak and Traver (2006, rev.).

CHAPTER 4

Nonmarket Valuation of Ecosystem Services and Environmental Resources

U nderstanding the economic benefits and costs of EBM helps ensure that decisions are fully informed and that policies improve (rather than reduce) social welfare. As detailed in previous chapters, assessment of benefits and costs is simplified when affected commodities are traded in markets. (The term "commodity" here encompasses all goods, services, and resources through which humans derive value or benefit.) That is, market exchange with observable prices facilitates straightforward assessment of economic benefits and costs. However, market exchange is not required in order to quantify economic value. As Freeman (2003) stated, "the basis of deriving measures of the economic value of changes in resource-environment systems is the effects of the changes on human welfare."[1] Chapter 2 describes how both market commodities and commodities that are not traded on markets influence human welfare (or well-being). The latter are broadly characterized as nonmarket commodities, and when ecosystem processes provide them, they are often called nonmarket ecosystem services.

This idea is not new; economists have long sought to quantify the human benefits derived from nonmarket commodities, including goods, services, and natural resources. Methods through which this quantification is accomplished come under the general category of nonmarket valuation.[2] Simply put, nonmarket valuation seeks to quantify the effects of nonmarket commodities—or commodities that are not exchanged in organized markets—on human well-being. These effects are usually monetized (expressed in monetary units) to allow straightforward aggregation or comparison of these effects across different individuals or groups, and to allow comparison to policy costs, which often appear in monetary terms.

As described in chapter 2, economists' ability to monetize market or nonmarket benefits relies on the concept of substitution—that the welfare gained through increases in one market or nonmarket commodity can be offset by decreases in other commodities. Nonmarket values are often expressed in terms

73

of willingness to pay (WTP). This is the maximum amount of money that a person would be willing to give up voluntarily (or substitute) in exchange for a commodity rather than go without. Drawing on the concept of substitution, this implies that the welfare provided by the commodity in question is identical to the welfare provided by that amount of money (or by the bundle of goods and services that would be purchased with that money). In other words, WTP is a measure of the value of the commodity to the individual and also reflects the welfare that the commodity provides. WTP may be measured for individuals, households, or groups.

Nonmarket valuation usually is required to quantify the full range of economic benefits and costs related to ocean and coastal management. As noted previously in this book, much of what people value in ocean and coastal systems—for example, natural commodities such as open space, attractive views, good beaches, and good water quality, and living resources such as marine mammals—is not bought and sold in markets. In other cases, commodities that are bought and sold in markets in some forms (e.g., fish and shellfish) may also provide values through nonmarket channels (e.g., recreational fishing or oystering). Market analysis does not capture the full value of these ecosystem goods and services. In environmental policy contexts, such as EBM, it is not unusual for nonmarket values to constitute the majority of total economic (market plus nonmarket) value. Hence, in the absence of nonmarket valuation, the value that the public holds for environmental and natural resource commodities affected by EBM may be underappreciated, ignored, or assumed to be zero. As a result, policy decisions may not reflect the true value of natural systems to the public. In many cases, ignoring the nonmarket economic values associated with (often less tangible) ecosystem goods and services may inappropriately favor activities that promote development or market activity and degrade natural resources.

Measuring nonmarket values is not always easy. Given the diversity of resource issues in coastal and marine environments, multiple nonmarket studies are often required to assess the full range of relevant nonmarket values. When considering activities such as swimming, boating, and recreational fishing, for example, comprehensive estimation of net benefits requires measurement of the economic values associated with nonmarket recreational uses. In other cases, coastal resources may provide aesthetic or other location-specific amenities (such as unobstructed ocean views) or disamenities (such as mosquito nuisance from coastal wetlands or flood risk),[3] which may be reflected in local property values. Residents or visitors may also benefit from the simple knowledge that resources such as shellfish beds, migratory fish runs, salt marshes, threatened species, or other resources are preserved or restored, whether or not they directly use these resources. Given these and many other sources of nonmarket benefits associated with ocean and coastal resources, no single valuation methodology can measure and distinguish all aspects of economic value. As a result, CBA that informs EBM often includes a combination of different methodologies, each designed to measure a different aspect of non-market value. (See chapter 2 for additional discussion of this topic.)

For example (as discussed in case study 2 in appendix A), sand mining and beach nourishment may have a number of effects on beach recreation (such as changes in beach size), commercial and recreational fisheries (such as damage to fish habitat at offshore sand-mining sites), property values (such as erosion of beachside property or increased attractiveness of nearby beaches), and other sources of market and nonmarket value. No single market or non-market valuation method can measure the total economic benefits and costs associated with all of these potential effects. Although individual methods may provide valuable information on specific aspects of benefits or costs, they may also create the false impression that resources or values that are not addressed have negligible economic value. In contrast, a carefully coordinated combination of different nonmarket valuation methods can often provide a more complete understanding of economic values.[4] However, researchers must exercise caution when aggregating benefits generated by different types of nonmarket valuation methods because these values often overlap. As a result, simple summation of values across different studies may double count some components of nonmarket value (i.e., count the same value twice).

Although nonmarket valuation methods provide important economic information that is not available through other means, applications of these methods can be challenging and sometimes controversial. In some cases, government agencies have been reluctant to assign monetary values to goods or services that they view as intangible. For example, some individuals may derive welfare simply from the knowledge that certain resources—endangered marine mammals, for example—exist in natural ecosystems. The value of coastal recreation can be enhanced by difficult to quantify changes in ecosystem conditions or the abundance of wildlife. Appropriate valuation may also require that one identify and quantify linkages between ecosystem processes (or properties) and human welfare—linkages that may be poorly understood in some instances.

For example, reducing the nutrient loading in estuaries may have myriad effects on ecosystem goods and services valued by people, many of which may be difficult to track and quantify accurately through ecological systems. Similarly, damage to benthic habitat (the bottom of the sea, including the organisms that live there) due to dredging or fishing activities may affect many different resources that convey benefits both in and outside markets (e.g., different fish species that are valued both for commercial and recreational purposes). However, it is not always easy to link changes in habitat to quantifiable changes in fish or other affected resources. Although this challenge is largely due to the difficulty of quantifying *ecological* relationships, it nonetheless influences economists' ability to estimate the values that are derived from these systems. Despite these and other challenges, many economists believe that it is both practical and defensible to estimate nonmarket values for ecosystem goods and services and, moreover, that the development of well-informed policy *requires* at least some insight into these values. Because of these and other factors, nonmarket valuation has become a vital component of environmental CBA.[5]

Appropriate nonmarket valuation analyses can be costly in terms of both time and money. For some small-scale policy changes, investing tens or hundreds of thousands of dollars in an appropriate suite of nonmarket valuation studies may not make sense. In other instances, investing in such studies—although costly at the outset—may prevent the misallocation of resources or otherwise poor decisionmaking that could result in social losses that are far greater than the cost of the studies. Hence, when deciding whether to conduct nonmarket valuation research, policymakers must consider the size of the policy in relation to the likely impacts on nonmarket goods and services, as well as the cost of the required data collection.

When considering whether to engage in nonmarket valuation, the decisionmaker typically has four options:

1) Conduct primary studies to estimate all or the most significant nonmarket values associated with the policy.
2) Conduct primary studies to estimate a targeted set of nonmarket values that are likely the most significant in the policy context.
3) Use benefit transfer—the use of values estimated in a different policy context and based on research conducted elsewhere—to approximate some or all nonmarket values.
4) Not to estimate nonmarket values.

Of these options, the first is sometimes prohibitively costly, and the fourth risks substantial welfare losses to society, that is, the losses of economic benefits due to poorly conceived policy. The decision to use benefit transfer or conduct a set of targeted primary studies often depends on 1) the availability of data for the policy or site in question, 2) the availability of high-quality studies that have been conducted for similar policies and sites elsewhere, and 3) whether policymakers require exact, tailored values or can make do with approximations from benefit transfer. In some instances, policymakers may choose primary research studies to estimate some nonmarket benefits and use benefit transfer to measure others. Despite the potential for nontrivial valuation errors associated with benefit transfer, it is among the most commonly applied methods for nonmarket valuation by government agencies.[6]

The remainder of this chapter summarizes the nonmarket valuation techniques that are most applicable to the types of policies encountered as part of EBM. For each method, the chapter includes discussion of the types of values estimated and the data required. It also explains the basics of benefit transfer—or the use of value estimates measured elsewhere to approximate values in a particular policy context that are not the target of the original study—as well as the tradeoffs made when choosing between benefit transfer and original studies.[7]

Types of Nonmarket Values and Valuation Methods

Ecosystem services and related commodities can be direct (beaches, fish, or other commodities subject to direct human use) or indirect (the contribution of coastal wetlands to the natural production of fish harvested elsewhere). These commodities may be traded in traditional markets with market prices and values (e.g., fish or shellfish harvested commercially and sold to consumers). They may also be available outside traditional markets, so that nonmarket approaches are needed to estimate economic values (e.g., uses such as recreational fishing and wildlife viewing). The social relevance of economic values is *not* related to whether values are realized in markets or are otherwise related to money transactions—nonmarket values are just as relevant and real as market values.

Market values are almost always *use values*, or values related to some observable human use of the resource or service in question. Nonmarket values, in contrast, may include both use and nonuse values. *Nonuse values* are improvements in human welfare that are not linked to any present or planned future use. Examples of nonuse values are *existence values* and *bequest values*. Existence values relate purely to the existence of a natural resource (e.g., being willing to pay to sustain a viable population of north Atlantic right whales simply because one values their existence). Bequest values come from the desire to pass on resources, goods, or services to future generations. Nonuse values also include those conveyed by altruism in some instances (e.g., being willing to pay for resource improvements because they contribute to others' use or enjoyment). Unlike use values, which usually require some proximity to the nonmarket commodity in question (i.e., in order to use the commodity), nonuse values can be held by respondents regardless of their physical location. For example, one can value the continued existence of specific species of sea turtles regardless of where one lives or whether one ever has the opportunity to experience these animals.

The type of values that are likely to be present determines the choice of nonmarket valuation method. *Revealed preference methods*, also called indirect methods, are based on analyses of observed human behavior or use of a resource. Such methods can only measure use values. *Stated preference methods* are based on the analysis of responses to carefully designed survey questions. These methods, while sometimes more controversial because of their reliance on survey responses, are able to measure both use and nonuse values. There are also *hybrid* methods that do not fit neatly into either category. Table 4.1 briefly compares the more common nonmarket valuation methods in these three categories.

TABLE 4.1 MAJOR NONMARKET VALUATION TECHNIQUES AND EXAMPLES

Type of method	Method	Measures nonuse values?	Description	Example application
Revealed preference				
	Recreation-demand models	No	Analyzes recreational behavior (site choice and/or number of trips) used to estimate recreational use values.	Layman et al. (1996) estimated the recreational value of the Gulkana River (Alaska) Chinook salmon fishery to anglers under current management conditions.
	Hedonic property value methods	No	Analyzes observed property values used to estimate location-dependent use values related to quality of life in particular areas.	Leggett and Bockstael (2000) estimated the effect of water quality on residential property values along Chesapeake Bay.
	Hedonic wage methods	No	Analyzes observed wages used to estimate location-dependent use values related to quality of life in particular areas.	Viscusi (1993) used wage differentials to assess the value of risk reductions to workers.
	Defensive behavior methods	No	Analyzes costs required to avoid or avert damages associated with losses of ecosystem services or environmental quality, including replacement-cost methods. In most cases, defensive behavior methods do *not* provide valid, exact measures of value (see discussion below).	Abdalla et al. (1992) used household avoidance costs to estimate economic losses resulting from groundwater contamination in a southeastern Pennsylvania community.
Stated preference				
	Contingent valuation	Yes	Analyzes open-ended willingness-to-pay survey questions.	Roberts and Leitch (1997) calculated the value of recreation, aesthetics, and habitat of Mud Lake (Minnesota–South Dakota).

Continued

TABLE 4.1   MAJOR NONMARKET VALUATION TECHNIQUES AND EXAMPLES (Cont.)

Contingent choice/ ranking	Yes	Analyzes surveys presenting referendum- or voting-type choice (or ranking) questions to respondents.	Johnston (2006) estimated residents' willingness to pay for public water supply improvements in Scituate, RI.
Choice experiments/ modeling	Yes	Analyzes surveys presenting choices across multi-attribute goods or policies.	Johnston et al. (2002b; 2005) estimated Rhode Island residents' willingness to pay for multiple-attribute salt marsh restoration programs in the state.
Other/hybrid			
Ecological productivity methods	Sometimes	Methods are distinguished by the combination of a natural science model of ecological productivity with an economic model estimating values of increased/ decreased production. Economic model component may be a market model, revealed preference method, stated preference method, or other.	Johnston et al. (2002a) estimated the economic value of eelgrass, salt marshes, and sand/mud bottoms in the Peconic Estuary of Long Island, NY, based on the value of the fish, shellfish, and bird species produced by these ecosystems.
Revealed/stated preference techniques	Sometimes	Methods combine observations of behavior (revealed methods) with survey questions that assess responses to hypothetical situations (stated methods) to estimate use and/or nonuse values.	Layman et al. (1996) combined revealed and stated data to contrast the recreational value of the Gulkana River (Alaska) Chinook salmon fishery under current and hypothetical management conditions.
Benefit transfer	Sometimes	Approximates of site- or policy-specific values using data or models generated for other sites and/or policies, often based on findings in the published literature.	Morrison and Bennett (2004) used benefit transfer to approximate values associated with ecological river improvements in New South Wales, Australia.

Revealed Preference Methods

Revealed preference or indirect valuation methods use data on observable human behavior to estimate economic value where no markets exist for the ecosystem resources, goods, or services under study. These methods provide value estimates that are conceptually identical to market values but must be measured using alternative approaches because market data are unavailable. These methods analyze data on human uses or behavior and so cannot measure nonuse values (because nonuse values are by definition unrelated to observable uses).[8]

There are many potential applications of revealed preference methods to ocean and coastal policies. For example, models of recreational behavior can be used to quantify recreational use values associated with beach nourishment, water-quality improvements, changes in fish abundance, or other EBM outcomes. Hedonic property value models can estimate potential welfare impacts on coastal residents related to changes in coastal aesthetics, water quality, flood risk, or other policy changes that affect residents' quality of life. Defensive behavior and damage cost models analyze data on costs and behavior used to mitigate or avoid losses due to environmental changes, or monetized damages caused by environmental events; unlike other revealed preference methods, these methods usually provide only approximations or upper and lower bounds of total value. They can, nonetheless, provide defensible and otherwise unavailable estimates of value for some types of coastal and ocean policies.

Recreation Demand Models

Outdoor recreation is a major activity in coastal and marine areas, and the economic value associated with recreation is substantial. Human impacts (e.g., pollution or overfishing) on the natural resources that support coastal and marine recreation can impose significant economic losses on different user groups. Coastal resources, such as beaches, marine parks, and coral reefs, are usually open to the public for recreation free of charge or for a nominal fee. As a result, although these resources are valued for recreational use, the lack of free-market price information prevents value estimation using market methods. For example, one cannot purchase a "beach day" or a good ocean fishing spot at the market. However, individuals do engage in costly travel and other observable behavior in order to obtain recreation benefits, and data on these behaviors can be used to indirectly estimate associated economic values. This is the basis of revealed preference methods for recreational valuation, often called recreation demand models.

Recreation demand models provide a means to assess the demand for resources used for recreation and to estimate the value associated with their use. These models are often applied to resource-dependent activities, such as

fishing, boating, swimming and other beach activities, clamming and oystering, hiking and walking, birding, and so on. These models were first conceptualized in the 1940s and have been used extensively since the early 1960s to assess the value of recreational resources that are not traded in formal markets.[9]
They are among the most commonly applied nonmarket valuation methods.

As stated by the U.S. EPA (2000), "recreation demand models focus on the
choice of trips or visits to sites for recreation purposes. The basic tradeoff to be
considered is between the satisfaction gained from participating in an activity
at a site and the value of money and time given up."[10] The basic premise underlying these models is that the costs required to travel to a recreation site (travel
costs) are treated as a price of access to the site. Visitors travel (either actually
or potentially) from different places to visit a site of interest. Often the site has
recreational value because of a particular natural resource, such as clean water
at a beach or fish populations in a river or stream. Because individuals incur
different travel costs to visit the site (i.e., it is more costly for some people to
visit the site than for others, largely because they travel varying distances), one
would expect to see different visitation rates.

This variation of visitation rates, as influenced by travel costs, defines the
estimated demand relationships through which values are estimated. As the
quality of a recreational site improves, one would expect to see an increase
in the demand for visits to that site (the number of trips) or an increase in
individuals' willingness to engage in costly travel to reach that site. Different
versions of the recreation demand model assess such relationships using different theoretical and empirical approaches, but the basic concept is similar.
For example, some approaches are based on observing the number of trips that
individuals take to a single site (or set of sites), while others analyze choices between alternative sites. (Chapter 3 provides additional detail.) Based on these
estimated relationships, researchers can calculate visitation rates and resource
values related to the use of a natural resource (or site), or changes in values
caused by changes in environmental or other conditions.

As a straightforward example, consider the difference in the number of
beach visits (demand) that pollution from polychlorinated biphenyls (PCBs)
in a specific coastal area might cause. A simple individual travel cost model
might calculate two demand curves for each beach: a demand curve for visits in the absence of pollution (or prior to a polluting event) and a demand
curve for the identical but polluted beach. As a result of the shift in demand
due to pollution, the number of annual visits by an average individual would
decline from X_1 to X_2. The difference between the consumer surplus estimates
generated from these two demand curves would be the economic recreation
value lost due to the PCB pollution.[11] This difference is shown as area *ABCD*
in figure 4.1.

Two main classes of recreation demand model are used in contemporary
analysis: the *individual travel cost* model (both one site and multiple sites) and
the *random utility* (or *discrete choice*) *travel cost* model.[12] Individual travel cost

FIGURE 4.1 CONSUMER SURPLUS LOSS DUE TO HAZARDOUS WASTE POLLUTION

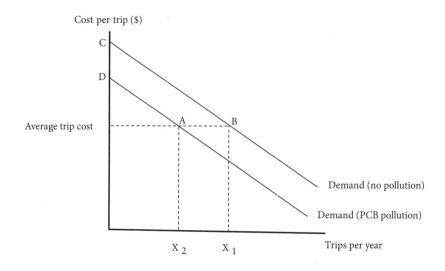

models assess recreational behavior through surveys and observed behavior of individual visitors. Using survey questions, researchers estimate the number of trips and travel costs incurred by individuals, focusing either on trips to a single site of interest (the single-site model), or several different (substitute) sites (multiple-site models). These data are used to estimate the average demand for visits to particular sites, often as a function of environmental quality variables or other policy goals. Discrete choice (also called random utility) travel cost models address travel behavior that is noncontinuous, or that involves a choice between different sites, rather than decisions regarding the number of trips to a single site. That is, the variable of interest is no longer the number of trips but the discrete choice of whether to visit or not to visit particular sites of interest. As a generalization, individual travel cost models are most appropriate for sites that receive many visits per season from each visitor (e.g., a local beach), where the fundamental question is not where to go, but how many times to go to a particular site. Discrete choice models are often best suited to sites that are visited less often per season, where the fundamental choice is among competing sites with similar activities, for example, traveling to different pristine rivers for salmon fishing. Discrete choice, or random utility, recreation demand modeling is discussed in greater detail in chapter 3.

Like all nonmarket valuation methods, recreation demand models require a variety of assumptions and face a number of challenges. These include methods used to estimate individuals' _opportunity cost of time_[13] (necessary to calculate travel costs) and the ways that models allocate travel costs across multipurpose trips (i.e., to quantify the travel cost associated with a single site or purpose when observed trips have multiple purposes). The opportunity cost of time is crucial to recreation demand models because it reflects the value of the time that individuals sacrifice in order to visit a recreation site (and, hence, is an important component of total travel cost). Because the opportunity cost of time is not directly observable, researchers have developed a variety of methods to estimate it. A common approximation is that the opportunity cost of time is equivalent to a fraction of the observable wage rate (one-third of the wage rate is frequently used), although more sophisticated approaches are also used. These approaches account for the fact that different individuals are able to trade off time and money at different rates, and that these rates may not be equal to a fixed proportion of an observable wage.[14] There is an extensive research literature that addresses these and many other technical issues in recreation demand modeling. Much of this literature emphasizes resources relevant to coastal EBM, including beaches and recreational fishing sites.

Box 4.1   Estimation of Estuary Management and Recreational Fishing Benefits

Bergstrom et al. (2004) created a straightforward, individual travel cost model to quantify the relationship between fishing trips and fish caught in the lower Atchafalaya River basin estuary along the Gulf of Mexico. The model also calculated associated economic values. It was based on the equation here that predicts the fishing trips of individual i to site j:

$$TRIPS_{ij} = f(TC_{ij}, CATCH_i, INCOME_i, H_i),$$

where $TRIPS_{ij}$ is the number of trips by individual i to site j; TC_{ij} is the round-trip travel cost for individual i to site j; $CATCH_i$ is the fish catch per trip for individual I; $INCOME_j$ is the household income of individual I; and vector H_j includes demographic and preference attributes of individual i.

Travel costs per individual were calculated as a function of the distance traveled (miles), average cost per mile, travel time to the site, the opportunity cost of time (calculated as one-third of the wage rate), and the size of the group traveling together per trip.

The study area included the 1,965-square-mile area of the lower Atchafalaya River basin, with data gathered from 381 onsite, personal interviews of saltwater anglers at various sites within the basin. The model was estimated using generalized least squares (GLS) regression with a linear-log functional form. The model showed statistically significant impacts of both travel cost and fish catch on angler trips. Interpreting these results, Bergstrom et al. calculated that a 1% increase in fish catch (redfish and speckled trout) would lead to a 0.079% increase in trips for an average angler.

The limited response of trips to travel cost and catch is explained by such factors as the high catch rates of anglers in this region (a small change in catch rate would not have a large impact on overall trip quality) and the importance of noncatch quality factors (such as camaraderie and enjoyment of the outdoors) on angler satisfaction. The authors investigated different specifications of equation (1) and, depending on model assumptions, consumer surplus (or economic value) per angler ranged from $31 to $59 per trip, or between $493 and $948 per year (in 1999 dollars). These results are similar to those reported in similar travel cost studies conducted elsewhere.[15]

Hedonic Property Value Models

Hedonic property value models estimate the impact of land use or other environmental attributes (or characteristics of the property, structure, neighborhood, and location) on the observed value (selling price) of local property. These results reveal what purchasers are willing to pay on the margin for increased levels of particular attributes, which is the implicit price, or marginal value, of these attributes. For example, assume that, holding other factors constant, an average house with an unobstructed ocean view sells for $50,000 more than otherwise identical houses without such a view. The implicit price of an unobstructed ocean view is thus $50,000 and reflects what buyers in that housing market are willing to pay on the margin to obtain an unobstructed ocean view. Alternatively, hedonic property value models can reveal people's willingness to pay to *avoid* attributes that are not desired (e.g., proximity to an airport's flight path or land zoned for industrial use). These models are an accepted and well-established means of estimating the value of residents' use of certain types of environmental changes. For example, one of the arguments that some people make against ocean wind farms is that these installations detract from ocean views and, hence, reduce oceanfront property values. Hedonic property value models can be used to quantify the magnitude of such effects and assess whether such claims are accurate.

The hedonic property value technique is based on the premise that environmental and other amenities (or the attributes) of a residential location provide valued services that increase the welfare of residents nearby, making properties with a high level of valued amenities more attractive, and therefore more valuable, than similar properties with a lower level of such amenities. As stated by the U.S. EPA (2000), "hedonic property value studies assert that individuals perceive housing units as bundles of attributes and derive different levels of utility from different combinations of these attributes. When individuals make transaction decisions, they are making tradeoffs between money and attributes. These tradeoffs reveal the marginal values of these attributes and are central to hedonic property value studies. Hedonic property value studies use statistical regression methods and data from real estate markets to examine the increments in property values associated with different attributes."[16]

A hedonic statistical model simultaneously compares a large number of properties with different prices and attributes, such as site, neighborhood, and environmental characteristics (e.g., a yard that has shade trees or a house that overlooks a valley). Attributes may include, for example, the size of the house or lot; the number of bedrooms, bathrooms, or fireplaces; the year the house was built; the location or look of the neighborhood; and many other characteristics that one would expect to influence the price of residential property. Also, modern hedonic models often include methods that incorporate the effects of spatial patterns on property values (e.g., that higher valued properties tend to be found next to each other, all else being constant). The analyst then estimates the average change in property value related to changes in each particular attribute, controlling for the other attributes. For example, a hedonic model might estimate that the presence of undrinkable groundwater (for properties with wells) reduces property value by either x percent or by y dollars, depending on how the statistical model is specified.

When the hedonic model is applied to an environmental amenity, it estimates the value of the services that the amenity provides to nearby residents. This is measured as the willingness to pay to buy a property with the environmental amenity (e.g., an undisturbed ocean view), compared to an otherwise identical property that does not have (or has less of) the amenity in question. For example, consider developments that affect ocean views, such as an oceanfront high-rise apartment building. Using hedonic methods, one can estimate the marginal impact of this building on property values in the affected area. Distance and location are often crucial factors in these relationships. For example, the effect of a positive amenity on property value (e.g., an attractive beach with clean water) will often be highest for homes adjacent to the amenity and will decline gradually for homes at an increasing distance. After a certain distance, the effect becomes so small that it cannot be estimated. Other patterns are possible, however. For example, the effect of some amenities depends not on physical distance but rather on whether it is possible to see them from a particular location (i.e., the landscape).

Hedonic property value models assume that analyzed real estate markets function smoothly and are in equilibrium. (There is not an excess supply of or demand for houses at current prices.) These models also assume that purchasers have full and reliable information about the presence, absence, and/or level of amenities that might influence their decision to purchase. When conducting such analysis, the quality and completeness of the data are critical; omitted variables and inappropriate model specifications are common challenges in these analyses. Note, too, that values estimated by recreation demand models and hedonic approaches may overlap because a portion of the recreational-use value of certain coastal resources may also be reflected in residents' willingness to pay to live near those resources.[17] Given this potential overlap, hedonic and travel cost estimates of value cannot simply be "added up" in many cases, even though they address mostly distinct elements of value. Finally, some resources will not have significant impacts on property values, but will have values realized through other pathways. For example, some residents might have nonuse values for the preservation of historic New England fishing ports but might have no desire to live near these areas. In such cases, hedonic methods are not appropriate tools for valuation or, at best, provide only a partial perspective.[18]

Box 4.2   Estimation of Property Value Impacts of Preserved Coastal Open Space in Southold, NY

The town of Southold on the north shore of the Peconic Estuary on Long Island (NY) was the focus of a case study for a hedonic property value analysis of scenic and other amenity resource services. The model compiled sales data from Southold property records for all real estate parcels sold in Southold in 1996 and combined these data with land-use and other data from the geographic information system maintained by the Suffolk County Planning Department. Altogether, the data included full information on 374 parcels of land. The model used a standard hedonic regression.

Model results provided insight into the economic gains and losses associated with various policies for future consideration, including preservation of open space, rezoning, and highway construction in the coastal zone. The principal findings of the analysis included:

A parcel of land located adjacent to preserved open space had, on average, a 12.8% higher per-acre value than a similar parcel located elsewhere.

A parcel of land located next to a major area highway had, on average, a 16.2% lower per-acre value than a similar parcel located elsewhere.

A parcel of land located within a district zoned R-80 (two-acre zoning) or R-120 (three-acre zoning) had, on average, a 16.7% higher per-acre value than a similar parcel located elsewhere.

Model results indicated that environmental policies in the Peconic Estuary affect local quality of life, as reflected in residents' willingness to pay to live in specific areas with specific ecosystem services and land-use attributes. These results also provided a framework for forecasting property value impacts of specific land-use changes, as incorporated in an overall estuary management plan. For example, results of the study suggested that zoning variances or rezoning for denser development in current R-80 or R-120 zones would negatively influence per-acre property values.[19]

Defensive Behavior Methods

When the environment is damaged, individuals engage in various activities to offset the negative impact on their welfare. These activities may include defensive behavior (also called *averting behavior* or *cost avoidance behavior*), designed to reduce the exposure to a pollutant or loss of environmental quality. Such behaviors often involve changing activities or purchasing goods to reduce exposure. Examples might include reducing time outdoors to avoid exposure to air pollution, purchasing a water filter to avoid impacts of water contaminants on health, or building a seawall to prevent property damage from flooding. Another class of defensive activity is *mitigating behavior*, or behavior designed to minimize the adverse effects of exposure. For the case of pollutants influencing health, this often involves the purchase of medical care.

In some cases, defensive behavior methods may provide information on the value of environmental improvements (or preventing environmental losses). A related method is the *damage cost method*, in which one simply computes the cost of damages (often medical bills or costs) caused by an environmental loss and uses this as a measure of economic value. However, one might also apply such methods to damages (or preventing damages) from natural events, such as coastal storms. Per the U.S. EPA (2000), "the economic theory underlying the averting behavior method rests on a model of household production. In these models, households produce health benefits by combining an exogenous level of environmental quality with inputs, such as defensive behaviors. The underlying theory predicts that a person will continue to take protective action as long as the perceived benefit exceeds the cost of doing so."[20] Hence, defensive behaviors provide information that may be used, in some instances, to impute values of environmental changes.

Although the information embedded in observations of defensive behaviors can provide insight into human preferences and welfare, these methods (both defensive behavior and damage cost methods) rarely provide theoretically appropriate, exact measures of economic value. Because they are easy to calculate, however, one often encounters them in CBA. Such use is not entirely unjustified; in some cases, averting or mitigating cost methods can provide useful approximations (upper or lower bounds) to true economic values. Although it is theoretically possible to estimate appropriate, theoretically exact economic values using averting or mitigating behavior methods, the data and assumptions required are often prohibitive. For example, in order to use defensive behaviors to estimate well-defined values, three elements are required: 1) expenditures on defensive behavior must be voluntary, 2) costs must be actually paid by the affected individual or group, and 3) there must be no joint production or additional utility (or disutility) associated with the defensive or replacement behavior. The third condition is particularly difficult to achieve; it implies that defensive behaviors must *exactly* and *perfectly* offset the benefits lost elsewhere (e.g., due to environmental damage), with no additional benefits or costs of any kind. Even when these conditions hold, it is not appropriate to use the gross amount of defensive expenditures as a measure of value. Instead, sophisticated models must be used to estimate values based on factors, such as the observed quantity, price (or cost) per unit, and effectiveness of the observed defensive behavior. In summary, observed defensive behaviors may sometimes be used to estimate well-defined economic values (or bounds on values), but the calculations and assumptions required to do so are often complex.

Damage cost methods, in contrast, cannot estimate theoretically appropriate values. For example, the cost required to rebuild a retaining wall damaged by a hurricane is not the same as the social value, or net economic benefits, lost due to the storm. Similarly, the net benefits of coastal wetlands for storm-surge prevention are not the same as the cost of providing similar protection using man-made structures—or the costs avoided by the presence of wetlands. The reason that such methods do not provide theoretically appropriate value estimates is simple: the cost of engaging in an action (e.g., rebuilding a retaining wall) is not the same as the benefit of that action. For example, the cost of building a coastal retaining wall in an unpopulated area could be substantial, but the value to the public would likely be minimal. Damage cost methods confuse costs and benefits.

Because there are both appropriate and inappropriate uses of data on defensive behavior, damage cost, and cost avoided to estimate economic values, one must interpret value estimates derived from defensive behavior and damage cost methods with caution. Inappropriate interpretation and use of defensive and/or damage cost estimates can lead to misguided policy and a loss of social welfare. Defensive behavior and damage cost methods are most often applied to the valuation of reductions in pollutants. Much rarer are applications to policy contexts, such as those encountered in EBM; perhaps the most common applications are to coastal hazards, such as flooding or coastal erosion.[21]

Stated Preference Methods

Stated preference methods, also called direct valuation techniques, use carefully designed surveys to estimate values that individuals hold for well-defined changes in the quantity or quality of a nonmarket good, service, or natural resource. These surveys create a hypothetical market where none exists through survey questions that, in effect, allow respondents to "purchase" nonmarket commodities in hypothetical situations. Answers to stated preference survey questions—they may be monetary amounts, voting or market-type choices, ratings or rankings, or other preference indications—are analyzed with economic models to estimate various measures of nonmarket economic value (or benefit). These models most often estimate a representative household's willingness to pay for environmental changes or policies that affect valued nonmarket commodities.

Stated preference methods arose from the need for ways to assess passive use or nonuse values generated by natural resources. (Recall that nonuse values cannot be measured by analyzing observed market or other behavior.) These methods are among the most flexible of all valuation methods: they can estimate values associated with an almost limitless range of nonmarket commodities. They are also the only methods capable of measuring both use and nonuse values. Hence, if nonuse values are present in a particular policy context, failure to apply stated preference methods can result in a substantial understatement of total nonmarket value. Over the past three decades, there have been many thousands of applications of stated preference methods to assess values associated with different types of environmental and resource changes,[22] and these methods have been subject to intense scrutiny and testing. Stated preference methods have been used widely in both applied and academic work, have been accepted for use by U.S. government agencies and courts (federal, state, and local), and are widely used to inform policy choices. As stated by Stevens

(2005), "the accumulated evidence clearly suggests that [the stated preference method] is a very useful methodology for decisionmakers."[23]

Stated preference methods, however, are not without challenges or detractors. Because these methods rely on responses to survey questions—which, in some cases, have been subject to a variety of response biases—they can be more controversial than revealed preference valuation methods. It is now clear, however, that many of the potential response biases found in stated preference methods also occur in actual markets. This calls into question the validity of many critiques and suggests that some critics have held stated preference methods to higher standards than those applied to other forms of economic analysis.[24] Most important, however, such surveys often represent the only means of estimating public preferences and values for environmental policies, particularly in cases where there are no behavioral trails or observable use behaviors that are required for revealed preference methods. These advantages aside, anyone conducting or commissioning such studies should be aware of the potential biases that may occur, particularly in studies with inadequately developed surveys or research designs.[25] Careful survey design and testing is crucial to ensure the validity of stated preference results; unfortunately, stated preference surveys are often conducted with too little attention to these steps.

One of the principal challenges of stated preference analysis is the possibility of hypothetical bias. This is defined as a divergence between that which individuals indicate they would do in a survey, and what they would actually do in a parallel "real life" situation.[26] Research shows that some level of hypothetical bias occurs in many, but not all, stated preference analyses. There are also survey-based or statistical steps one can take to reduce or eliminate these biases. Anyone contemplating the use of stated preference methods should be aware of such issues and make sure that surveys include methods to minimize hypothetical bias. This again requires careful attention to survey design and testing—a point that cannot be emphasized too heavily.

Despite these and other challenges, there are numerous policies and related nonmarket commodities for which stated preference methods are the only practical option for measuring public willingness to pay or nonmarket value. For example, public values associated with preservation of a species, such as the north Atlantic right whale, comprise mostly nonuse values and can only be measured in a comprehensive manner using stated preference methods. In contexts such as this, in which nonuse values are likely significant, failure to use stated preference methods can result in misguided policy that ignores a significant portion of total economic value.[27] Hence, stated preference methods can be an important tool for EBM policy analysis.

Types of Stated Preference Methods

Different types of stated preference methods include 1) *contingent valuation*, 2) *contingent choice or ranking*, and 3) *choice experiments*. All of these methods can provide theoretically appropriate and valid measures of value, but each differs in the specific details of survey design and analysis.

Contingent Valuation

Contingent valuation—sometimes called open-ended contingent valuation—creates a constructed market for a nonmarket commodity of interest. The survey typically presents respondents with a single (or small number of) hypothetical good or policy change based on an actual good or service for which values are desired. Survey questions then ask respondents to answer open-ended (fill-in-the-blank) questions about the maximum amount that they would be willing to pay to obtain the good or policy rather than going without. Alternatively, respondents may be asked to choose a dollar value from a range of bids presented on a payment card or they may be asked iterative questions regarding whether their willingness to pay is equal to, greater than, or less than a specified amount.

Within all contingent valuation studies, individuals who state that they are willing to pay as much as x dollars for a program to preserve or provide a specific nonmarket commodity are viewed as having indicated that their value for the commodity is x dollars. That is, the individual is just as well off with the described nonmarket commodity and x dollars less money (the amount he has stated that he would pay) as the individual would be if he retained the x dollars and did not obtain the nonmarket commodity. The individual considers the exchange of x dollars and the environmental commodity to be an even trade, so that economists consider the value of the nonmarket commodity to be equal to x dollars. Stated willingness to pay (some dollar amount) usually depends on the characteristics of both the nonmarket commodity in question and the individual. For example, individuals with higher incomes may have a higher value for resource protection, if all else is constant.

Contingent valuation is the oldest and original form of stated preference valuation. The open-ended questions found in these surveys (i.e., respondents "fill in the blank" with a value for a specified change), however, can be difficult for respondents unaccustomed to such tasks. That is, many people are accustomed to purchasing goods at non-negotiable prices (i.e., choosing whether to buy at a fixed price) rather than stating a maximum willingness to pay for a good. Moreover, open-ended contingent valuation questions can provide incentives for individuals to provide strategic or untruthful answers.[28] For these and other reasons, recent valuation efforts, as well as guidance documents,[29] place greater emphasis on choice-based stated preference methods, namely contingent choice and choice experiments (described below).

Like all stated preference methods, contingent valuation surveys must be designed and tested carefully. They must contain sufficient information for respondents to understand the implications of policies or resource changes for their personal welfare. Surveys must also be designed to prevent or mitigate various types of potential response biases that can invalidate survey results. An example is scope insensitivity, in which survey responses do not demonstrate awareness of the magnitude of effects on nonmarket commodities. Another example is hypothetical bias, as described above. There is a substantial research literature that discusses these and other challenges in contingent valuation survey design and data analysis. Because the validity and reliability of contingent valuation require such careful attention to survey design and testing, a substantial investment of time and money is often required to implement this research appropriately.[30]

Contingent Choice or Ranking

Unlike the open-ended format of contingent valuation, contingent choice surveys ask respondents to make discrete choices between two or more policy alternatives, vote yes or no for a specific policy option, or rank a set of given alternatives. Contingent choice methods are frequently chosen over open-ended contingent valuation because respondents are more comfortable with choice questions, compared to open-ended questions. For example, many contingent choice questions are similar to those found in public referenda, a question format with which many respondents are familiar. The most common question format asks respondents to vote yes or no for a specific policy option (the *referendum format*) or to choose between alternative policy options that differ across physical, environmental, aesthetic, and/or money dimensions (the *paired-comparison format*). Respondents may also be asked to rank a set of competing policy proposals (*contingent ranking*) according to their preferences.

For example, in a paired-comparison format, respondents might compare two competing environmental policy proposals, each with a different impact on valued nonmarket commodities and a different money cost. Alternatively, in a referendum format, respondents might vote for or against a carefully defined coastal management proposal, compared to the status quo of no policy change. In such contexts, contingent choice surveys mimic public referenda, except that more information is provided by a contingent choice survey than is usually available to referendum voters. Moreover, unlike public referenda, different contingent choice surveys (shown to different households) will typically offer the same policy at different household costs. This allows the analyst to estimate the probability of voting for the policy as a function of its cost and is the basis for WTP calculation. This is described in more detail below.

A distinguishing aspect of contingent choice (as opposed to choice experiments, discussed below) is that the surveys usually illustrate, and respondents consider, a small number of policies whose characteristics (other than the stated cost of the program) do not change. As a result, contingent choice analyses typically provide value estimates for only a small number of whole policies (e.g., a single proposed policy to protect North Atlantic right whales, considered as a whole). These methods do not typically allow one to estimate values for the individual components or attributes that define each policy (e.g., number of whales saved per year, total resulting size of whale populations, effects on commercial fishing, etc.). Analysts desiring such results must use choice experiments. However, some researchers use the terms contingent choice and choice experiments interchangeably, so that some studies labeled contingent choice actually use choice experiment methods and vice versa.

In order to assess money-denominated welfare effects or WTP (i.e., non-market values) within a contingent choice study, the commodities or policies addressed in the survey must include a money (cost or revenue) component, called the *payment vehicle*. However, if one is solely interested in estimating rates of in-kind (resource for resource) tradeoffs or substitutions, then money elements need not be present. The tradeoff between the personal benefits that respondents expect to receive from the policy in question compared to the cost that they or their household would pay forms the basis of their survey choices and the subsequent estimation of values.

More specifically, the contingent choice method relies on the random utility model (see chapter 3). This approach models the probability that a respondent will choose or prefer a particular policy option at different costs. That is, the approach models the tradeoffs that respondents are willing to make when choosing between competing policies, at different household costs. Various types of statistical models may be applied to contingent choice survey data, each appropriate to different choice situations and survey types. Some approaches, for example, allow researchers to estimate how preferences and values vary across individuals or groups, while others provide results for an average or representative respondent.[31]

Among the advantages of contingent choice methods is an ability to avoid incentives for untruthful (or strategic) responses that can occur in open-ended contingent valuation. If respondents believe that survey results are *consequential* (i.e., have importance and will be used to inform policy) and hypothetical *payments are described as mandatory* or coercive (e.g., unavoidable household taxes or fees), then the contingent choice question format is typically *incentive compatible* when applied to public policies or goods. That is, this format provides incentives for respondents to answer hypothetical survey questions truthfully, in the same way that they would for actual, binding choices of actual goods in real-life contexts. When this occurs, responses reflect actual values, and there is no hypothetical bias. Past research has shown that carefully designed contingent choice surveys can closely predict votes that people would make in actual, binding elections on referenda—and, hence, the estimated values reflect actual willingness to pay. Other studies, however, have found evidence of hypothetical bias in contingent choice results. Taken together, these results suggest that the contingent choice survey format can help reduce hypothetical bias, and can sometimes eliminate this bias, but it is not a panacea.

Contingent choice methods can be applied to both preservation and development components of ocean and coastal policies. There are thousands of applications of these methods found in economic journals, books, theses/dissertations and technical reports. For example, Johnston (2006) used contingent choice methods to estimate public willingness to pay for new public drinking water sources, Whitehead (1993) used similar methods to assess willingness to pay for marine and coastal wildlife preservation, and Bergstrom et al. (1990) applied them to quantify willingness to pay for marsh protection.

Box 4.3   Contingent Choice Question Addressing Wetlands Protection

Bergstrom et al. (1990)[32] posed the following contingent choice questions about the protection of Louisiana marshes: "would you approve of the wetlands protection program, if it reduced your income by *x* dollars per year [this amount varied between $5 and $1,500 in different questionnaires], in order to have your game bag or fish catch preserved at current levels, rather than have your bag or catch reduced to zero because of continued marsh loss?" The value per acre estimated based on this question was $8.42 in 1986–87 dollars.

Choice Experiments

The primary difference between contingent choice methods and choice experiments[33] is that contingent choice asks respondents to consider a small number of policy options whose attributes are fixed. Choice experiments, on the other hand, define policy options as a collection of policy attributes. Within choice experiment surveys, possible levels for these different attributes are mixed and matched to allow respondents to choose from many different policy options. That is, choice experiments present individuals with an opportunity to select one from a set of available multi-attribute policy options or to reject all the presented options in favor of the status quo. Choice data from many sets of possible choice options, where each option is defined by component attribute levels, enables the probability of choice to be modeled as a function of attribute levels.

For example, a coastal land preservation program might be defined in terms of such attributes as the type of land preserved, the number of acres preserved, the location where land is preserved, the means of preserving the land, the risk of development on unpreserved lands, and so on. By mixing and matching possible levels (or outcomes) for each of these attributes, one can often illustrate hundreds if not thousands of potential attribute combinations that are possible in a given policy context. Although each individual choice experiment survey only includes a few of the many possible policy options, different survey versions (sent to different respondents) can combine to represent many different policy options. By analyzing different respondents' choices

FIGURE 4.2   CHOICE EXPERIMENT QUESTION ADDRESSING RIVER RESTORATION ALTERNATIVES

Effect of Restoration	Current Situation (no restoration)	Restoration Project A	Restoration Project B
 Fish Habitat	0% 0 of 4347 river acres accessible to fish	20% 225 of 4347 river acres accessible to fish	20% 225 of 4347 river acres accessible to fish
 Population Survival Score	0% Chance of 50-year survival	30% Chance of 50-year survival	30% Chance of 50-year survival
 Catchable Fish Abundance	80% 116 fish/hour found out of 145 possible	70% 102 fish/hour found out of 145 possible	90% 130 fish/hour found out of 145 possible
 Fish-Dependent Wildlife	55% 20 of 36 species native to RI are common	60% 22 of 36 species native to RI are common	80% 28 of 36 species native to RI are common
 Aquatic Ecological Condition Score	65% Natural condition out of 100% maximum	80% Natural condition out of 100% maximum	80% Natural condition out of 100% maximum
 Public Access	Public CANNOT walk and fish in area	Public CAN walk and fish in area	Public CANNOT walk and fish in area
$ Cost to your Household per Year	$0 Increase in Annual Taxes and Fees	$10 Increase in Annual Taxes and Fees	$15 Increase in Annual Taxes and Fees
HOW WOULD YOU VOTE? (CHOOSE ONE ONLY)	☐ I vote for NO RESTORATION	☐ I vote for PROJECT A	☐ I vote for PROJECT B

over hundreds or even thousands of different choice options, one can estimate values for each of the different possibilities.[34] In addition, it is possible to estimate the marginal value (or change in willingness to pay) associated with each individual attribute: this is the implicit price. For example, one could calculate the marginal willingness to pay for each additional acre of coastal land preservation, holding all else constant.

Choice experiments have several advantages, including a capacity to estimate values for a wide array of potential policies, a foundation in well-developed random utility theory, and a similarity of the discrete choice context to familiar referendum or voting formats. Choice experiments also provide a more flexible range of output than alternative stated preference methods (such as standard contingent choice methods). This flexibility stems largely from the ability of choice experiments to quantify values associated with each policy attribute (or component).

Choice experiments also present respondents with realistic choices in which policies are not always superior across all possible attributes or dimensions (e.g., one policy might preserve more coastal land, while another policy might preserve land in a more desirable location). That is, choice experiments ask that respondents make tradeoffs not only between household cost and environmental outcomes, but also between different types of environmental outcomes. As a result, choice experiments may reduce the potential for yea-saying and symbolic biases because the multi-attribute policy choices and tradeoffs found in these methods offer no obvious choice for a respondent who wishes to either express purely symbolic environmental motivations unrelated to policy characteristics (symbolic bias) or acquiesce to any proffered environmental policy regardless of cost (yea-saying). An additional advantage of such methods is that they permit straightforward assessments of the impact of resource scope (i.e., the size of program effects) on respondents' choices.

Although choice experiments provide more flexible and detailed results than contingent choice or contingent valuation methods, this comes at a cost of greater methodological complexity. That is, the design and analysis of choice experiments are much more complex than parallel methods for either contingent valuation or contingent choice.[35] In addition, because choice experiments often demand the production, distribution, and tracking of many different survey versions, they can be more costly than similar contingent valuation or contingent choice surveys. As a result, those contemplating the use of choice experiments for economic analysis must balance the additional information provided by these methods with the additional complexity and cost that may be involved.

Development and Implementation of Stated Preference Surveys

The validity of stated preference survey results depends on appropriate survey design. Because of this, stated preference surveys—whether contingent valuation, contingent choice, or choice experiments—require an intensive process of iterative design, testing, and revision, including the use of focus groups and pretests. This is necessary to reduce the potential for survey biases and show that respondents understand the policies and goods under consideration.[36] For example, focus groups can be used to verify whether respondents are aware of budget constraints, the scope of the resource changes under consideration, and the availability of substitute environmental resources. They also help ensure that respondents answer survey questions in ways that correspond to the norms of economic theory, so that responses may be interpreted as indications of underlying economic values.

Similar assessments may be conducted in one-on-one interviews with respondents. Although focus groups and individual interviews can provide related insights into survey performance, these insights are not always identical. For example, the interactive nature of focus groups can provide information that is not likely to be elicited in a one-on-one interview setting. In contrast, one-on-one interviews offer an opportunity to explore individual respondents' cognitive processes in ways that are not possible in a group setting. Because of this, stated preference survey design often includes both focus groups and individual interviews. Among the specific testing tools one can use within focus groups and individual pretest interviews is the *verbal protocol*, in which respondents describe aloud their mental processes as they make survey choices or respond to questions. With verbal protocol analysis, researchers can determine if respondents answer questions using expected cognitive processes.[37] Surveys conducted without such detailed preparation can produce invalid or misleading results. Despite a preponderance of published, well-designed stated preference surveys, there is a surprisingly large number of surveys—even in the peer-reviewed literature—conducted without adequate attention to development and testing.

Once designed and tested, stated preference surveys can be administered in person, by mail, by telephone, or via email and/or the Internet. The method used depends upon such factors as the complexity of the issue, its relevance and familiarity to respondents, and the available survey budget. For example, complex surveys that address unfamiliar issues may require extensive use of visual aids and verbal instructions, and hence may have to be administered in person using direct intercept surveys. These face-to-face interviews are sometimes preferred because it is easier to present complex information (with maps, pictures, graphs) and the dynamic interaction keeps respondents focused. Similar survey administration methods distribute written surveys to respondents through an onsite intercept. Sometimes these surveys include additional information materials (e.g., a video or information card shown to respondents), but the interviewer is otherwise not directly involved in questioning or verbally instructing the respondents. Despite the advantages of in-person interviews, this administration method is generally quite expensive. Moreover, interviewers may inadvertently influence responses through subtle cues.

Mail surveys are popular in lower-budget studies, for which larger samples are required, or in which it is difficult to obtain representative samples using in-person interviews (see discussion of representative samples below). Mail surveys are a cost-effective means of distributing surveys with more information than is possible over the telephone. However, low response rates and nonresponse bias are common challenges (e.g., only the most interested people may respond). Methods like those of Dillman (2000) can at least partially ameliorate these problems, as can survey designs that promote interest among a broad spectrum of potential respondents. Well-designed and well-implemented stated preference surveys can often achieve response rates of 30–50% or greater.[38] Telephone surveys may be an option for simpler stated preference questions and can be cost-effective for reaching large numbers of respondents. However, telephone surveys can only provide limited information to respondents, so for this reason telephone surveys are not appropriate for many types of stated preference applications. Finally, Internet surveys can combine the convenience of a telephone survey with the information capacity of in-person or mail surveys. Internet surveys often have low response rates, however, and a significant concern is whether the resulting sample of respondents is representative.

In all cases, sampling methods (how respondents are chosen from a population) are crucial to how representative a survey's results are (i.e., whether the sample of survey respondents is representative of the broader population of interest). In-person surveys typically use convenience sampling, meaning that they choose potential respondents from people who pass by a survey location. It is often difficult to obtain a random sample of a population using such methods, particularly when implemented at a single location. As a result, in-person surveys are often conducted at a number of different locations. In addition, certain locations, such as state motor vehicle departments and shopping malls, may offer better opportunities for reaching a more representative population sample than other locations. For mail surveys, it is important to obtain a random, representative mailing list of the population of interest. For telephone surveys, random samples can be encouraged by computerized random-digit dialing. Researchers may also wish to consider whether *stratified sampling* is appropriate. This involves dividing a heterogeneous population into more homogeneous subgroups before sampling each subgroup independently. For example, researchers conducting a survey over an entire state might wish to stratify the survey by community to ensure that representative, random samples are obtained for each community, as well as the entire state.

Increasingly, some survey researchers are turning to Internet survey sites, such as "SurveyMonkey," or preselected pools of respondents for Web-based surveys, such as those offered by the Knowledge Networks company. While there are some advantages to such approaches, including ease of implementation, researchers must take care that the resulting samples are indeed representative of the target population. Survey firms, for example, sometimes maintain preselected pools of demographically representative respondents who participate in perhaps dozens of surveys per year. Reasonable questions arise as to whether such respondents are truly representative of the broader public and whether they are "expert survey takers," whose responses do not reflect those of less experienced, more random survey respondents. These questions do not yet have definitive answers. Broader Internet surveys, in contrast, can result in nonrepresentative samples because the population of Internet users is not yet representative of the broader public. Given such concerns, researchers employing stated preference surveys must often balance the convenience of the Internet or other survey methods with the likelihood that these methods may or may not provide representative data.

Because of the many challenges involved in the development, testing, and implementation of stated preference surveys, consultation with trained

Box 4.4   The Peconic Estuary Resource Values Survey

The Peconic Estuary System (PES) Resource Value survey[39] used original choice-experiment survey results to estimate relative preferences of residents and second homeowners for preserving and restoring key PES natural and environmental resources. The primary goal of the survey was to learn about the public's preferences, priorities, and values for the environmental and natural resources of the Peconic Estuary that might be affected by preservation and restoration actions.

The survey was conducted over a six-month period in winter 1995, via an extensive process that included individual interviews, focus groups, and pretests of preliminary versions of the survey. To ensure coordination of the survey with existing scientific and technical studies and with potential policy actions, meetings with various groups of science and policy experts preceded the development of the survey. Based on input from focus groups and experts, the survey addressed five natural resources: 1) farmland, 2) undeveloped land, 3) wetlands, 4) shellfishing areas, and 5) eelgrass.

The objective of the survey was to determine respondents' values for improvements in natural resources above a specified baseline, defined as what would exist in the year 2020, if no action were taken to preserve or restore the resource. In the survey questions, each resource was included at three different levels: the projected level for 2020 (the "no new action," or baseline, scenario), and two other levels associated with hypothetical programs to preserve or restore the resource. Respondents chose which of these three policy options they preferred, given program cost and associated changes in PES resources.

Surveys consisted of random, in-person intercepts in the Suffolk County (Long Island, NY) communities of Brookhaven, Riverhead, Southold, Shelter Island, East Hampton, Sag Harbor, and Southampton. Survey locations included beaches, shopping centers, libraries, post offices, and other venues. In total, 968 surveys were collected from year-round and seasonal residents of Suffolk County.

Choice experiment model results indicated that the order of priorities for protection or restoration of resources was farmland, eelgrass, wetlands, shellfish, and undeveloped land. Estimated annual dollar values per acre (1995 dollars), per household, and per year ranged from $0.016 per acre for undeveloped land to $0.087 per acre for farmland. Multiplied by the number of households in the PES, total values per acre per year ranged from $1,203 per acre for undeveloped land to $6,398 per acre for farmland. Discounted over 25 years at a 7% discount rate (see discussion of discounting in chapter 2), the result was a total discounted value of $14,024 per acre for undeveloped land and $74,562 per acre for farmland. This reflected the total value of the preservation of these land types to PES residents, as represented by their willingness to pay for preservation. Within a cost-benefit analysis (see chapter 2), these numbers would be compared to the total cost of land preservation to determine whether preservation actions passed a benefit-cost test.

experts is paramount. For example, stated preference questions added to surveys designed for other purposes—with minimal attention to testing, design, and sampling details—are unlikely to provide valid or useful information. On the other hand, well-designed stated preference surveys can provide significant insight into public preferences and nonmarket values.

Other Valuation Methods

In addition to the revealed preference and stated preference methods summarized above, there are other valuation approaches that do not fit neatly into either category. These include ecological productivity methods, revealed/stated valuation methods, and benefit transfer. Each of these can play important roles in assessing the benefits and costs of EBM policies.

Ecological Productivity Methods

Coastal and ocean resources, such as eelgrass, salt marshes, and intertidal mud bottoms, provide many ecological or ecosystem services—direct and indirect—to the public. For example, they contribute to the production of commercial and recreational harvests of fish and shellfish and the hunting and viewing of birds and other wildlife. They also protect shoreline property from storm damage and erosion and filter nutrient runoff. Such coastal ecosystem services may occur on- or offsite and may or may not be valued in markets. Shellfish harvests, for example, occur onsite, while other cases—say, when fish or birds whose habitat is in eelgrass beds or intertidal salt marshes are caught or viewed many miles away—are realized offsite. Some of these services are valued in the marketplace (e.g., commercially harvested fish or shellfish), while others are not (e.g., birds for viewing and waterfowl for hunting). In addition, some coastal habitats contribute negatively valued commodities or "bads," such as mosquito nuisance and vector-borne disease, which can reduce social welfare.

Understanding the economic value of the various natural services—or the "production" of valued goods and services—supplied by coastal ecosystems can provide useful information for policy analyses concerning preservation and restoration decisions. For such purposes, the most useful information is often the value of a small change in coastal ecosystems, such as the marginal value of an acre of wetlands. Marginal values, rather than the total value of all systems, are important because most policies address relatively small changes in coastal habitats or ecological systems instead of whether to preserve (or not preserve) all such systems. Notice, too, that the value of ecological production is *not* equal to the cost of producing similar services through other methods (replacement costs), as discussed earlier.[40]

The hallmark of ecological productivity models is the linkage of two model components. The first is an ecological model that connects policy-induced (or other) changes to a consequent change in the production of valued ecosystem goods or services, and the second is an economic model that assesses the market and/or nonmarket value of the increment (small change) to ecosystem goods and services identified in the ecological model. A number of different models may be appropriate for both components, depending on the type of resources and human uses in question. Hence, the specific details of ecological

Box 4.5   Applying Ecological Productivity Methods in the Peconic Estuary System

An ecological productivity model by French and Shuttenberg (1998) was estimated for specific resources in collaboration with ecologists, as part of the Peconic Estuary System Resource Value study by Johnston et al. (2002b). The model considered two types of wetland productivity gains: 1) the increase in food produced by the habitat, which is utilized by higher trophic levels (organisms higher up the food chain, such as commercially harvested fish and shellfish) in the PES, and 2) the increase in the production of higher trophic levels (e.g., birds) brought about by the increased availability of habitat.

These biological gains from restoring or protecting increments of each wetland type (eelgrass, salt marsh, and intertidal mud flat), in turn, were assigned an economic value based on 1) the commercial value of the fish and shellfish, 2) the viewing value of birds, and 3) the hunting value of waterfowl ultimately "produced" by wetlands.

Although coastal wetlands may provide additional services, such as erosion control, this research focused solely on nursery and habitat services. The approach estimated wetland productivity using data specific to PES. The virtue of this approach is that it captures the underlying biological structure and productivity of PES wetlands, applying biological models and economic values specific to the region. However, the method also relies heavily upon professional judgment to derive estimates.

To estimate the economic value of food web effects, several pieces of information were required. First, it was necessary to quantify the amount of food produced by a habitat. Production rates for primary (plant) and bottom (amphipods, worms, etc., in and on the sediments) were estimated for PES wetland categories, using results from the ecological literature by French and Shuttenberg (1998). Then the fraction of the additional production that passed up through the food web was estimated. This additional production was translated into eventual commercial fish and shellfish production and landings, using average relationships estimated across numerous estuaries by Nixon (1982). Finally, the estimated fish and shellfish landings were valued using species-specific fishery values for PES landings.[42]

Habitat values were also estimated for bay scallops, blue crabs, softshell clams, and birds. These values were based on 1) the expected yield of fish or shellfish dependent upon the habitat and 2) the abundance of wildlife (birds) that utilized the habitat. Fish and shellfish values were commercial values, based on market sales. Wildlife values were related to nonmarket values of hunting (waterfowl) and viewing (wading birds). The marginal value of bird species' usage of the habitat was based on the benefits human receive from viewing or hunting waterfowl.

Based on model results, the marginal asset values of PES habitats were substantial (especially since other services that wetlands may provide, such as protection from erosion and storms, aesthetics, and existence value, were not considered). Productivity results also indicated substantial variance in ecological productivity values provided by different coastal ecosystem types. For example, study results indicated that eelgrass productivity values ($1,065 per acre per year) exceeded those for salt marshes ($338 per acre per year) by nearly a factor of three, and exceeded those for intertidal mud flats ($67 per acre per year) by greater than a factor of fifteen. Restored wetlands have a lower value than existing wetlands because it may take years for an existing wetland to become fully functional.[43]

productivity models may vary widely depending on the resource and policy context. Common applications in coastal or ocean contexts include models that estimate the value of habitat improvements from coastal habitat restoration to commercial or recreational fisheries, or the nonmarket value of birds or other wildlife whose "production" is enhanced by policies that restore or preserve coastal habitats.[41]

Because ecological productivity models have both ecological and economic components, they often require concerted interdisciplinary efforts. One of the greatest challenges of such models is identifying the specific increment to production that can result from specified policy changes. For example, it is often challenging to determine the specific increase in harvestable fish or shellfish populations that would result from a given amount of coastal habitat restoration. One should also recognize that ecological productivity values in some cases may overlap use values that are estimated with other valuation methods (e.g., hedonic models or recreational values estimated by travel cost approaches). In other instances, productivity values may represent a unique class of values not captured by alternative valuation methodologies. It is important to identify cases where one may add productivity values to values estimated via alternative methods versus cases where one cannot aggregate values in such a manner. The inappropriate aggregation of values from multiple valuation approaches risks *double counting* some components of value, or measuring the same benefits twice.

Revealed/Stated Valuation Methods

An alternative approach to valuation (largely developed since the early 1990s) combines data from both revealed and stated preference methods to enable valuation of resources for which revealed or stated preference valuation alone are either impractical or limited. Common applications of such methods include the use of *contingent behavior* questions to enrich the data available through standard observations of recreation or other behavior. Such questions present a hypothetical situation to individuals and ask how these individuals would change an observed behavior (e.g., number of recreational trips), should a specific event happen. For example, one might conduct a recreation demand (travel cost) model to assess the demand for visits to a certain beach, given current environmental quality. One might then supplement this observable (revealed) data with hypothetical (stated) data regarding how individuals might change their visitation behavior if environmental quality changed by a certain increment. A model combining these two sources of data to estimate the impact of environmental quality on value of beach visits is a revealed/stated preference approach. Its primary advantage, in this case, is the ability to estimate the impact of changes in environmental quality—even if actual data for visits for the quality level in question are not available.[44]

While such methods have great promise, a number of methodological challenges have hindered their widespread use. One of the most significant is ensuring that the revealed and stated data are consistent and can be appropriately combined into a single behavioral model. That is, are the responses, preferences, values, and behavioral patterns implied by the revealed data consistent with those from the stated data? Inconsistencies can lead to difficulties combining information from the two approaches into a single, consistent model.[45] As a result of these and other challenges, the number of revealed/stated valuation studies that have been conducted is smaller than the number of pure revealed or stated valuation studies.

As for the productivity models above, a wide range of different possibilities for revealed/stated preference models exists, depending on the specific types of revealed and stated valuation approaches that are combined. However, by far the most common revealed/stated valuation approaches combine recreation demand models with additional stated preference data on anticipated recreational behavior under new hypothetical circumstances. For the case of EBM, such methods provide a means to enrich revealed preference recreational data, to enable estimation of recreational values under a wider range of circumstances than would otherwise be possible.

Benefit Transfer

The preferred option for estimating nonmarket values is to conduct original or primary research—studies targeted at the specific resources and policy changes in question. Benefit transfer, in contrast, involves adopting or adapting research conducted for another purpose to address the policy questions at hand.[46] Because cost-benefit analysis of environmental regulations rarely affords sufficient time to develop original valuation research specific to policy effects, benefit transfer is often the only remaining option. Past assessments of transfer performance, however, are mixed; some assessments show modest or acceptable errors and others show large and unacceptable errors. Almost any type of valuation estimate can be transferred, although errors involved in the transfer vary depending on various factors.[47]

One advantage of benefit transfer is that it can estimate values cost-effectively when primary (original) valuation studies are either impractical or infeasible. A major disadvantage includes the potential for significant generalization or *transfer error*. Transfer error is the difference between the transferred values (benefit estimates from a study of one policy or site are "borrowed" to forecast benefits for a different policy) and actual, but generally unknown, values elsewhere. The likelihood and magnitude of such errors are critical to the validity and relevance of benefit transfer. As a general consensus, transfer errors are assumed to be smaller in cases where transfer and study sites are more similar and where researchers transfer adjustable value functions rather than simple fixed values. Transfers conducted between dissimilar sites or contexts—even

---

Box 4.6   Benefit Transfer of the Value of Land Preservation in Rhode Island

Johnston (2007) illustrated the use of benefit transfer in the context of coastal land preservation. Drawing from stated preference choice experiments conducted in different Rhode Island communities, this study assessed the validity of function-based benefit transfers across communities. The value in question was Rhode Island residents' willingness to pay for various types of land-use policy, including policies to preserve various types of undeveloped open space, as well as those that imposed more stringent development restrictions. More specifically, Johnston (2007) assessed the transferability of community households' willingness to pay: 1) to preserve open space isolated from housing developments, 2) to preserve open space adjacent to housing developments, 3) to prevent additional houses (new development) in the community, and 4) to prevent additional housing density in planned developments. For example, one might ask whether survey results from the town of Burrillville could successfully approximate the willingness of Exeter residents to pay to preserve open space adjacent to new housing developments in their own community.

Johnston's (2007) results are generally supportive of the transfer validity of willingness to pay for land-use attributes, and had average transfer errors across communities of 38%. However, results varied across communities and resources, with errors for some resources exceeding 100% in rare cases. The most successful transfers were conducted across the two most similar communities, Exeter and West Greenwich. Drawing from these results, one could argue that policymakers might accept the appropriateness of benefit transfer in this case, if errors of approximately 38% were deemed acceptable in a given policy context. If that is the case, then such survey results could provide an inexpensive, practical means to estimate values for land-use policy in Rhode Island communities.

---

if they address willingness to pay for otherwise similar resources—are often treated with skepticism. Transfer validity is also related to the quality of the original study—the quality of a transferred estimate cannot exceed the quality of the study from which it originated.[48]

Given the likelihood that some degree of error will occur with any benefit transfer, the appropriateness of such an approach for policy assessment often depends on the extent of transfer errors that policymakers consider acceptable. The U.S. EPA (2000) stated, "of concern to the analyst [when deciding whether to apply benefit transfer] is whether more accurate benefits information makes a difference in the decisionmaking process. There are many situations in which a benefit transfer may provide adequate information. For example, if the entire range of benefit estimates from the transfer exercise falls well above or below the costs of the policy being considered, more accurate estimates will probably not alter [the results of the benefit cost analysis]."[49] The intended use of transfer estimates is also a consideration. If, for example, the primary goal of a benefit transfer is to demonstrate that a certain resource has a significant, nonzero value, then benefit transfer may provide a perfectly acceptable means to demonstrate this contention. If, on the other

Box 4.7   Benefit Transfer of Willingness to Pay for Water-Quality Improvements using Meta-analysis

In cases where researchers have access to a large number of earlier studies that estimate values for a particular natural resource in other locations or policy contexts, it is possible to estimate benefit functions using statistical analysis that synthesizes and combines findings from these studies. This method is called meta-analysis, characterized by Glass (1976)[51] as "the statistical analysis of a large collection of results for individual studies for the purposes of integrating the findings." In some cases, the estimated valuation or benefit function can allow researchers to more accurately adjust willingness to pay estimates, providing an improved mechanism for benefit transfer. Johnston and Besedin (2009) described the use of meta-analysis for applied, function-based benefit transfer and illustrated an application to water-quality improvements in aquatic habitats. They applied an estimated benefit function to forecast willingness to pay associated with water-quality improvements that benefited fish habitat in a northeastern U.S. estuary. Water quality was presumed to be at level 5 on a standardized 10-point water-quality scale and to improve to 7 on the same scale. Nonfishing uses were assumed to be unaffected by the policy change and the resulting gain in fish populations was not expected to exceed 50%. Household income for the affected region was assumed to be at median level from the 2002 census in the northeast United States. The meta-analytic benefit transfer forecasted a willingness to pay value of $18.09 (2002 dollars) per household for the specified policy change. This result could approximate household willingness to pay for the specified change in cases where a primary study is unfeasible.[52]

hand, policymaking requires highly accurate estimates of value, benefit transfer might be a less appropriate choice.

Often, the realities of the policy process dictate that benefit transfer is the only option for assessing certain types of benefits. In such cases, the choice facing policymakers is simple—one can apply benefit transfer drawn from the most appropriate studies in the literature to obtain an approximation of resource value or provide no valuation estimates and risk the unstated assumption that the value of the resource in question is zero. Based on experience, it is likely that the majority of valuation results used for most EBM policy deliberations will come from benefit transfers of some type. Fortunately, the large number of well-designed valuation studies on coastal and marine resources improves the prospects for high quality benefit transfer in EBM policy contexts.[50]

Conclusion

Although nonmarket values are often more challenging to quantify than market values, they are no less valid or relevant for policy. Public benefits received from nonmarket commodities are no less real or important than benefits from goods purchased in markets. This chapter has summarized some of the most common methods for nonmarket valuation available to policy analysts, with a particular focus on issues related to EBM. Ocean and coastal management often has numerous direct or indirect impacts on natural resources or ecosystem services valued by the public. In many cases, affected goods, services, or resources are not traded in organized markets. Nonmarket valuation methodologies can measure a wide range of related values that do not appear in more typical, market-based analyses. In doing so, they can ensure that policy decisions appropriately consider both market and nonmarket benefits.

Many different methods for valuation are available. Different methodologies will often provide estimates of different aspects of nonmarket values. Improved knowledge of the existence, assumptions, outputs, and limitations of different valuation methodologies can help managers assess whether and how nonmarket valuation methods can provide relevant information and identify the specific approaches most appropriate to any given policy context. Although combinations of multiple studies (such as the suite of studies conducted for the Peconic Estuary by Johnston et al. [2002b]) often provide the broadest scope of economic information, funding considerations often prevent such large-scale research. Given scarce time and resources, policymakers must often choose economic analysis methods carefully to provide relevant and cost-effective insight.

Even for a specific type of nonmarket value, there may be various options for measurement, each with different costs and levels of accuracy. For example, analysts can choose between conducting a primary research study to estimate values tailored to a specific policy context, using benefit transfer to approximate these values based on research conducted elsewhere, or omit valuation entirely and risk that decisions will overlook the economic value of affected natural resources. Although valuation can be costly in terms of both time and money, decisions based on inappropriate assumptions regarding economic values can lead to misguided policy, inappropriate resource uses, and actions that diminish the sustainable benefits that the public derives from coastal and ocean resources. Managers must therefore balance information needs with the cost of conducting various types of analysis when choosing the most appropriate research agenda and valuation approach for a given policy context. Moreover, as emphasized in chapter 2, it is important to avoid common misuses or misinterpretation of economic information that can hinder appropriate policy development.

Over the last three decades, valuation methods have experienced significant advances. The valuation toolbox includes many approaches that can help develop EBM policies that better recognize the benefits humans derive from coastal and ocean environments. Public databases make many valuation results available to the broader policy community, and an expanding battery of instructional texts detail theory and methods for appropriate economic valuation. While economic valuation is rarely simple, well-developed methods now exist to measure many of the types of nonmarket economic values related to changes in ocean and coastal policy.

Endnotes

1. Freeman (2003, 7).
2. A variety of sources explain different aspects of nonmarket valuation at various levels of technical difficulty. These include Freeman (2003), Champ et al. (2003), Lipton and Wellman (1995), Garrod and Willis (1999), and Haab and McConnell (2002), among others.
3. Amenities are characteristics of a particular location that enhance human well-being and disamenities are characteristics that reduce well-being. Individuals are willing to pay for amenities (e.g., pay more for a house that has more desirable amenities, such as ocean views), but they are also willing to pay to avoid disamenities. Johnston et al. (2005b), for example, quantified willingness to pay to avoid mosquito disamenities associated with salt marshes.
4. For examples of such coordinated assessments in a coastal management context, see Johnston et al. (2002b) and Opaluch et al. (1999).
5. Both Freeman (2003) and Champ et al. (2003) provide excellent discussions of these issues.
6. The applicability of benefit transfer depends on, among other things, the size of error in value estimates that policymakers consider acceptable in specific policy contexts. For discussions of the use of the use of benefit transfer to guide policy, see U.S. EPA (2002a) and Griffiths and Wheeler (2005), for example.
7. Readers should also see Lipton and Wellman (1995) and Edwards (1987), who provide a number of uncomplicated case studies illustrating the application of various methods of nonmarket valuation in coastal policy contexts.
8. Revealed preference methods are less flexible than stated preference methods, both in terms of the policy contexts to which they may be applied and in terms of the types of values they are able to estimate. Numerous works discuss methodological details of various indirect valuation methods, including Freeman (2003), Herriges and Kling (1999), Haab and McConnell (2002), Lipton and Wellman (1995), and Champ et al. (2003), among many others. Of these, the presentations of Lipton and Wellman (1995) and Champ et al. (2003) are particularly well suited for those less familiar with economic valuation.
9. See Hotelling (1949) for the earliest concepts.
10. U.S. EPA (2000, 73).
11. This example comes from McConnell (1987), who used methods such as this to estimate economic damages cause by hazardous waste pollution of beaches near New Bedford, MA. Based on travel cost demand equations and regional population projections, the study estimated discounted pollution damages at $11 million in 1986 dollars ($20.8 million in 2007 dollars).
12. A third approach, the zonal travel cost method, was common in the 1970s and 1980s but now is rarely used.
13. The opportunity cost of time is defined as the value of time in the next best alternative use that is sacrificed in order to engage in any activity.
14. See Freeman (2003) and Haab and McConnell (2002), among others, for discussion and details of these other approaches.
15. For example, Johnston et al. (2002b) calculated an average value of approximately $44 per person per trip (in 1999 dollars, or $54.76 in 2007 dollars) for recreational fishing in the Peconic Estuary of Long Island, NY.

16. U.S. EPA (2000, *77*).

17. For an example of using hedonic methodology in a policy context that is particularly relevant to EBM, see Boyle et al. (1999), who calculated values associated with reductions in eutrophication and resultant losses in visibility in selected Maine lakes. (Eutrophication is the presence of excessive nutrients in a lake or other body of water, usually caused by runoff of nutrients, such as animal waste, fertilizers, or sewage, from the land.) In another relevant example, Leggett and Bockstael (2000) estimated the effect of water quality on residential property values along the Chesapeake Bay. Freeman (2003) and Champ et al. (2003) offer additional details and examples of such methods. See also Irwin (2002).

18. Another approach, hedonic wage model, uses the same underlying concepts as hedonic property value models. Hedonic wage studies most often assess benefits or costs associated with policies that change job risks. (See table 4.1 for a comparison with other nonmarket valuation techniques.) They are also used to estimate the "value of a statistical life" (VSL) in broader cost-benefit analyses (Freeman 2003; Champ et al. 2003). However, according to the U.S. EPA (2000, *76*), "because they are narrowly focused on labor market tradeoffs, hedonic wage studies are not generally well-suited to measure the benefits of environmental regulation directly." Moreover, applications of hedonic wage models in the past often faced numerous challenges, including difficulties isolating the full range of factors that influence wages in various regions. As a result, hedonic wage models are not commonly applied to coastal management policy contexts, such as those encountered in EBM decisionmaking. Where policies such as EBM are expected to have direct or indirect influences on human mortality or morbidity, however, VSL or similar estimates from prior studies may be "transferred" for use within a broader benefit cost analysis (e.g., Viscusi 1993).

19. Information and details for the discussion in box 4.2 came from Johnston et al. (2001).

20. U.S. EPA (2000, *80*). For an example, see Abdalla et al. (1992).

21. For more details on these methods, including the numerous associated challenges, see Cropper and Freeman (1991) and Freeman (2003), for example.

22. Many applications of stated preference methods may be found in centralized databases, such as the Environmental Value Reference Inventory (EVRI), at www.evri.ca/.

23. Stevens (2005, *192*).

24. See Hanemann (1994) for a discussion of some of these critiques.

25. For discussions, see Mitchell and Carson (1989), Bateman et al. (2002), Arrow et al. (1993), and Freeman (2003), among others.

26. For reviews of the literature of such issues, see Murphy and Stevens (2004), List and Gallet (2001), and Little and Berrens (2004). Also see Johnston (2006), Champ and Bishop (2001), Smith and Mansfield (1998), Vossler and Kerkvliet (2003), and Johannesson (1997) for examples where no hypothetical bias is found. Sinden's (1988) assessment of 17 cases found no statistical evidence of differences between stated preference and actual willingness to pay.

27. For example, portions of nonmarket value related solely to whale watching can be measured using recreation-demand models, but this is likely only a small proportion of the total value associated with the preservation of this species.

28. See Carson and Groves (2007).

29. For example, Arrow et al. (1993).

30. Mitchell and Carson (1989) and Bateman et al. (2002) provide good summaries of contingent valuation methods. Lipton and Wellman (1995, *54*) provide a simple example of the application of contingent valuation methodology to the valuation of coastal development impacts.

31. In this utility specification, or RUM, individual utility is divided into observable and random (unobservable) components (Hanemann 1984). RUMs allow estimation of contingent choice models using specific types of statistical models (discrete choice models), as described by Greene (2003), Maddala (1983), and Haab and McConnell (2002), among others.

32. Bergstrom et al. (1990, *146*).

33. Choice experiments are the most recent development in stated preference survey methods, with early applications by researchers such as Opaluch et al. (1993) and Adamowicz et al. (1998). They were derived from methods originally developed for transportation and marketing research (Louviere et al. 2000).

34. Note that each individual respondent considers only a small number of voting choices (often 3–6), but often hundreds of different survey versions are sent to different respondents. Hence, in total, one obtains data on voting choices over many hundreds of different policy options, defined by their attributes.

35. For additional details of choice experiments, see Bennett and Blamey (2001). For more on yea-saying and symbolic biases, see Blamey et al. (1999) and Mitchell and Carson (1989). For additional details on choice experiment methodology (also called choice modeling), see Adamowicz et al. (1998) and Louviere et al. (2000).

36. As Arrow et al. (1993, *4605*) stated, "if [stated preference] surveys are to elicit useful information about willingness to pay, respondents must understand exactly what it is they are being asked to value." See also Mitchell and Carson (1989), Bateman et al. (2002), and Johnston et al. (1995).

    For details on focus groups used for stated preference survey design, see Desvousges et al. (1984), Desvousges and Smith (1988), Johnston et al. (1995), and Chilton and Hutchinson (1999).

37. See Schkade and Payne (1994) and Kaplowitz et al. (2004). Powe (2007) also provides an excellent summary of these and other qualitative methods used to assist in the design of high-quality survey instruments for stated preference valuation.

38. Johnston (2006), for example, obtained a 79% response rate in his contingent choice survey that addressed water supply.

39. The discussion in box 4.5 (and further details) of the Peconic Estuary System Resource Value survey is found in Johnston et al. (2002b).

40. For more on marginal values versus "values" for whole systems, see Bockstael et al. (2000). The common misperception that the value of ecological production does not equal the cost of producing similar services is seen in the inappropriate but commonly cited valuation methods of Costanza et al. (1997) and others, as noted by Bockstael et al. (2000) and U.S. EPA (2000).

41. For more details, see Barbier (1994) and Johnston et al. (2002b).

42. Two assumptions are critical to food web and habitat-productivity analysis. The first is that food and habitat are biologically limiting factors for the species considered—that is, fish, shellfish, and birds depend on the availability of wetlands, so that small changes in wetlands will cause changes in the populations of these

species. The second critical assumption concerns effort and its cost. Fishing, viewing, or hunting requires the use of labor, capital, and other inputs, so the net gain from these activities is the benefit (e.g., value of fish landings) minus the costs of the effort required. However, very small changes in the abundance of fish, shellfish, or birds from a small change in wetland areas will lead to only a very slight increase in harvests per unit of effort. Accordingly, to simplify the model, marginal changes in the availability of each wetland category due to preservation or restoration actions are presumed to be small enough that fishing, hunting, or viewing effort (and, hence, cost) remains the same. As a result, the change in revenue from fishery landings, for example, may be interpreted as a change in economic benefits because costs are assumed constant.

43. For additional details, see Opaluch et al. (1999) and Johnston et al. (2002b).

44. For examples of the revealed/stated preference approach applied to recreational values, see Bergstrom et al. (2004) and Layman et al. (1996), as well as Adamowicz et al. (1994, 1997), Huang et al. (1997), and Kling (1997).

45. Huang et al. (1997), among others, discuss such issues.

46. See Bergstrom and De Civita (1999). Smith et al. (2002, *134*) describe benefit transfer as the "practice of taking and adapting value estimates from past research . . . and using them . . . to assess the value of a similar, but separate, change in a different resource." Johnston and Rosenberger (2009) provide a broad summary of benefit transfer issues, methods, and controversies. Rosenberger and Loomis (2003) provide a good introduction to benefit transfer methods.

47. The consensus in the literature is that function transfers (transferring a valuation function that can be updated with information available from the policy site) typically outperform unit value transfers (transferring a fixed value), although contrary or nonconclusive findings have been reported (e.g., Brouwer and Bateman 2005), particularly for certain resource types (e.g., value of statistical life estimates, or VSLs). As a result, researchers are increasingly considering benefit-transfer approaches that allow welfare measures to be adjusted for characteristics of the transfer site or policy context. These include functions derived from such techniques as meta-analysis (Bergstrom and Taylor 2006), choice experiments (Morrison and Bergland 2006), and preference calibration methods that combine results from prior studies within a predefined utility theoretic structure (Smith et al. 2002). Because of the common use of benefit transfer in policy analysis, it has gained much attention among researchers in recent years. For example, *Ecological Economics* devoted an entire special issue to an assessment of the current practice of benefit transfer (Wilson and Hoehn 2006).

48. For more on transfer error, see Rosenberger and Stanley (2006).

49. U.S. EPA (2000, *86*).

50. Examples of benefit transfer applied to coastal and/or aquatic resources include Morrison and Bennett (2004), Morrison et al. (2002), Hanley et al. (2006a, 2006b), Jiang et al. (2005), Johnston et al. (2005a), and others.

51. Glass (1976, *3*).

52. Like all valuation methods, the accuracy and validity of meta-analysis benefit transfer depends on many factors, including the quality of the underlying data, the statistical methods used, and the linkages to utility theory. See Bergstrom and Taylor (2006), Nelson and Kennedy (2009), Rosenberger and Johnston (2009), and Smith and Pattanayak (2002).

CHAPTER 5

Incorporating Uncertainty into Economic Decision Frameworks

The previous chapters in this book have presented a variety of methods that can help predict the economic outcomes of (EBM) and ensure that it has the desired long-term effects. These chapters primarily focused on conditions in which the components affecting policy outcomes are assumed to be known with certainty. In most cases, however, policy decisions must be made under conditions of significant economic or ecological *uncertainty*. For example, analysts' ability to predict environmental policy outcomes are confounded by such factors as future weather and oceanographic events—how these events will affect various species populations and how the policy and other factors will affect the actions of resource users, among many others. Similarly, estimates of the benefits associated with various policy outcomes may be subject to uncertainty about future human preferences (e.g., whether and how demand for various ecosystem services will change). Without incorporating (or, at the very least, acknowledging) these and other areas of uncertainty, policy analysis can provide misleading results.

Uncertainty is not unique to economic models; any model used to inform EBM involves either implicit or explicit treatment of—or assumptions regarding—uncertainty. Many models suppress explicit information regarding uncertainty, and in some cases this may be appropriate—for example, where uncertainty is low or model predictions are broadly recognized to be *expected values* (i.e., the policy outcome that is expected on average).[1] Sometimes, in contrast, lack of formal treatments of uncertainty can contribute to misleading inferences. Even though not all models will explicitly address various types of uncertainty, policymakers should be cognizant of the important role of uncertainty in the prediction of policy outcomes and the various types of approaches to incorporating information regarding uncertainty into economic or ecological models.

Basic Concepts of Risk and Uncertainty

While the terms *risk* and *uncertainty* are often used interchangeably, there have been historical distinctions between the two concepts in decision theory.

The distinction is attributed to Knight (1921), who characterized uncertainty as the case in which there is no reliable probabilistic depiction of possible outcomes, and risk as the case in which there is a probability distribution of possible outcomes. This distinction has become blurred more recently.[2] In an analytical context, it is important to note that *risks are not synonymous with bad or negative outcomes*. In common parlance, decisionmakers often speak of "managing risks" in the context of negative outcomes, such as invasive species, fires, hurricanes, and floods. In more formal economic terms, however, risk and uncertainty relate not to good versus bad events, but rather to cases in which the future is not known with certainty.

For expositional reasons, this section follows the NRC (2004) report on ecosystem services and classifies the case in which there is no reliable information or data on which to estimate probabilities as *ambiguity*. In contrast, *risk* is classified as the case in which probabilities are known or may be estimated, and uncertainty is classified as the more general case that encompasses either risk or ambiguity.[3] For example, analysts might know that water quality and the mortality of fish populations are related but lack any basis for making claims about the likelihood of any one particular relationship. Therefore, the ability to map the impact of water policy on fish populations is more difficult because this missing information or inability to understand—a case of ambiguity—prohibits assigning estimated probabilities to different outcomes. In this case, quantitative-based decisionmaking is still possible with the use of subjective probabilities (e.g., expert opinion), which include as much information about the likelihood of the process as possible. It is also possible to learn about the relationships between fish production and water quality over time. Incorporating the potential value of learning is one way that such ambiguities can be acknowledged and addressed within policy analysis.

Unlike ambiguities, risks can be assigned *reliable* probabilistic information on outcomes and relationships. This information is usually based on past empirical studies or observed patterns. For example, if analysts know the ways in which water quality and mortality of fish populations are related (e.g., experts might have models that predict the probability of a large fish kill when water quality falls below some threshold), they might be able to quantify the ways in which different regulations of nitrogen and phosphorus pollution would affect the probability of a eutrophication-related event. In this case, the decisionmaker would be able to incorporate the risk to fish populations when determining water quality standards and regulations.

Given that analysts and decisionmakers commonly face situations in which uncertainty—either ambiguity or risk—is associated with an EBM decision, a natural question arises as to how these factors can be incorporated into economic decision frameworks, particularly cost-benefit analysis. The following sections address this general question. Moreover, because many conservationists and officials argue for a precautionary approach and/or adaptive management strategies in the presence of uncertainty, this chapter also discusses ways in which these concepts are related to economic decisionmaking under uncertainty.[4]

This chapter is not an exhaustive discussion of decision theory or the many complexities that may arise when modeling uncertain situations.[5] The main paradigm in decision theory, and the one adopted here, is *expected value analysis*, where each alternative is assigned a weighted average of some benefit, cost, or utility function, and where the weights represent the probabilities that certain states of nature will occur. This general model encompasses a wide range of different measures and approaches that are used by economists to address the impact of uncertain outcomes on behavior and measures of economic value.[6] Issues that are common to all approaches include the definition of alternatives (e.g., policy A or policy B), states of nature with probabilistic weightings (e.g., probability that a fish population will be equal to 75% of its target level), and the linkage of alternatives via states of nature to outcomes. These commonalities are reflected in the discussions below. When possible, the compilation of these factors is outlined in a decision matrix that shows the relationships between policy decisions and possible—but uncertain—outcomes.

Incorporating Uncertainty into Policy Frameworks

In EBM decisions, some outcomes and the probability that they will occur may be directly associated with management actions, but often variability in potential outcomes is due to factors outside a manager's control. That is, policymakers may face both *endogenous* (i.e., affected by management actions) and *exogenous* (i.e., not affected by management actions) risks.[7] For example, managers might influence the likelihood of a species collapse by reducing the conversion of critical habitat to a less ecologically suitable use (for example, by permitting fewer acres of sea bottom to be mined for sand than originally planned). However, since the probability of collapse is also affected by exogenous factors, or drivers, such as changes in sea-surface temperatures, frequency of upwelling events, and rainfall, it may also be necessary to evaluate how the management strategy will perform under a variety of different possible natural states. For instance, the expected (but unpredictable) frequency and severity of storm surges will likely influence the expected net present value of beach nourishment projects. Analysis of such risks would assess the range of possible outcomes for net benefits associated with different storm surge possibilities. Similarly, local wetland restoration strategies might consider the likelihood of future marsh drowning from a climate change–induced rise in the sea level—an element of risk that is outside local control.

Given that ocean and coastal resources are susceptible to uncertain conditions, how can they be managed? Previous studies suggest that both the magnitude and type of uncertainty, whether exogenous or endogenous, can have important implications for policy. As shown by Johnston and Sutinen (1996), in a case of species collapse and biomass shift, for example, the type of uncertainty facing managers can affect renewable resource management. Some types of uncertainty can lead optimal management strategies to accelerate exploitation of an affected resource (e.g., fish species subject to uncertain collapse due to changes in ocean conditions). Other types of uncertainty, in contrast, can cause optimal policy to reduce exploitation. As a result, there is no simple rule of thumb for addressing uncertainty in ocean and coastal management. Analysts seeking to incorporate uncertainty into policy decisions must not only attempt to measure the magnitude of uncertainty but must also characterize the type of risks and ambiguities that are present.

Although formal treatments of uncertainty are often mathematically complex, they are generally grounded in a relatively simple set of initial building blocks. Quantitative modeling of risks associated with any policy decision begins with two steps. First, one must define the range of possible outcomes associated with different actions. For example, an outcome from building a dam on a river might be the change by some percent of the recreational catch of diadromous fish (species that use both salt- and freshwater habitats during their life cycle), such as river herring. Second, one must determine probability distributions across the different consequences. For example, there might be a 50% probability that the recreational catch will be reduced by half and a 50% probability that it will be left unchanged. Alternatively, a more rigorous treatment would be the estimation of a range of probabilities (e.g., continuous probability density function) reflecting the likelihood of a range of different outcomes for recreational catch. Subsequent analysis may be either simple or complex, but is almost always grounded in this initial definition of outcomes and estimation of probabilities.

How does one define probabilities for management outcomes? When there is a long history of observations on relationships between outcomes and factors that affect those outcomes, probability distributions can often be computed using relatively simple statistical methods. For example, from statistical distributions, the moments of the distribution, such as the mean and standard deviation of the probability of each possible outcome, can be easily calculated. In many environmental settings, however, there are insufficient data to quantitatively estimate probabilities using such techniques. In this case, subjective probabilities can be used (although there are some complicated issues with regard to how such probabilities conform to formal theories of decisionmaking).[8]

In many cases, some type of information will be available from which analysts can calculate at least approximate probabilities. For example, information could be derived from a small sample of observed data and/or expert opinion. Some issues that arise in such analyses are the need to disentangle personal beliefs from scientifically based opinions, weighing the likely differences of opinions from expert panels and devising a robust set of questions that minimize the potential biases inherent in the framing of the problem.[9] Thus, using expert opinion requires additional research to assess what the likely impact of incomplete information is on outcomes of the analysis.

Incorporating Risks into Economic Frameworks

Once uncertain outcomes and their probabilities have been characterized and quantified, there is a variety of mechanisms through which this information may enter economic policy analysis. This section sketches the basic framework for *expected value analysis*, which is the most frequently used method to include uncertainties in policy analysis. Expected value analysis is easily amenable to CBA where instead of focusing on the net benefits of a particular project, the decision criterion depends on the expected net benefits.

In particular, expected net benefits, E[NB], of a policy are given by

$$E[NB] = p_1(B_1 - C_1) + p_2(B_2 - C_2) + \ldots + p_n(B_n - C_n),$$

where $i = 1, \ldots n$ represents the n different possible contingencies or outcomes of the policy in question, B_1 represents benefits under contingency i, C_1 represents costs under contingency i, p_1 is the probability of contingency i occurring, the probabilities sum to 1 (i.e., all contingencies are accounted for), and E[*] is the expected value operator.

To provide a simple example, assume that a beach nourishment project will cost $10 million. The benefits of the larger beach will be $8 million if a hurricane does *not* strike the affected region within the next 20 years, and $70 million if a hurricane does strike the region. Assume that forecasters estimate a 5% chance that a hurricane will strike during the relevant time period, and thus a 95% chance that a hurricane will not strike. The expected value of net benefits is calculated as

$$E[NB] = \underbrace{0.05}_{\substack{\text{Probability} \\ \text{that} \\ \text{hurricane} \\ \text{will hit}}} * \underbrace{(70-10)}_{\substack{\text{Net benefits} \\ \text{if a} \\ \text{hurricane} \\ \text{will hit}}} + \underbrace{0.95}_{\substack{\text{Probability} \\ \text{that} \\ \text{hurricane} \\ \text{will not hit}}} * \underbrace{(8-10)}_{\substack{\text{Net} \\ \text{benefits} \\ \text{if a} \\ \text{hurricane} \\ \text{will not hit}}} = \underbrace{\$1.1}_{\substack{\text{Expected} \\ \text{net} \\ \text{benefits}}} > 0$$

In this example, the decision would be to move forward with the beach nourishment project, (E[NB]>0).

Although the basic framework for expected value analysis is straightforward, analysts who seek to apply expected values to policy analysis should be aware of a number of implicit assumptions and related caveats. First, the use of expected values, particularly for policy outcomes, generally presumes *risk neutrality* (a condition in which society is indifferent to the degree of risk associated)—that is, it presumes that individuals only care about the average outcome and not the relative degree of risk involved. While risk neutrality is sometimes an acceptable assumption for society, oftentimes experimental and field evidence show that individuals behave as if they were risk-averse (an individual's or society's willingness to pay to avoid an uncertain outcome). For example, individuals will often purchase health insurance even though the expected value of such insurance is, on average, negative. The reason is that insurance reduces risk—a valued result for many individuals. Recognizing this fact, it is often more appropriate to utilize an expected utility criterion in which the degree of risk aversion can be incorporated explicitly for individual choices.

Second, expected value analysis reports the average value, which is the value that is most likely to arise when the action is repeated many times. In policy analysis, however, the alternatives under consideration and the parties affected by the decision do not have the luxury of playing out the analysis multiple times. There will be one outcome, and the ability to average unfavorable outcomes with favorable ones, for example, is not applicable. Third, expected value analysis assumes that the decisionmaker applies equal weight to positive and negative outcomes.

Despite these limitations, expected value methods dominate practical applications of decisionmaking under uncertainty, including the vast majority of applications within CBA. This is largely due to the fact that the data required for more complex treatments of uncertainty are rarely available.

Box 5.1   Sources of Uncertainty in Beach Nourishment Projects

There are several sources of uncertain outcomes in the prediction of benefits and costs of beach nourishment projects. The benefits are likely to be affected by variables such as rates of beach erosion after nourishment and the intensity of future storms. Benefits will also be affected by future development that creates higher potential for storm damage.

The costs of future beach nourishment projects are also uncertain. It may be possible to predict the associated engineering costs with care, but predicting the cost of sand may not be straightforward. This is especially true if the sand has to be obtained from commercial upland sources as opposed to offshore sources in public waters.

Monte Carlo Analysis

In the end, there is no single, theoretically correct way to weight different policies that does not introduce subjective judgments or assumptions into the analysis. A prudent analysis, therefore, considers implications of the degree of society's risk aversion to these potential outcomes and devises a transparent weighting scheme based on those preferences. For example, a risk-averse decisionmaker would likely choose a policy with a lower expected payoff and lower variance, everything else being equal. A risk-neutral decisionmaker would likely choose the opposite. Choosing the degree of risk aversion to include in the analysis, however, is not an easy task. As the NRC (2004) report stated, "in a heterogeneous population, the analyst will have to make an assumption about the degree of risk aversion that is appropriate for the group as a whole."[10] It is also prudent to incorporate a sensitivity analysis on the level of risk aversion to develop an understanding of how important this assumption is to the outcome of analysis.

One way to avoid some of the potential issues associated with providing a single estimate of expected value or utility is to undertake a *sensitivity, or Monte Carlo, analysis* that provides decisionmakers with information on the range and probability of different outcomes that might actually occur. Such an approach calculates the distributions of the net present value associated with different management scenarios, as opposed to simply reporting the average outcome.[11] The advantage of such approaches is that they allow policymakers to view the entire range of possible outcomes rather than merely the expected value.

Using the example of the beach nourishment project, this is how an analyst could develop a distribution of expected net benefits. For simplicity, assume that the distribution of benefits, costs, and probability of a hurricane are uniform, where the mean of the uniform distribution equals the (maximum + minimum)/2. Assume too that the means of the distributions match the numbers used above, for example, the mean of the benefits with the nourishment project is $70 million. These assumptions imply that the expected value analysis from these distributions results in the same answer as discussed above. The distribution of benefits without the storm, for example, has an upper bound of $120 million and a lower bound of $40 million.[12]

The two panels in figure 5.1 represent two possible types of levy projects. In this figure, the height of each blue bar (on the *y* axis) represents the relative likelihood of a particular net benefit, where the net benefit is quantified on the *x* axis in millions of dollars. For example, the figures show that the most likely outcomes for both projects are net benefits between $0 and $5 million, and that the likelihood of net benefits in excess of $10 million is relatively small. However, since both the mean and variance are lower for the project depicted in panel A, it represents a project with a lower expected value, but also less risk. The project depicted in panel B has a higher expected value and includes both possibilities of higher or more negative benefits being realized, relative to the project in panel A.

As seen in figure 5.1, the distribution of net benefits provides a probability for a range of outcomes in response to a given regulatory initiative. The distribution can and does, in this example, have negative benefits over some range (left of the white line) and positive benefits over another range (right of the white line). With this information, the decisionmaker can expressly consider the potential for both negative and positive outcomes and the relative risk of

FIGURE 5.1   DISTRIBUTION OF EXPECTED NET BENEFITS

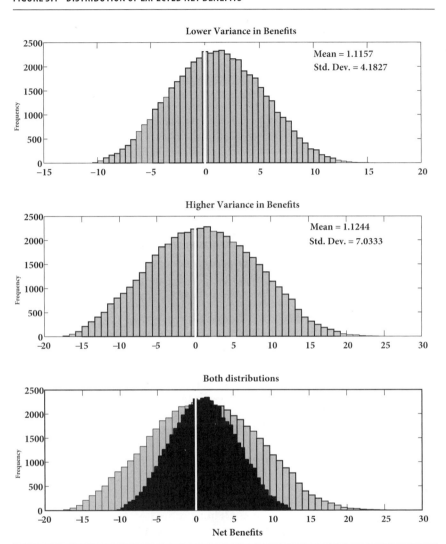

It is assumed that the benefits in both states of the world, costs, and the probability of a hurricane were drawn from a uniform distribution, where the means were equal to the levels used in the calculation in the figure. Specifying a uniform distribution requires choosing upper and lower bounds (minimum, maximum) of the distribution. By increasing the spread between the two bounds while maintaining the same mean level, the potential variance in outcomes is increased. In panel B, the same example is modeled with identical (analytical) means, but the policy has higher variance in the expected net benefits both with and without the project. Both cases had 50,000 trials run.

The white line corresponds to the case where expected net benefits are equal to zero. Panel C superimposes both distributions where the one outlined in red corresponds to panel A.

the alternative approaches, rather than just being informed that expected net benefits are positive. The use of the Monte Carlo simulation approach, when feasible, is regarded by many as more superior than simply reporting the expected value of a given policy because it provides policymakers with a richer description of the possible range of outcomes.[13] In practice, the full representation of uncertain outcomes is often ignored in favor of more ad hoc approaches, such as the representation of some output variables by "low," "middle," and "high" values. These are then paired with corresponding values from the other stages of the analysis. The result is a set of "low," "middle," and "high" values for the final output (e.g., the benefits of locating a wind farm in area Z) that does not correspond to a rigorous quantification of the nature of the risks and uncertain outcomes. As a result, this type of analysis can be misleading, especially when the classification uses different judgments and methods within a single analysis.

Regardless of how risk is incorporated into the decision process, there are a number of good practices that should be followed. First, the analyst should appropriately describe the variation in input data, equation parameters, and other features of the analysis with probability distributions. Second, to the extent possible, the process should separate the description of the risks in the CBA from the decisionmakers' judgments about the degree of risk aversion to unfavorable outcomes (or the willingness to take risks to obtain more favorable outcomes), appropriate to a given public policy decision. Finally, the uncertain outcomes and the probabilities that they may occur (likelihood) should be described quantitatively to the extent possible. In general, the analyst should make the treatment of uncertainty as transparent as possible and distinguish between objective analysis and subjective judgments.

Inclusion of Ambiguities

Up to now, this discussion has focused on incorporating risk into the decision process. EBM, however, also includes ambiguities, which are more difficult to include in a quantitative analysis. All hope is not lost, however. A Bayesian approach to decisionmaking, which is based on probability theory, is one technique that can incorporate ambiguities into formal decisionmaking in a rigorous manner (see endnotes 2 and 3). These techniques are especially appropriate when there is incomplete information or it is not possible to gather enough information to reduce uncertainties. In addition, one could adopt *maximin* (maximizing the minimum possible payback) decision criteria, whereby the analyst would only need to classify the magnitude of the potentially worst outcome and not the probabilities of all possible outcomes. Such a criterion works by identifying the worst possible outcome (minimum) and choosing the policy options that minimizes this outcome (maximum).[14] It should be emphasized, however, that this is not equivalent to the maximization of net benefits, as discussed in chapter 2. Concepts related to the maximin criteria that are often discussed in the presence of risks and ambiguities are the precautionary approach and safe minimum standard.

Model and Parameter Uncertainty

Approaches to the quantification of uncertainty that are broadly applicable are often applied only to the final outcomes of a given policy. Uncertainties, however, can show up in many areas of policy analysis, including those that precede measurement of final outcomes. The basis of many decisions in EBM, for example, will be a scenario analysis built on predictive models. These models follow economic and ecological causal chains (such as how different levels of fishing and conversion of coastal habitat affect the population of fish) to predict the likelihood of various natural and social outcomes of particular policy choices. The appropriate structure of these models, however, is rarely known with certainty. In predictive models, the ecological and socioeconomic interrelationships can include *model* and/or *parameter uncertainty*. Each of these types of uncertainties can be addressed, and an appropriate CBA or behavioral model would make transparent both the presence and treatment of uncertainty.

Model uncertainty captures the case in which there is a relationship between two or more variables, but the specific functional relationship between the variables is not known with certainty. That is, experts do not know the mathematical "shape" of the relationship between two variables. For instance, a general functional relationship that maps levels of X (e.g., variables that affect a policy outcome) into levels of Y (a policy outcome) is:

$$Y = f(X, \beta) \, ,$$

where Y is the outcome, X can include a number of different variables, and β represents the parameters that define the relationship.[15] For example, suppose one wants to quantify the benefits of reducing the footprint of a wind farm by 25%. (For a discussion of the benefits and costs of a similar example, see case study 1 in appendix A.) If one could easily predict the changes in net benefits (Y) that would result from different footprints (X), the analysis of benefits would be straightforward.

But what if this information is not available? More specifically, what if even the general shape of the mathematical relationship is not known? In such cases, model uncertainty can influence optimal policy decisions, as the stylized model in figure 5.2 illustrates. Begin by assuming that the benefit from the wind farm is Y and that it is related to (is a function of) the footprint of the wind farm, X. Three possible functional relationships are shown. Assume also that for small projects the benefits are negative, which is equivalent to the reasonable assumption that wind farm projects require sufficient scale before benefits become positive.

Recall that the point of this exercise is to map a 25% change in the size of a footprint of the wind farm (X) and to model how this might impact

FIGURE 5.2 POTENTIAL RELATIONSHIPS BETWEEN THE BENEFIT AND FOOTPRINT OF A WIND FARM

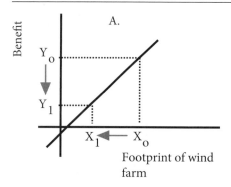

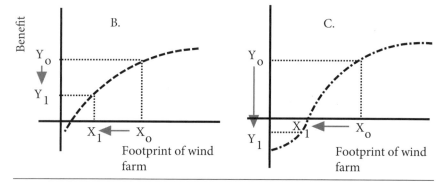

Panel A illustrates a linear relationship, panel B is illustrates a relationship where benefits increase at a decreasing rate as the footprint increases, and panel C illustrates a relationship where there is an inflection point. The pair (X_0, Y_0) represents the base case. The change in X is represented by the difference between X_0 and X_1, and the change in Y is represented by the difference between Y_0 and Y_1.

the economic value of the project (Y). This change is illustrated in figure 5.2 with X_0 and X_1, where 0 represents the base case and 1 represents the level after the change. Starting with the linear relationship (panel A), we see that the reduction in Y is equal to the difference between Y_0 and Y_1. In this case, the benefits are still positive and, therefore, one would still proceed with the wind farm even at the smaller size. In panel B, there is only a slight reduction in the benefits. Comparing this to panel A, the reduction is lower, everything else being equal. One potential implication is that if one believed that the relationship was more like that in panel B than in panel A, then the decision in favor of the smaller wind farm would be even more likely because it only has a small reduction in benefits. On the other hand, if the relationship is as depicted in panel C, then the benefits are negative for a wind farm that is 25% smaller. In this case, there is a dramatic reduction in benefits, and one might then be more inclined to reject the smaller wind farm.

How might an analyst take such uncertainty into account? Without the data necessary to distinguish these differences and choose a particular model, one could employ a number of techniques. First, the analyst could use different relationships and compare the differences across the formulations. If, for example, the differences are small, then the results can be considered robust to model uncertainty. Another possibility is for analysts to use their own expert judgment or convene an expert panel (subjective probability) to either choose the most likely form or to put relative weights on what they consider the closest likelihood. In the latter case, the analyst could use this information to develop an expected reduction in value by running many different scenarios weighting the responses from the different representations accordingly. Putting equal weight on each of the models (weighting by 0.33) would simply result in an "average" of three reductions to be reported out.[16]

Parameter uncertainty, which is often considered a subset of model uncertainty, is the situation where the functional representation is known but the rates of the responses are unknown. In the simplest case, panel A in figure 5.2, the equation describing the relationship is equal to $Y = \beta X$, where β is the slope of the line. One can approach the uncertainty in α in the same way that model uncertainty was approached. If the data exists the analyst can estimate the mean and variance of β, using econometric techniques (see chapter 4). Without sufficient data, a subjective value could be used, which (as described later) could be followed with a sensitivity or Monte Carlo analysis. In general, compared to model uncertainty, parameter uncertainty is easier to address within economic models. The primary reason for this is that model uncertainly involves lack of knowledge concerning both the fundamental shape of the relationship and parameter values, whereas parameter uncertainty only involves lack of knowledge of parameter values.[17]

In summary, the treatment of model and parameter uncertainty capitalizes on many of the same tools (e.g., expected values, probability distributions, sensitivity analysis) used to address risk in model outcomes. The primary difference is the specific area in the model within which uncertainty is addressed. This highlights one of the challenges facing analysts who seek to incorporate uncertainty into policy models: there is no single correct way to address uncertainty. Policy analysts must consider a range of factors, including information needs, types and magnitudes of uncertainty involved, and the cost of conducting various types of analysis, when choosing the treatment of uncertainty that is most appropriate for a given policy context.

Learning, Irreversibility, and Option Value

As implied above, uncertainty results from a lack of perfect information about the future. A corollary to this observation is that information received in the future can help alleviate current uncertainty about policy outcomes. The related value of this future information can provide a rationale for delaying irreversible actions. How might decisionmakers incorporate into today's management decisions the prospect of learning about uncertainty in the future? Economists have long considered the question of how to best incorporate the prospect of learning about uncertainties into today's decisions.[18]

A classic example in natural resource economics of ways that learning might affect a decision is the case where an irreversible development of a wilderness area might reduce the potential (uncertain) benefits from the area. The benefits of maintaining the recreation area in its current state include preserving species habitat, healthy ecological systems, and the potential pharmaceutical benefits of a species. But an additional value, known as a *quasi-option value*, should be considered in the development decision, which is the value from waiting and *learning* about the uncertain future benefits that raise the *opportunity cost* of developing the area today.[19] That is, by waiting to develop—developing wilderness is an irreversible choice—policymakers gain valuable information related to the true value of the undeveloped site. The loss of the opportunity to obtain this valued information represents an added cost of development. In some cases, the higher opportunity cost can lead to postponing the decision to develop to the next period. In this example, the value of the information on future benefits is conditional on maintaining the option to preserve or develop the wilderness area in the future.[20]

It is possible to represent such a situation with a simple decision matrix with two periods, today and the future, and two possible states of the world in the future to which a probability is assigned. This is illustrated in table 5.1. In the future, one state of the world includes "low" preservation benefits and the other includes "high" preservation benefits. In the current time, no one knows which will occur. By postponing irreversible development, however, one can obtain information on whether these preservation values are "low" or "high." To simplify the example, assume that the development decision is "all or nothing," that is, one must either develop the entire area or none of it. This assumption can be relaxed to consider partial development, but this creates in a more complex model. (Appendix B presents a mathematical example that illustrates how to derive quasi-option value). The matrix of the decisions is show in table 5.1.

If the decision is to develop today, then there is no further decision: the wilderness area is gone. If, on the other hand, the decision is to preserve the area in the first period, then policymakers can gather more information and learn about the value of the preserved wilderness area in the second period. In the second period, one can again make the decision whether to develop or not. Maintaining the *option* to develop in the second period, when there is better information on the state of the world, is the intuition behind quasi-option value. If policymakers do not consider the possible benefit today of delaying the irreversible action and learning more in the future, then the estimates of

TABLE 5.1   DECISION MATRIX TO DEVELOP OR PRESERVE

		Future *(t = 1)*	
		State of the world with low preservation benefits	*State of the world with high preservation benefits*
Today *(t = 0)*	Develop today	No decision necessary	No decision necessary
	Preserve today	Develop	Preserve

benefits from preservation in the first period are too low. If one ignores quasi-option value—or the value of information that helps allay uncertainty—the decision is more likely to favor developing the wilderness area today in a cost-benefit analysis, everything else being equal.

While the concept of quasi-option value is a powerful idea, it does not always support delaying an environmentally destructive practice. There are many instances in which, even after accounting for the potential value of learning, the benefits of environmental preservation will not outweigh the associated costs. For example, as shown by Chichilnisky and Heal (1993), positive quasi-option value requires that the initial decision be irreversible and that, with the passage of time, there be the possibility of learning. If instead the project is reversible, then it would always be optimal to invest (or develop in this example) in the first period (if the net returns are positive). One can recover the costs in the second period if it turns out, with new information, that the value of the returns with preservation is high. Similarly, there may be some instances in which quasi-option value is positive but too low to influence policy decisions.

Learning in much of the research on quasi-option value is passive; that is, the research does not consider possible investments in learning. Active learning, in contrast, implies that one can improve the estimate of the probabilities that a particular event will occur, either through direct investment in science, management actions, or limited experiences with the good or project in question. For example, in some cases, active learning would be an investment in some development (not a decision on whether to develop or not to develop). The notion of active learning is related to *adaptive management*, as proposed by Walters (1986). In its primitive form, adaptive management concerns experimentation and learning by doing through the application of different policy choices. As such, it is an active way to learn more about ambiguities and risks. Some analysts even make the argument that the quasi-option value related to conservation increases in adaptive management settings because of the greater rate of learning.[21] Although adaptive management has been discussed for many years, it is often not implemented by regulators. There are a number of reasons for the paucity of true adaptive management applications. First and most important is the political and distributional difficulties of experimenting with people's livelihoods. Second, adaptive management (as envisioned by Walters 1986) is based on rigorous scientific, economic, and ecological models that often are not incorporated directly into the decisionmaking process.

Bayesian Belief Networks

Another framework for modeling the occurrence of uncertainty in economic and ecological states and the nature of the feedbacks is known as Bayesian belief networks (BBNs). Bayesian belief networks or belief nets are models based on graphical representations of nodes, which represent different variables that typically have a set of discrete outcomes or states and an associated probability of occurring. For example, Hammond and Ellis (2002) used a BBN for fish stock assessments, where the different states are levels of the fish population, each of which has a probability of occurring. Conditional probability tables then relate nodes using Bayesian statistical methods to predict their relationship.

Illustrated in figure 5.3 is a highly stylized BBN that maps water quality to the value of recreational fishing on a prey species. It assumes that the prey is fished and not the predator. Using such frameworks, one can track the probabilistic impact of policy or other exogenous changes through an economic or ecological system.[22]

An advantage of BBNs is that they can incorporate both qualitative and quantitative information that can be applied to problems involving complex relationships among variables. BBNs are also important as an interface for communication between scientists, stakeholders, and decisionmakers. The simple graphical nature of BBNs allows scenarios to be sketched out quickly, so that the probabilities of outcomes are known.[23] For these reasons, BBNs are gaining in popularity among academics and policymakers. However, it is important to recognize that the insights gained through BBNs are only as valid as the information from which the conditional probabilities are determined. This, of course, is true of any formal treatment of uncertainty in economic modeling and analysis.

Precautionary Principle and Safe Minimum Standard

Although there are ways to address uncertainty in economic policy analysis, some policymakers and scientists favor policy responses, based not on formal treatments of uncertainty, but on precautionary rules of thumb. The *precautionary principle* is both one of the most commonly "applied" decision rules in environmental policy and one of the most controversial. The principle was first defined in article 15 of the Rio Declaration and states, "where there are

FIGURE 5.3   A SIMPLE BAYESIAN BELIEF NETWORK MAPPING WATER QUALITY TO THE VALUE OF RECREATIONAL FISHING

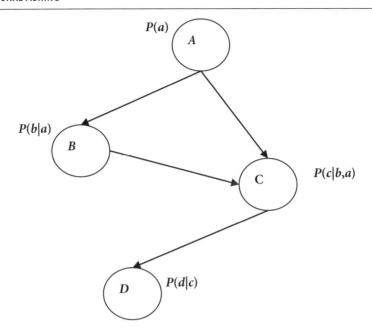

Variables (nodes)	States
A Water quality	A = {high, medium, low}
B Predator population	B = {high, medium, low}
C Prey population	C = {high, medium, low}
D Value of recreational fishing	D = {high, medium, low}

The different nodes (A, B, C, D) correspond to the different variables, and the lowercase variables represent the possible states of these variables. To simplify the example, assume that the states are discrete and are all classified as high, medium, and low, although actual applications may be far more complex. In this example, P(a) is the probability associated with the different states of water quality. P(b|a) is the (conditional) probability that the predator population will be high, medium, or low, given the level of water quality. P(c|b,a) is the (conditional) probability of the different levels of the prey population, conditional on the level of the predator population (b) and water quality (a). P(d|c) is the (conditional) probability of the value of the recreational catch, given the prey population.

threats of serious and irreversible damage, lack of full scientific certainty shall not be used as a reason for postponing cost-effective measures to prevent environmental degradation."[24]

In other words, one does not need to fully understand the damages that might occur in the future to begin investing in prevention today. From a practical perspective, the principle is more of a general guide or rule of thumb than a *decision rule* that can be implemented consistently across many different decisions. The precautionary principle does have appeal and in many ways is consistent with the frameworks presented earlier in this chapter. In some applications, however, the principle is used as a justification for a particular predetermined view of how society's resources should be used, rather than as an analytical framework through which the optimal choices are determined. Unfortunately, these normative undertones—while rendering the concept a ubiquitous part of many policy dialogues—have also given the idea a strongly negative connotation with many stakeholders.

Most economists would argue that the precautionary principle, as stated in the Rio Declaration, is related to learning and the value of information and is not formally grounded in economic theory.[25] However, in some cases, economic analysis can lead to solutions that are similar to those associated with the precautionary principle. For instance, the outcome of the example above (developing or preserving a wilderness area) on quasi-option value is consistent with a more precautionary approach. In most instances, the prospect of increasing information over time biases decisions in favor of more flexibility.[26] In summary, there are some instances in which both economic analysis and the precautionary principle suggest the same types of actions. In general, however, most economists believe that precaution should be an outcome or the result of a rigorous analysis, rather than an ex ante rule or guide for making decisions. The reason is that, within formal economic models, losses result from actions that are either "too precautionary" or "not precautionary enough"; there is no a priori reason that a bias toward precaution will increase expected or sustainable social benefits.

Another important concept relating to uncertainty is the *safe minimum standard*.[27] In the case of an activity with a positive probability of an irreversible impact of unknown value, it may not be possible to determine the optimal level of the activity. An alternative is to set a safe minimum standard believed sufficient to ensure that the loss is not incurred, yet does not allow that standard to be breached, unless the costs of doing so are catastrophic. Ciriacy-Wantrup and Phillips (1970) explained that "here the objective is not to maximize a definite quantitative net gain but to choose premium payments and losses in such a way that maximum possible losses are minimized."[28] This concept is intuitively appealing to many but has been found to be somewhat flawed from an economic logic and philosophical perspective.

Despite these flaws, the safe minimum standard approach is reflected in numerous policies, including the Endangered Species Act. To the extent that particular fishing practices or other marine activities create a significant risk of the extinction of a particular species, for example, the Endangered Species Act would be the pertinent legislation, and the applicable restrictions would be largely based on a safe minimum standard criterion. Reliance on a safe minimum standard approach, however, might be less defensible for general habitat protections oriented to ecosystem protection or protection of biodiversity, where there are not specific species or unique objects at risk.

Box 5.2   Use of a Margin of Safety in the Setting of Total Daily Maximum Loads in Watershed Management

The total daily maximum load (TDML) can be represented as the sum of the present and near future load of pollutants from point, nonpoint, and background sources flowing into receiving water bodies, plus an adequate margin of safety (MOS) needed to attain water quality standards. According to the NRC (2001) report, "the MOS is sometimes a controversial component of the TDML equation because it is meant to protect against potential water-quality standard violations, but does so at the expense of possibly unnecessary pollution controls. Because of the natural variability in water-quality parameters and the limits of predictability, a small MOS may result in not attaining the water quality goal; however, a large MOS may be inefficient and costly. The MOS *should* account for uncertainties in the data that were used for water-quality assessment and for the variability of background (natural) water-quality contributions. It should also reflect the reliability of the models used for estimating load capacity."[29] As the NRC (2001) report goes on to discuss, the margin of safety used is most often an arbitrary number when a quantitative estimate is provided.

Conclusion

All coastal and ocean management contexts involve risks and ambiguities. Any policy analysis implies assumptions about uncertain future outcomes, although these assumptions are often hidden. Such common approaches notwithstanding, the treatment of uncertainty can have critical impacts for policy guidance—and more specifically the ability of economic models to provide appropriate insight. As noted above, there is no single best way to incorporate uncertainty, and the most suitable approach in any EBM context will likely depend on the details of the policies under consideration and the extent of available data.

There are distinct philosophies on the treatment of uncertainty that may differ from a strict adherence to economic theory. In some cases, the philosophical or ethical attractiveness of such approaches, such as a safe minimum standard, may cause them to be selected over policies that might generate greater net benefits on average. For policymakers and analysis, however, the primary concern is that the treatment of uncertainty is transparent—so that people reviewing policy analyses and associated decisions are aware of how the uncertainty is addressed and what assumptions were made. The NRC (2004) report recommended that, "under conditions of uncertainty, irreversibility, and learning, there should be a clear preference for environmental policy measures that are flexible and minimize the commitment of fixed capital or that can be implemented on a small scale on a pilot or trial basis."[30] In other words, admit that the future cannot be perfectly predicted, and follow the best course, which is to maintain the flexibility to adapt to changes that may or may not be foreseen.

Endnotes

1. Situations assuming that the model represents average outcomes might not be appropriate, for example, in the presence of threshold effects and/or the presence of cumulative impacts. In general, these conditions are likely to be present in coastal and marine ecosystem–based management, which implies that decisionmakers should take into account the variance of the outcome and not just the expected value associated with any action.

2. Freeman (2003). In a Bayesian view of the world, where the quantity of information available is summarized by a prior distribution of outcomes, the difference between these two concepts is a matter of the degree of information available (Berger 1985).

3. Another term that is often used to describe ambiguities is ignorance. As stated in endnote 2, a Bayesian would not make these distinctions. In this view, ambiguities, while having less informative priors than risks, can still be accounted for in a formal quantitative approach to decisionmaking. The NRC (2004) report and the terminology here are due to Ellsberg (1961).

4. Additional technical details of such issues are presented in many texts, including NRC (2004) and Freeman (2003). For more formal, technically advanced treatments of these topics, the interested reader might consult Maler and Fisher (2005), Graham-Tomasi (1995), and Machina (1987), among others.

5. Important issues beyond the scope of this chapter include the advantages and disadvantages of employing one school of thought (such as Bayesian, classical economic treatments, or behavioral economics) over another with regard to how to model individual and society decisionmaking under uncertainty.

6. For example, net benefits associated with probabilistic outcomes may be expressed either in terms of option prices or expected surpluses. Option prices represent ex ante willingness to pay for a policy or situation whose outcome is subject to risk (see connection with quasi-option values in endnote 19), and expected surpluses represent willingness to pay for the expected value of the outcome. The distinctions between option prices and expected surpluses, while subtle, can have important implications for CBA (Boardman et al. 2001).

7. Johnston and Sutinen (1996).

8. Savage (1972) and Machina and Schmeidler (1992) provide a rigorous mathematical foundation for the use of subjective probability in decisionmaking.

9. When including risks (with very little objective information about their levels of risk) in CBA, the question arises as to whether the risks should be the risks perceived by those who will be directly impacted by the policy or the risks as perceived by an expert or policymaker. See Portney (1992) and Freeman (2003) for a discussion of these issues. See, too, Berger (1985), for example, for the impact of incomplete information. Also, the literature on the pros and cons of expert opinion analysis is extensive and beyond the scope of this chapter. See, for example, Cooke (1991), and Johnston et al. (2002b).

10. NRC (2004, *222*).

11. Monte Carlo techniques involve characterizing the range of possible outcomes and levels in input data, equation parameters, and other features of the analysis with probability distributions. The steps include taking random samples of each of these distributions in the designated calculations to generate a set of observations and using them to form probability distributions of the output variables. Point estimates use sample data to calculate a single value (known as a statistic), which serves as a "best guess" for an unknown (fixed or random) population parameter.

12. The other distributions for the variables used in the base case are the probability of a storm hitting, u[.00001, .09999]; the benefits with the storm, u[40,100]; and the costs, u[5,15].

13. According to the NRC (2004) report, these approaches have been incorporated into decisionmaking at U.S. EPA. A paper by Jaffe and Stavins (2004) contains a review of these approaches.

14. See Reckhow (2003) for more on techniques with incomplete information. The NRC (2004) report discusses how adoption of *maximin* decision criteria is justified in cases where society has a very high degree of risk aversion. The maximin decision criteria and their economic logic are presented in Arrow and Hurwicz (1972) and Maskin (1979).

15. In general, Y and X can capture a biophysical, ecological, or economic relationship.

16. If one attempted to estimate the relationships in figure 5.2, the data necessary to distinguish between the different forms would need to cover the range of X values presented. If, for example, there were only observations on (Y, X) at levels above X_0, then the statistician will likely not be able to statistically differentiate between the three possible cases. Therefore, not only is the existence of an extensive frequency of observations important, but also the existence of observations in the relevant range necessary for extrapolations.

17. When undertaking a regression analysis, there are statistics that can help in model selection, such as Akaike's information criteria. Another more formal and mathematically complex technique for dealing with model uncertainty in statistical analysis is *model averaging*, where instead of choosing a particular model for forecasting, the forecasts are weighted averages across the models (Hoeting et al. 1999). A formal discussion of these techniques is beyond the scope of the chapter.

18. See, for example, the research by Arrow and Fischer (1974), Henry (1974), Maskin (1979), Bishop (1978, 1979), Smith and Krutilla (1979), Conrad (1980), and Epstein (1980).

19. This is the quasi-option value, as defined by Arrow and Fisher (1974) and Henry (1974).

20. Often when discussing quasi-option values, another conceptually related concept, *option price* is discussed. Whether and when the option price might be positive or negative has been discussed in the literature for more than 30 years and is still controversial. The thinking on option price is that it represents the amount of money that affected individuals would be willing to pay for a project with risky outcomes, prior to knowing what contingency will actually occur. See, for example, Boardman et al. (2001) and Freeman (2003) for further discussions on the merits and measurement of option prices.

21. See Freeman (2003), Gollier and Treich (2003), and NRC (2004) for a discussion of these issues, as well as NRC (2004) for discussion that the quasi-option value increases in adaptive management settings in conservation.

22. For example, assume that for each variable in figure 5.3 there is an equal probability that each of the three states can occur. Specifically, it is assumed that $P(a) = \{1/3, 1/3, 1/3\}$ and $P(b|a) = \{1/3,1/3,1/3\}$, and $P(A$ and $B) = P(a)P(b|a)$ are used. In other words, given a policy intervention to reduce runoff, there is an equal chance that the water will be high, medium, or low quality. In this example, the probability that the predator population is low and the water quality is high (P(predatory population is low and water quality is high)) is equal to $1/3*1/3 =1/9$. Furthermore, the probability that the prey population is low, predatory population is low, and the water quality is high is equal to $1/27$ (e.g., $P(c,b,a) = P(c|b,a)*P(b|c)*P(a)$).

    Some recent applications of BBNs with EBM include analysis of land-management decisions (Marcot et al. 2001), fish stock assessments (Hammond and Ellis 2002), and impact of logging on bird and mammal species in rain forests (Crome et al. 1996). Analyses using BBNs start with a hypothesized model that often can be updated as additional information becomes available. The models involve large uncertainties, and often they pool information from different data sets, including expert judgment (Orme-Zavaleta and Munns 2007).

23. Reckhow (2003).

24. See the UN Environmental Programme's "Rio Declaration on Environment and Development," which came out of the UN Conference on Environment and Development (informally known as the Earth Summit) in June 1992. The Rio Declaration has 27 principles to guide future sustainable development around the world. www.unep.org/Documents.Multilingual/Default.asp?DocumentID=78&ArticleID=1163.

25. Doremus (2007) discusses the relationships, from the legal and decisionmaking perspectives, between precaution and learning by doing (active learning). She argues that, in some cases, active learning can generate policies that both capture the notion of precaution and the need for proof of causation between actions and environmental harm.

26. See, for example, Epstein (1980). Freixas and Laffont (1984) showed, however, that this—gathering information over time induces flexibility—might not hold if the society's welfare depends directly on the first period decision. Studies by Gollier, Jullien, and Treich (2000) and Gollier and Treich (2003), however, illustrated that, under some limited conditions, there is a possible economic interpretation to the principle. In their analysis, which included active learning, scientific

uncertainties can justify an immediate reduction of consumption of a potentially toxic substance.

27. Ciriacy-Wantrup and Phillips (1970, *28*). Ciriacy-Wantrup introduced the idea of safe minimum standard in his classic 1952 work, *Resource Conservation.* See, too, Ready and Bishop (1991) for a discussion of the flaws in the concept of safe minimum standard.

28. Ibid.

29. NRC (2001, *109*).

30. NRC (2004, *235*).

CHAPTER 6

Regulatory Methods and Governance

H istorically, the most common regulatory approach to managing marine resources and impacts on them has been a command-and-control approach, which regulates (controls) inputs and activities (e.g., how much fishing is allowed, where, and with what gear, or what substances can be dumped into the ocean and where). In some cases, however, it may be more effective to regulate and manage outputs or the consequences of activities directly, for example, how much fish can be caught, how much disturbance of habitat will be allowed, or what level of nutrient loading is permissible. The approach chosen depends on a variety of factors, and no single approach will be best in all cases.

Market-based approaches (such as taxes and cap-and-trade systems) that use economic incentives to influence outcomes and allocate ecosystem resources or services will sometimes be more effective and efficient than command-and-control approaches. Market-based approaches can help regulate either inputs (e.g., trap limits) or outputs (e.g., catch levels), although they are more commonly applied to outputs. Their advantages include incentives for resource users to encourage them to develop methods, information, and technology that minimize unwanted impacts associated with resource use, and allocation of resources (through trading) to those who can generate the most value with them.

Managing Environmental Impacts on the Marine Environment: Inputs versus Outputs

The most common approach to managing marine resource use and environmental impacts on marine ecosystems has been to impose input controls that prescribe which activities are allowed, when and where they are allowed, how they can be undertaken, what technologies can or must be used, and who can participate. For example, most fisheries have traditionally been managed with limits on the number of vessels that can fish. Often constraints on vessel size, type of gear, and locations where fishing can take place are added in an attempt to indirectly control the total catch. Environmental impacts on fishing have also been managed with input-oriented approaches. For example, take-reduction plans[1] for marine mammals in the United States have relied primarily on seasonal area closures, gear restrictions, and other technological requirements (e.g., sonic pingers on gill nets[2] to drive away porpoises or breakaway buoys and sinking ropes to reduce whale entanglements in lobster traps). Sewage treatment plants and industries that release pollutants into the ocean are typically required to have permits and use specific technologies to treat effluent and meet prescribed standards before dumping it.

The primary alternative is to manage outputs directly, such as limiting the total catch or bycatch, amount of habitat damage, pollution, etc. Outputs may be managed in aggregate (e.g., when a total catch limit is reached, the fishery is closed) or quotas may be allocated to individuals or groups. However, allocating outputs to groups can be problematic and result in a loss of the economic value generated from ecosystem resources if the groups are unable to coordinate use. For example, when an annual total allowable catch is set for a fleet of vessels, they may race against each other to catch it and expend resources on larger and faster vessels, which can increase the costs of harvest. Allocating outputs to individuals or smaller groups capable of coordinating activities allows them to generate the most economic benefit for their allocation.

Both input- and output-oriented approaches to managing resource use and environmental impacts have advantages and disadvantages. Neither is superior in all cases, but different situations are better suited to one approach or the other. The relative benefits depend on a number of factors, including the information held by the regulators and those being regulated, cost of monitoring, the degree to which the cost of reducing impacts differ among users, and the economic and technical characteristics of the activity or environmental effect (see table 6.1 and Holland 2007).

A key question when choosing between approaches is whether regulators have sufficient information about the relationship between inputs and outputs to determine the input controls or technology standards that will lead to the desired output levels and environmental outcomes. If, for example, areas where marine mammals are entangled by fishing gear are well identified and do not shift from year to year, an area closure may be effective. However, if these areas shift over time and fishermen are aware of the presence of marine mammals in real time—and regulators are not—direct limits on bycatch may be more effective than closures. Similarly, if there is a close relationship between particular agricultural practices (e.g., quantities and types of fertilizer used, cultivation methods) and nutrient runoff, it may be sensible to focus regulation (or economic incentives) directly on farming practices, rather than measuring and regulating runoff or its impacts. If, on the other hand, there is a very uncertain and variable relationship between farming practices and nutrient runoff, and if

---

Box 6.1   Reducing Interactions between North Atlantic Right Whales and Fixed Fishing Gear

North Atlantic right whales (NARW) are the rarest of all large whale species and among the rarest of all marine mammal species, with a total population of around 300 in the North Atlantic. A recent model predicts that, under current conditions, they will be extinct in less than 200 years.[3] The two most probable causes of injury and mortality of NARW are ship strikes and entanglements in lobster traps and gillnets. Critical habitat includes areas of Massachusetts Bay and Cape Cod Bay during specific times of year. There is no acceptable level of whale take, so an output-oriented management approach is not an option. Specific regulations focus on reducing whale entanglements in these areas during the times the whales are present. For example, gillnets are prohibited in Cape Cod Bay between January 1 and May 15, and certain modifications to how lobster pots are deployed are in effect during this period to reduce the number of vertical lines in the water, prohibit floating lines between pots, and ensure that pots that do become entangled break away.

---

farmers develop specialized information on how to reduce runoff, then it may be more effective to focus regulation on outcomes (e.g., measures of pollutants in runoff or groundwater).

The information requirements for effective input-oriented management extend beyond knowledge of the relative environmental damage that will be caused by one activity or another. Input controls are likely to change behavior. Regulating farming methods, for example, may affect areas where specific plants are cultivated. While this may reduce a specific impact, the opposite can also occur: the impact increases or problems may be diverted to other areas. Also, the economic impact of the action may be more severe than expected, if the behavioral response is not considered. The distribution and methods of fishing effort, for example, may change considerably, either as a result of direct exclusion from some areas or changes in relative profitability. A requirement to use a bycatch reduction device (such as a turtle excluder) in a particular area might reduce profitability and push fishing effort to other locations or fisheries. Understanding the indirect effects of input measures is necessary to avoid unintended consequences. (Chapter 3 has more discussion on the economic methods for predicting behavioral responses.)

The relative advantage of an output-oriented approach is likely to be higher if impact reduction is achieved though behavioral as opposed to purely technological adaptations (e.g., fishing in a different location versus modifying fishing gear). It should be noted that, to be effective, impact-reducing technologies may require performance-based incentives if deliberate misuse of the technology is hard to detect and increases profitability.

The potentially high costs of actively monitoring and enforcing input- and output-oriented regulations (e.g., at sea) are an important consideration. An active at-sea monitoring presence is extremely costly, but technological advances are making remote monitoring much more effective, which can greatly reduce enforcement costs. Vessel monitoring systems that track vessel locations and speed via satellites make it possible to monitor compliance in distant and irregularly shaped closed areas or track the amount of fishing by individual vessels in particular areas. Depth sensors on gear can monitor adherence of fishing activities to vertical, horizontal, and even temporal zones.

Direct monitoring of bycatch and habitat impacts, however, poses a greater challenge. Bycatch can sometimes be effectively policed by placing observers aboard vessels to monitor compliance or log bycatch, but this is expensive and impractical for smaller vessels. Randomly assigned observers may be adequate for monitoring bycatch of a group of vessels, but insufficient if impacts are regulated at the individual level. Even with group controls, concentrated coverage may be required if impacts are rare or irregular, such as bycatch of marine mammals, turtles, or endangered seabirds. Monitoring bycatch with tamper-proof video cameras may less expensive (and has proven effective for monitoring seabird bycatch).[4] Monitoring impacts to marine habitat is most challenging because it occurs below the surface.

For some outputs not easily observed (e.g., habitat impacts of fishing gear or nutrient loading of ground or surface water), one can use a model coupled with monitoring systems to more accurately measure impacts and track their causes. For example, models of groundwater flows or surface runoff combined with monitoring stations at key locations may be able to impute the sources of the contaminants. Model-based systems have improved how water trading is monitored. For example, a water-use and water-trading system in Colorado Springs integrates real-time satellite monitoring of water diversions and river stages (levels of water), real-time tracking of flows and storage within its water-delivery system, models of groundwater return flows, and models of travel times for exchange of water releases downstream. (See box 6.2 for a model-based system to monitor habitat impacts in fisheries.)

Market-Based Regulatory Approaches

Market-based regulatory approaches that create incentives for users to operate more efficiently can be designed to achieve desired physical or biological outcomes while increasing benefits to society. Generally market-based approaches utilize taxes or fees on outputs or grant transferable rights to outputs (e.g., the maximum quantity of fish that can be caught or the quantity of a pollutant a plant can discharge). They can also be applied to inputs (e.g., transferable limits on fishing efforts or fuel taxes).

Liability for damages is another form of regulating outputs that utilizes economic incentives. It is sometimes used in conjunction with input controls as an additional incentive for individuals and firms to take precautions that avoid environmental damage. Although most of the literature in this

TABLE 6.1   FACTORS INFLUENCING THE NET BENEFITS OF INPUT- VERSUS OUTPUT-ORIENTED APPROACHES TO FISHERY MANAGEMENT

Favor input approach	Favor output approach
Regulators clearly understand relationship between the activity and output or impact.	Individuals or firms understand relationship between activities and output or impact, but regulators do not.
Output or impact can most easily be controlled by technological adaptations.	Output or impact can most easily be controlled by behavioral adaptations.
Output or impact is temporally and spatially consistent.	Output or impact is spatially or temporally dynamic.
Monitoring inputs is feasible and cost-effective.	Monitoring of output or impact is feasible and cost-effective.
Activities and impacts are widely dispersed in remote areas, or with a large number of participants, making direct observation of outputs costly.	Activities and impacts are concentrated spatially or there are few participants making direct observation of outputs cost-effective.

area relates to pollution, parallel concepts apply to any undesirable activity in the marine and coastal environment or any activity that imposes costs upon others.

In his seminal work, Pigou (1920) showed that a fee or tax on the amount of pollution that a firm generates could be used to motivate its owners or managers to reduce pollution to socially optimal levels and, under certain circumstances, at a minimum cost. Taxes also help achieve efficient levels of resource use as a disincentive for excessive resource exploitation. An alternative to taxes or fees is the cap-and-trade concept, in which the overall amount of impact (e.g., emissions of a particular pollutant) by all firms is limited (the cap) and firms are allocated tradable permits (measured in units) for a share of the total allowable emissions. Trade of these emissions permits among firms (per economic theory) minimizes the individual cost of complying with the overall emissions constraint. (Firms become less polluting—by beating the target emissions level—and have permits to sell, while firms that pollute over the limit can buy unused permits and avoid more costly penalties or renovations.) Cap and trade can also help manage resource use, such as fishery harvests. It not only limits harvests to a desired level but also (through trading) allocates harvest rights to those who can generate the greatest net value with them.

Both taxes and cap-and-trade systems allow individuals or firms flexibility in their levels of environmental impact or resource use and in how they reduce their impact or utilize resources. The gains from allowing individual flexibility in meeting a desired output target (via a tax or cap-and-trade system) are likely to be greater if there is substantial heterogeneity among individuals or firms causing the impact. The gains from cap and trade will also be higher if there is a relatively deep market for permits trading and few restrictions.

When trades are restricted spatially, temporally, or between sectors for techni-cal or social reasons, it may reduce the cost-savings advantage over an input-oriented approach because there are likely to be fewer allowable trades that generate value. Nevertheless an output-oriented approach may be less costly or more effective since it provides flexibility in how to reduce impacts. While the relevant economics literature mainly focuses on tradable permits at the individual firm level, controls applied to a group of firms could achieve similar economies if the group can coordinate internally to achieve the desired out-come cost-effectively.

Market-based approaches (primarily cap and trade) have frequently been used to manage catches of target species in commercial fisheries (mostly out-side the United States). These approaches are not only efficient but have been effective in preventing overfishing and rebuilding overfished stocks.[5] There has been limited use of market-based approaches to regulate environmental impacts of fishing, such as bycatch. Setting bycatch caps for fleets of vessels has spurred the development of cost-effective bycatch reduction strategies when the fleets were able to cooperate and had appropriate technology to communi-cate with and monitor individual vessels.

Regulators need substantive, detailed information (costly to obtain) to de-sign efficient, effective ways to reduce negative environmental impacts. These information needs are often less with market-based approaches. Given eco-nomic incentives, firms may come up with their own solutions to reduce their impact. Also, when the target level of impact (the cap) is controlled directly, the regulator need not predict the relationship between input use and the re-sulting environmental impacts, which also helps avoid ineffective or overly strict regulation. This information advantage may not hold for a tax-based approach since the regulator must understand how different tax rates will af-fect production decisions and resulting environmental impacts. Adjusting the tax may partially solve this information problem,[6] but if the costs of reducing impacts and the benefits (associated with a related fishing activity, for exam-ple) vary over time, as is common, it may be difficult to identify a tax rate that achieves the desired aggregate level of impacts.

On the other hand, a tax-based approach may avoid unduly strict regu-lation when the cost of limiting environmental impact is uncertain. Under cap-and-trade systems with strict output limits, the marginal cost of reaching the target may be much higher than the value of the benefit of doing so. If the regulator has relatively good information about the marginal benefits curve but poor information about the costs of reducing impacts, a tax on outputs may be a better way to achieve the economically optimal level of impact.

When individuals or firms lack information or face substantial uncertainty regarding the relationship between their actions and resulting environmental impacts, it can undermine the effectiveness and efficiency of an output-orient-ed, market-based strategy. For example, if individual fishermen do not know how to avoid bycatch but regulators have identified chronic problem areas, then closing these areas may prove more effective than economic penalties on bycatch alone. However, if regulators have pertinent information that can be effectively conveyed to fishermen, then economic incentives may be highly effective. (The advantages of this approach over closures will be much greater if the areas where bycatch is a problem change over time, since it may not be possible to adjust closures quickly enough.)

Some proponents have argued that perhaps the greatest benefit from a market-based, output-oriented approach for managing environmental impacts is its incentive to users to develop innovative, cost-effective ways of reducing impacts (or production practices that avoid them). A firm that can lower its cost of reducing the regulated impact (or create a production method that avoids it) can reduce its environmental tax burden. With cap and trade, it can sell permits to another firm and improve its profitability and competitive position. In contrast, uniform technology standards tend to freeze development of technologies, impel even more regulatory control, and provide no financial incentives for businesses to do better than the target levels.[7]

Despite their many advantages, market-based approaches have certain disadvantages that can tip the balance in favor of an input-oriented, or command-and-control, approach. One critical consideration is the cost of monitoring. A market-based regulatory approach typically sets outputs or impacts at individual or firm levels. Such monitoring can be costly when users and locations of resource or impact are dispersed over large areas, are the result of actions by large numbers of people, or are difficult to observe and measure. Nonpoint source pollution (pollution from several different or unidentifiable sources, such as pollutants in runoff water) and environmental impacts of fishing share these characteristics: it can be expensive to monitor the flow of pollutants and map them back to their sources or to monitor large numbers of fishing vessels, which constantly move and operate over sizable areas.

Impact on marine habitat can be particularly difficult to monitor because it requires observation and measurements of harm under the surface of the water, for example, on the sea bottom after a dredge or trawl has passed through. But a model-based system can track habitat impacts at the individual vessel level (see box 6.2).

There may be situations where the technical and economic nature of the fishing activities and associated environmental impacts make gear restrictions or zoning more efficient, regardless of monitoring costs. Incentive-based approaches may be poorly suited for location-specific problems or problems with threshold (nonlinear) damage functions.[8] The advantages of an output-oriented approach will also be less if it is important to control where or when impacts occur, which would require separate caps on impacts for different areas or time periods. This curbs the flexibility in how environmental impacts are reduced and increases the costs of achieving an overall reduction in impacts.[9]

Box 6.2   Individual Quotas for Habitat Impacts

Holland and Schnier (2006) proposed a model-based cap-and-trade system for managing habitat impacts using a virtual habitat fish "stock." A proxy for habitat impacts, habitat impacts units (HIUs), would represent the marginal damage that the habitat incurs from discrete fishing events. They would vary depending on the ecological characteristics of the location fished, as well as the amount of fishing that had recently occurred at the location. A model of the virtual habitat stock would be maintained and updated with information on fishing activity and natural regeneration. Fishermen would get individual quotas of HIUs. Because the marginal damage of fishing in areas that have recently been fished is less (the first cut is the deepest), they would be charged fewer HIUs for fishing in areas that have been more heavily and recently fished and incur higher HIU charges for fishing in pristine areas or areas that have not been fished for some time. Individual fishermen would make the decision whether fishing in a given area with a higher HIU charge was compensated by higher catch rates. The system would harness the private knowledge of fishermen on the location of fish to achieve a cost-effective means of providing a given level of habitat protection.

Conclusions

A number of factors are crucial when evaluating whether to use input- or output-oriented management of a particular resource use or environmental impact, and whether to apply a market-based approach. A key question when choosing an input- or output-oriented approach is whether regulators have sufficient information about the relationship between inputs and the resulting resource use or environmental impact to set input levels or technology standards that will effectively achieve the desired outcome, but are not too strict. If regulators do not have sufficient information, or if resource users can find ways around regulatory constraints, an output-oriented approach may be a more effective means of reaching a target outcome. A market-based approach, such as cap and trade, may also achieve desired outcomes efficiently and can harness the information and innovation of those being regulated. However, market-based approaches are not a panacea, and they may often be more useful in conjunction with some input controls, such as technology standards and area closures.

Political and philosophical factors are also critical and possibly decisive in favor of input-oriented approaches to environmental impacts, particularly for emotional issues, such as marine mammal bycatch. However, there appears to be increasing acceptance of output-oriented controls using market-based approaches to manage land pollution and catches of target species in fisheries. Technological improvements in remote automated monitoring should increase the feasibility and reduce the cost of output-oriented approaches. Greater use of output-oriented approaches should, in turn, fuel innovation that decreases the costs of monitoring and reducing environmental impacts.

Endnotes

1. Take-reduction plans have an immediate goal of reducing the incidental serious injury or mortality of marine mammals from commercial fishing.
2. A gill net is a curtain of net that hangs in the water at various depths (held in place by floats, weights, and anchors). The mesh openings are large enough for the fish's head to squeeze through, but not the body. If the fish tries to back out, its gills catch in the mesh. A gill net's mesh comes in different sizes, depending on the type of fish it will catch.
3. NMFS (2006b).
4. Ames et al. (2005).
5. Costello et al. (2008).
6. Sanchirico (2003).
7. Jaffe et al. (2002).
8. This refers to cases where a small increase in damages that exceeds a critical threshold creates a large increase in total damages. For example, this might be a critical population level below which a population is unable to recover and may go extinct.
9. Hahn and Stavins (1992). These arguments are often applied to mercury pollution, where damages are localized and where the ability to develop outcome-oriented approaches, such as a permit market, at the correct scale is often not feasible (e.g., the market size is too small for the market to function competitively).

CHAPTER 7

Spatially Refined Management and Zoning of the Coastal Marine Ecosystem

In addition to choosing an appropriate policy mechanism (chapter 6), there are questions about the temporal and spatial scale over which to apply the policies. Because the marine environment varies so vastly in both dimensions and because these characteristics, in conjunction with location, affect the value of ecosystem services, there are opportunities to increase the human benefits from ecosystem services by crafting policies that vary over time and space. Some areas are better suited to certain activities and are not so good for others. Some activities result in negative impacts only at certain times (e.g., bycatch may only be a problem at a certain time of year when migrating marine mammals are present).

In the terrestrial environment, spatially refined management—including zoning rules and an array of regulations that allow or prohibit various uses and activities in a defined area—is often applied to both private and public property. Certain areas, for example, are zoned for industrial or agricultural use. Others are limited to residential use or may prohibit any sort of development. Regulations can dictate, among other things, alteration to and construction on land, waste storage and disposal, noise levels, hunting limits and seasons (or not), and so on. Regulations and prohibitions vary, depending on the characteristics of an area and its surroundings, such as its endemic qualities (e.g., wetland or forest), proximity to residential areas, historical use, etc. The frequent use of spatial management in terrestrial environments nationwide implies widespread acceptance among residents and policymakers that it makes sense to segregate and control uses and activities spatially, even when this may restrict the rights of property owners. This is not to say that zoning land is not controversial or that it always results in benefits to society, but it is common, and some kind of zoning is generally accepted in most areas.

Oddly enough, explicit spatial regulation of activities on public lands can be more controversial than for private land. For example, prohibiting hunting or motorized vehicles in areas of national forests denies use to some in favor of others, even though everyone has access to them. Nonetheless, spatial separation of conflicting activities and bans on certain activities in specific types of areas are widespread on public lands. In publicly owned marine areas, explicit spatial regulation is less common, but this is changing as demands on marine areas increase. Aside from near-shore or enclosed areas (such as estuaries and tidal rivers), management regimes that precisely describe which activities are allowed or prohibited in specific areas are rare.[1] Rather, the norm (particularly in federal waters) permits a range of often competing activities over vast areas, with little attempt to separate incompatible activities and little thought on how to optimize use over space. Through use of marine protected areas and closures of areas to specific fishing activities, managers of public marine resources are attempting to realize some of the gains that explicit spatial management of human activities in the marine environment can generate. However, with few exceptions (mostly outside the United States), spatial management in marine settings consists of ad hoc attempts to address specific problems, rather than development of a comprehensive zoning approach that could actively regulate the spatial and temporal distribution of activities in ways that increase overall benefits or reduce conflicts.[2]

Better understanding of the spatial heterogeneity and dynamics of the marine ecosystem and technological progress that facilitates monitoring of marine areas has improved the ability to implement effective spatial management, while growing demands on the marine environment increasingly require it. The environmental community, in particular, recommends a comprehensive program of ocean resource management and protection based on marine zoning "that reduces conflict, uncertainty, and costs by separating incompatible uses and specifying how areas may be used."[3] But before deciding to zone the oceans, one should consider the reasons for the historical lack of coordinated spatial management of the marine environment and the constraints that still exist.

The Economic Rationale for Explicit Spatial Management and Zoning

Consider the case where two activities take place in close proximity to each other, such that one or both of the activities increase the costs or decrease the benefits of the other activity. Economists call this a negative externality[4]— when different individuals undertake activities and benefit from their own activities, but are not affected by the negative impact they have on the others. For example, plowed fields at water's edge can increase nutrient runoff, which leads to greater algal production, making the water cloudier and decreasing the benefits to divers in an adjacent marine park. The farmer presumably benefits from plowing his fields, but it imposes a cost on the divers for which he does not have to compensate them. Of course, another activity may create a positive externality, such as an adjacent mussel farm that increases water quality and clarity in the marine park, offsetting the damage from the agricultural runoff. Here the divers benefit from the mussel farmer's action, but she does not capture those benefits, and thus they may not enter into her decision of where to site the mussel farm there or how many mussels to grow.

To optimize the overall level of interdependent activities, one must consider the external costs and benefits. To ignore them in the fields versus marine park example would lead to excessive nutrient runoff because the maximum total net benefits—after subtracting the external costs to the marine park— might preclude plowing near the water's edge. Some reduction in runoff would benefit divers more than it would cost to reduce the runoff, but the farmer does not consider the effects of the runoff in weighing the benefits of plowing. In the example of the mussel farm, benefits to divers might justify a higher level of production of shellfish than what maximizes profits for the shellfish farm, but if the mussel farmer has no way of capturing these benefits, she is unlikely to consider them in operating her business.

To illustrate, consider both the negative and positive activities together. The mussels in the marine farm filter the water, which may allow the marine park to maintain an acceptable level of water clarity, even with a higher level of nutrient runoff from the plowing. Of course, the mussel farm may also have negative externalities, such as bringing a visual blight to the seascape. A single private owner of the three areas—the marine park, the mussel farm, and the adjacent coastal farmland—would presumably internalize these cross-activity benefits and costs and choose the levels of the three activities that generate the highest total benefits. Separate private owners might negotiate agreements with each other to do the same, with side payments that distribute the net gains from cooperation equitably. However, transactions costs (the costs involved in reaching an agreement or conducting the required transactions and enforcing the agreement) might (and often do) prevent such bargaining solutions.

For publicly owned or managed activities, or a combination of public and private activities, regulations of various forms can be used to achieve optimal outcomes (or at least closer to optimal solutions). Per chapter 6, these regulations might explicitly dictate the level of activities or prohibit some. For example, the farmer might be prohibited from plowing more than 100 feet from the water's edge. Alternatively, one could use economic incentives that internalize the external costs or benefits, such that private parties participating in the various activities incur the full costs and benefits associated with these activities. For example, the farmer might be charged a fee for increased runoff that is equal to the damage done to users of the marine park. Alternatively, the users of the marine park might be assessed a fee to subsidize the operation of the mussel farm.

Many marine areas are multipurpose, used by different groups, each of which includes large numbers of individuals making independent use decisions (e.g., whale watching, various commercial and recreational fishing, sailing, ship transit, etc.). Some of these activities tend to be incompatible in the sense that undertaking them in the same place and time decreases their benefits or perhaps makes it impossible to undertake both. For example, fishing with lobster pots in the same area that trawlers use is likely to result in loss and damage to lobster pots as well as trawling gear. In such cases, the benefits of separating activities may exceed the costs in terms of lost production from the excluded activity. If the spatial exclusion needs to be in place only part of the time (e.g., seasonally) or can be configured at a fine spatial scale, this may help limit the cost in terms of lost production from the excluded activity. While it is possible for lobstermen and trawlers to voluntarily coordinate when and where they fish to avoid gear conflicts, this can be difficult and costly, given the large number of independent fishermen in both groups and the need to get agreement from all parties. This suggests the need for marine zoning that specifies which activities are allowed in which areas, or seasonal or year-round prohibitions of certain activities in specific areas.

Note, however, that if the conflicts between activities decrease as the volume or intensity of an activity is reduced, then it may be sufficient and preferable to limit the level of the activity rather than completely prohibit it. For example, limited recreational fishing inside part of a marine park might provide benefits to anglers that exceed any decrease in benefits the park generates for divers who come to look at fish. However, too much fishing might reduce the value of the park to divers more than the value generated by fishing. Specifying the levels of various activities that equilibrate costs and benefits at the margin may require information not available to regulators. Allowing some limited level of activity can produce information about the value of the activity that would otherwise be unknown, although it may take trial and error to find the appropriate level.

Even when some level of competing activities appears optimal, the costs of determining the optimal level and policing it may exceed the benefits of allowing these activities, even on a small scale. Sometimes the optimal level of certain activities is zero. Allowing boats to transit through the mussel farm or engage in bottom trawling in the marine park are potential examples. In such cases, the appropriate regulatory response would be some form of exclusive zoning, where certain types of activities are excluded altogether or only a single activity is allowed in a given area.

If exclusive zoning is desirable, then one has to determine the optimal design of these areas. A number of questions arise: how big should the area (or areas) be; where should it be located; what activities should be allowed and prohibited? The answers depend on the objectives of the zoning restrictions. Because these design questions are likely to be interdependent, they should be considered jointly, and consideration must be given to what activities are allowed in surrounding areas and where displaced users may go.

In general, one expects that, if the area set aside for some use is enlarged, the benefits from that use will increase—but at a decreasing rate, at least after reaching some critical minimum size. For example, the added value of an additional hundred meters of public beach may decline once the beach gets beyond a certain size. Similarly, the costs of excluding certain activities may be low within a small closed area (placed outside favored areas for the banned activity), but the costs may increase as more and more area is closed.

The optimal size of the zoned area occurs when the additional benefits from further expansion fall below the additional costs associated with the excluded activities. However, the changes in benefits (costs) associated with allowed (excluded) activities also depend on which areas are closed. The benefits and costs of excluding activities in an area must also be addressed in the context of the larger system. It depends on whether there are substitute areas available for the excluded activity. A cost-benefit analysis of closing a particular area should account for whether and where associated activities will be diverted and how that will affect other areas.

Consider the myriad considerations that can affect spatial management choices, as illustrated by designing a marine protected area that excludes some or all fishing. Costs (to those excluded) when increasing the size of this protected zone may be reduced by locating it where fishing is more costly because it is further from major ports. Closing marine areas near the shore and near population centers may be more costly to anglers than to commercial fishermen (depending on the fishery). Closing an area that contains primarily juvenile fish (perhaps because of habitat type) may represent a small cost or even a benefit to a fishery, if adults tend to migrate out of the area. An irregularly shaped marine protected area or one consisting of a network of small closed zones may protect benthic habitat with less impact on fisheries, since fish are likely to move in and out of a closed area and thus be available to the fishery. Allowing some fishing activities with minimal impacts on benthic habitat may also result in cost savings, but fishing may not be the only activity of concern. If the objective of an area is to preserve biodiversity, then one may need to expressly choose a location and exclude activities that reduce other threats, such as pollution or damage from anchoring.

Spatial Aspects of Utilizing Marine Ecosystem Services and Resources

The challenge—and the motivation—for explicit spatial management of the marine ecosystem arise from the high degree of interconnectedness, due to the movement of water and organisms in the marine environment. It is generally not possible to control ocean currents that transfer sediments and contaminants over geographic space. With the exception of aquaculture sites, it is generally neither possible nor desirable to control the movement of marine organisms directly. One can control when and where human activities add or extract substances or organisms in the water column or the benthos, but often there is little control and limited knowledge of how these activities will affect the environment and populations of organisms in other areas. It can also be very expensive to monitor and enforce regulations in marine areas that are far from shore or remote from populated areas.

Nevertheless, because the marine environment is highly heterogeneous, it makes sense to account for and take advantage of this heterogeneity in managing human activities. The physical characteristics of the ocean bottom, the water column, and the associated ecological communities can vary dramatically over short distances. Proximity to land also affects both costs and benefits of various activities (e.g., how far someone has to travel to fish or the effect of aquaculture or a wind farm on coastal property values). This spatial heterogeneity offers opportunities to increase the benefits derived from ecosystem resources and services and to decrease negative impacts of various activities by directly controlling where and when they take place or by creating economic incentives that lead to the desired spatial and temporal distribution of activities. Simply put, the heterogeneity of coastal and marine environments implies that some areas will be relatively better suited to some types of activities and less well suited to others. This type of spatial "comparative advantage" creates possibilities for increasing social benefits, if activities can be located in areas where they are most productive and limited or prohibited in areas where they cause undesirable impacts.

As implied by the above discussions, the economics of spatial management are often place and activity specific. Hence, it helps to consider a variety of different activities that occur in marine areas and how they may interfere with, or perhaps complement, one another in ways that create opportunities for gains with more explicit spatial management. It may be possible to substantially increase the benefits that humans derive from marine ecosystems through explicit spatial management of fisheries, aquaculture, and other activities that negatively affect the marine environment.

Perhaps the most actively managed activity in the marine environment is fishing. The spatial heterogeneity in the distribution and productivity of fish stocks presents both opportunities and risks for fishery management. However, the question of optimal management of fisheries to capitalize on spatial heterogeneity is only recently beginning to receive attention. Sanchirico and Wilen (2005), for example, showed that explicit spatial management of catch or effort is necessary to achieve optimal management when the productivity of the fish stock or harvest costs vary over space. Source-sink[5] processes, where the fish population in one area (the source) tends to contribute to the growth in another area (the sink), may contribute to suboptimal outcomes in those fisheries managed without explicit spatial controls. It may be more beneficial to forgo harvests in source areas in order to increase recruitment in others.[6] Higher exploitation rates might be justified in areas that are sinks for recruits[7] but do not appear to be sources for other areas.[8] When a fishery has multiple species, the fishes have different spatial distributions. In this case, spatially structured regulations provide a means of increasing the selectivity of harvest and are especially beneficial when species interact ecologically.[9]

While there may be good reasons to try to control the spatial distribution of fish catch, doing so is likely to be costly and require more information. In the absence of good information, spatial management can actually do more harm than good. For example, a misplaced closure of an area or a poorly determined spatial quota might end up diverting fishing effort into habitats that are more sensitive or have a weaker fish stock. Management and decisionmaking should explicitly consider this uncertainty.

One reason for spatial management of fisheries is to reduce conflicts between different types of fishing. If these conflicts lead to costly disruptions of fishing and gear losses, explicit separation of incompatible fishing gears may yield net benefits. It may only be necessary to prohibit specific gear at certain times, if conflicts are not problematic year-round. Restrictions that are carefully targeted, both spatially and temporally, may be able to resolve problems at much lower cost than year-round exclusions of particular types of gear over large areas. A prominent example of competition for the same resource in Massachusetts waters is the competition over bluefin tuna in Cape Cod Bay between commercial purse seiners[10] and "general category" fishermen using harpoons and rod and reel. At issue is not the total amount of tuna allocated to each user group but rather the belief that the activity of purse seining for tuna depletes the resource locally, which reduces catch rates and consequently total catch for general category and recreational fishers in Cape Cod Bay.

One aspect of fishery management where spatial controls have been widely applied is in habitat protection. In 1996, the U.S. Congress added new habitat conservation provisions to the Magnuson-Stevens Fishery Conservation and Management Act. To the extent that protections of essential fish habitat close areas to fishing or restrict certain fishing practices and gear types to mitigate these impacts, they are likely to increase harvest costs. Cost increases may be offset in the long run, if habitat protection increases the productivity of fish stocks. This will increase the availability of fish, but there is considerable uncertainty as to what effects protective actions will actually have on habitat and how long recovery of damaged habitat will take. In the absence of sufficient information to determine the optimal level and form of habitat protection, it may be more useful to concentrate on designing systems that protect a given amount of habitat of varying types in a cost-effective manner. In many cases, incremental damage to habitat will decline with successive passes of fishing gear simply because much of the potential damage occurs on the first pass. In that case, concentrating fishing in areas that have already been fished will result in less habitat damage for a given amount of fishing effort.

Marine aquaculture in the United States is quite limited. However, demands for seafood continue to grow while wild capacity does not, and this is likely to increase demands to place aquaculture facilities in coastal waters. Growth of aquaculture in coastal waters has been inhibited by the complexity of permitting policies, the lack of clear guidelines for siting aquaculture facilities, and concerns that aquaculture will interfere with commercial and recreational fisheries.[11] Similar issues have stalled development of offshore aquaculture in federal waters, but this may begin to change. There is little argument

Box 7.1　Seasonal Gear Restrictions in the Cape Cod Bay Bluefin Tuna Fishery

Migrating bluefin tuna arrive in the Gulf of Maine and Cape Cod Bay each June to feed for the summer and then depart in October. Anglers prize bluefin tuna as a game fish, but it is also one of the most valuable commercially fished species on a per-pound basis. The catch in U.S. waters is allocated among several user groups and gear types, including a commercial purse seine category and both commercial and recreational hand-gear categories using harpoons and hook and line.

Participants in the hand-gear fisheries argue that purse seiners' catches can cause local depletion, which reduces catch rates for hand-gear fishermen and anglers and undermines the quality of their fishing experience. In deference to these concerns, purse seining for bluefin has been prohibited in certain areas of the bay at all times and in most of the bay on weekends during September, until the general category quota is reached.[12] This policy, however, has not eliminated the conflict.

The State of Massachusetts prohibited all purse seining for bluefin tuna in Cape Cod Bay for the 2006 season and again in 2008. The time-area closures for tuna purse seining do not explicitly change the allocation of fish between sectors of the fishery. However, they clearly affect the potential producer surplus of the purse seine fleet because they exclude it from a preferred fishing ground and may increase catches for hand-gear fishermen and anglers.

Since neither sector of the fishery has caught its full allocation in recent years, an action that excludes one group from a preferred fishing area is likely to further reduce its catch and act as a de facto re-allocation. To calculate the change in net benefits associated with an exclusion of purse seining in Cape Cod Bay, one would need to estimate how the producer surplus of the excluded purse seiners is affected and compare this to the gains by other user groups. The benefits to the general category sector can be partially estimated by considering the projected increase in catch and effort and subtracting increased costs of effort from increased revenues. However, this may underestimate general category benefits because of the quasi-recreational nature of the fishery. Some general-category fishermen may enjoy the consumer surplus associated with the improved fishing conditions and increased catches, in addition to the producer surplus associated with sale of catches.

that aquaculture can have negative impacts on the marine environment and can conflict with other users, but appropriate siting and regulation of aquaculture facilities can minimize these impacts and balance them with benefits generated by aquaculture.

Aquaculture operations typically occupy relatively little space, so offshore operations that are properly sited should not interfere substantially with fishing. However, the physical impacts of installations and pollution associated with feed and waste discharges could lead to serious environmental impacts. There may be some advantage to designating zones for aquaculture in advance of specific applications. This can streamline the regulatory process and reduce the costs of permitting. Potential conflicts can be identified beforehand so that the process of permitting becomes quicker and less costly. This will not

Box 7.2 Offshore Wind Farm

Wind energy is among the more economically viable sources of renewable energy. Historically, wind turbines have been built on land, but wind speeds are higher and less variable in some ocean areas. Although many offshore wind energy farms exist in other parts of the world (especially Europe), it is a relatively new phenomenon in the United States. In fact, the Cape Wind project proposed for Nantucket Sound would be the first offshore wind energy installation in the United States.

The Cape Wind project plans to erect 130 wind turbine generators in an area of about 25 square miles. Despite the potential benefits of electricity generation with offshore wind energy, proposed projects (including Cape Wind) have faced resistance from the local coastal population and from some environmental groups. The former group often expresses concerns about the impairment of the ocean view (because, in many cases, the wind turbines are visible on the horizon) and attendant adverse impacts on property values and tourism. There are also concerns about potential impacts on commercial and recreational fisheries and boating, and potential navigational hazards related to the placement of large structures in coastal waters.

While many environmental groups support offshore wind energy proposals, some oppose these projects because they fear damage to marine life from turbine construction and electrical cables, and injury to birds by turbine blades. Siting wind farms farther offshore might reduce some adverse impacts (particularly on amenity values), but this must be balanced against the increased costs of building the installations in deep water and longer transmission lines.

eliminate the need to evaluate individual proposals, however, and it may be difficult to identify in advance the preferred areas for aquaculture since the methods and technology are still evolving.

There is increasing demand to site industrial installations, such as wind farms and offshore terminals for unloading liquefied natural gas tankers, in the ocean. While these installations take up only a tiny fraction of the space in coastal waters, they have generally been highly controversial. This is partly due to strong public resistance to allowing any one entity to have exclusive use of ocean areas, stemming from a long tradition of maintaining open public access to marine areas. However, once a location is chosen, specific conflicts with other uses and users often arise, which may represent real costs to be considered along with the project development costs in a cost-benefit analysis of the project.

The net benefits associated with alternative locations for these projects are dictated by various physical characteristics of the location, including proximity to land or population centers; water depth; presence or absence of wind, waves, or currents, etc., that can affect the benefit stream from the completed project and construction and maintenance costs. The external costs of the installations (in terms of impacts on other uses and users) may also vary substantially, depending on location. If the facility is visible from shore or sited in an area subject to intensive recreational use, the visual impact of the project may be important. Some projects may substantially reduce coastal property values, as well as cause losses in utility to recreational users. These facilities may have negative impacts on marine habitat and productivity of fisheries. Optimal location of a facility requires balancing site characteristics that are favorable for the installation with negative impacts on existing users and ecosystem services. Determining the relative costs and benefits of siting facilities in alternative locations will often require nonmarket valuation methods to determine costs, such as exclusion of recreational activities or loss of amenity values associated with unsightly installations.

Coastal waters absorb a substantial amount of contaminants from terrestrial sources, both from point sources (such as sewerage outfalls) and from nonpoint sources (such as nutrients in runoff from agriculture land and lawns that enter the coastal waters directly or through rivers that drain into coastal waters). The ocean has immense capacity to absorb this pollution, with apparently limited consequences, when the contaminants are diluted and dispersed sufficiently. However, localized impacts and even impacts over large areas can be significant.

In most cases, it is neither possible nor economically optimal to eliminate pollution completely from terrestrial sources entering the sea. Potentially costly measures, such as prohibiting septic tanks in favor of sewerage treatment or strict controls on use of fertilizers or pesticides, may be justified in some locations but not in others. The physical and ecological characteristics of a marine area, as well as the activities undertaken there, will affect the impacts of pollution from terrestrial sources, as well as the damage associated with them. For example, currents and tides may rapidly disperse contaminants and transport them to the open ocean in some areas, while in other areas contaminants may persist for longer periods or settle into the sediment. In such areas, it may be necessary and worthwhile to impose stricter and more costly controls on activities that pollute. The benefits of these controls will depend also on the ecological impacts of the pollution and human use of the area. Some marine ecological communities may be highly sensitive to pollution, while others may be less so. Pollution in areas that are important for fishing or recreation may cause more economic damage and validate stronger mitigation measures.

Determining the economically optimal level of pollution control may require a combination of physical, ecological, and economic modeling (see chapter 3) that relates pollution flows to ecological impacts and then maps ecological impacts to human benefits. It may be important to account for how humans respond not only to measures designed to reduce pollution but also to negative or positive changes that result from changes in pollution levels.

Conclusions

Although the appropriate scale of management is not clearly specified, most definitions of an ecosystem approach to fisheries suggest a spatial, or "place-

Box 7.3   Controlling Runoff from Nonpoint Source Pollutants

Many times, storm water runoff contains nonpoint source pollutants, such as suspended solids and fecal coliform bacteria. These pollutants have been responsible for closing shellfish beds and public beaches in Massachusetts, for example. One possible remedy is to build infiltration structures designed to hold and treat storm water (or sewerage) runoff—especially the first half inch or so of precipitation. Infiltration structures should be located just before the points where the storm water is released into the ocean.

The towns of Wareham and Tisbury in Massachusetts built infiltration structures to reduce bacterial and other pollutants in the storm water flowing from their towns into the adjacent water bodies.[13] Their structures successfully removed not only fecal coliform bacteria from storm water but also other nonpoint source pollutants, such as petroleum oil, grease, hydrocarbons, zinc, barium, chromium, and lead. Consequently, the shellfish beds near the towns' shores are now open much longer during the year. It is only after heavy rains that a shellfish bed may be closed. Estimating the construction and maintenance (over the expected lifetime) costs of the infiltration structures is relatively straightforward, but valuing the benefits may not be. Two potential benefits of this project mean that shellfish beds remain open for harvesting for a much longer period and public access beaches are not closed as often.

based," approach to management.[14] The ostensive purpose of EBM is to maintain the integrity of overall marine communities, rather than simply focusing on particular species. Because the ranges of different species in these communities vary, with some swimming widely and others staying more localized, it will almost certainly be necessary to design nested management structures that incorporate local-scale management into larger-scale management. A decision to prohibit or segregate certain activities in marine areas leaves open the question of how to design these areas. Size, shape, location, and the mixture of activities permitted will all affect the benefits and costs of zoning policies. These design issues are interdependent and must be considered jointly to maximize the benefits of zoning.

Many factors constrain the ability to implement effective spatial management of marine areas. Humans have little or no control over movement of living resources across whatever boundaries might be designated and quite limited knowledge of the spatial dynamics of these resources (e.g., species migration, meta-population structures, importance of different habitats, quality of those habitats, etc.). These factors tend to increase the expense and reduce the benefits of imposing explicit spatial management. Not only is more knowledge of the spatial dynamics of the marine ecosystem needed, improved methods of managing human activities that explicitly account for (and are robust to) uncertainty must be developed (see chapter 5). The ability to ensure that users adhere to regulations is often limited, particularly in areas far offshore. However, monitoring technology, such as satellite transponders and video monitoring systems, is becoming more common, more effective, and less costly, which should help managers implement effective and efficient spatial management of offshore activities.

Policies in the marine and coastal environment are designed in a political and often contentious process, and spatial policies are no exception. The implication is that it is often possible for rent-seeking behavior[15] to alter the design of a policy from one that "on paper" increases social benefits to one that "in the water" does not. Overall, the design of governance institutions (e.g., the management organizations and policy-development processes for creating regulations) should make these behaviors transparent and, where possible, try to minimize them. One potential mechanism might be the inclusion of a rule that ensures that winners must compensate losers when those negatively affected can demonstrate how they are harmed by the policy change.

Endnotes

1. Wilen (2004).
2. Crowder et al. (2006), Edwards (2007).
3. Norse (2005, 433).
4. An externality (or spillover) of an activity is an impact on a party not directly involved in the activity. The impact may cause harm to that party (negative externality) or benefit it (positive externality).
5. Source-sink is an ecological process in which the population in one area (the source) augments the population in another area (the sink). It can occur through active emigration of adults from the source area to the sink, or by passive transport of eggs or larvae to the sink by ocean currents. Eggs that are spawned in the sink areas settle and grow there.
6. Brown and Roughgarden (1997).
7. Recruits are juvenile fish grown old enough or large enough to be counted in the fish stock.
8. Holland (2004).
9. Herrera (2006).
10. A purse seine is a large wall of netting that encircles a school of fish. A smaller boat lays out the net and brings the end back to the fishing boat, completing the circle. Fishermen pull the bottom of the netting closed (like a drawstring purse), which moves the fish into the center of the net, and then drag the net into the boat or scoop the fish out with smaller nets or pumps.
11. Massachusetts Aquaculture White Paper (1995).
12. 322 CMR (Code of Massachusetts Regulations) 4.01 and 6.04.
13. U.S. EPA (2002b).
14. Murawski (2007).
15. Rent seeking here refers to the use of political means by an individual or group to ensure that regulations benefit them to the exclusion of others. Rent seeking can result in substantial expenditures of resources on lobbying and lawsuits, which does not necessarily lead to a more efficient outcome and often leads to the opposite.

CHAPTER 8

Integrating Economics into Coastal Policy: Guidelines and Case Studies

There is growing consensus among policymakers, stakeholders, and researchers that integrated multi-use ocean management can yield substantial benefits. Current management systems often fail to account for the interconnectedness of the marine ecosystem and its components, the cumulative impacts of different activities, and associated spatial heterogeneity. Implementation of integrated management, however, raises numerous questions, such as what criteria should be used to determine the activities allowed in specific locations and the limits on how these activities are undertaken. These decisions have traditionally been made on an ad hoc basis that (not surprisingly) fails to yield the greatest net benefits to society.

This book discusses a number of economic approaches that can provide policy-relevant information to policymakers and resource managers. It includes frameworks for evaluating the economic merits of projects and policies, methods for predicting behavior and measuring value, and approaches that use insights from economic theory to improve policy design and inform management. These methods and tools are not mutually exclusive; rather, they are interrelated and are typically used in combination. For example, cost-benefit analysis (CBA) or cost-efficiency analysis (CEA) often requires economic behavioral models and valuation techniques to quantify and value the expected outcomes of alternative policy choices. Models to predict behavior can often be used for valuation or other purposes as well. Expected policy outcomes and associated costs or benefits are frequently uncertain; in most cases, this uncertainty should be explicitly considered in the decision-making process and when conducting economic analysis. Moreover, while economic analyses may be contingent upon a predefined set of policy alternatives identified by policymakers or stakeholders, economics can be useful in identifying or designing the alternatives to be considered.

This last point is worthy of additional emphasis: while rigorous evaluations of the costs and benefits of alternative uses of marine resources or policies that affect human activities are important, many times these evaluations, or those of other economic models, are too narrowly defined. This often occurs due to the fragmented (and sometimes conflicting) jurisdiction of different regulatory agencies that manage human activities in the coastal marine ecosystem. That is, agencies tend to request analyses that address their particular regulatory or policy mandates, or related research interests. Analyses of broader issues are often given much less emphasis. To best inform integrated multi-use ocean management, however, analysis of particular actions and policies should attempt to identify and quantify the economic, ecological, and social spillover effects that reach beyond the scale and scope of the primary issue at hand. This can provide information that allows managers to better control or mitigate the harmful effects of these spillovers or even encourage positive spillover effects. Expanding the scope of analysis, however, depends on reforms to the broader governance system to mandate a more coordinated approach to managing human activities and impacts.

Economic Analysis: Asking the Right Questions and Choosing the Right Tools

The economic frameworks and tools most appropriate to any given policy analysis depend first and foremost on the questions asked (or that should be asked) by decisionmakers. Each of the evaluative frameworks discussed in chapter 2, including CBA, CEA, and EIA, answer different types of questions. For example, CBA addresses questions regarding the social benefits and costs of different policy alternatives and related outcomes, whereas CEA addresses more limited questions on the costs of alternative mechanisms that could achieve predefined policy goals. An economic impact analysis provides information about the number of jobs and other economic impacts that are generated by a project or policy, but does not reveal net social benefits. Although CBA can sometimes be controversial (especially to those who object to quantifying values associated with ecological resources), it is considered by many—including most economists—to be the most applicable analytical framework to guide policy. For this reason, methods that contribute to defensible CBA applications in ocean and coastal policy contexts have received greater attention in this book. Other models and approaches, however, can be equally or more relevant in particular circumstances, depending on the primary questions at hand.

In addition to choosing the appropriate analytical framework, policy analysts must make a number of decisions regarding which benefits, costs, and/or impacts to include in the analysis. These choices often require decisions about the geographical regions and human populations to consider, the economic outcomes to be measured (or omitted), and other considerations that define the analysis. To as great an extent as possible, these decisions should take into account the relevance of different groups, areas, or considerations to the models in question and final outcome (i.e., whether the inclusion of certain groups or areas might change recommended policies, for example). If the answer is that group A in area B will not likely be affected significantly, nor will including their costs and benefits change the decision, then this might be a basis for omitting these groups from the analysis. This is an important point: analysis that informs integrated multi-use coastal and ocean management does not require that analysts model every sector that occupies or uses some resource in affected areas. Rather, the analyst must strike the right balance between including sufficient sectors to adequately represent the cumulative and spillover impacts of decisions, as well as cost-effective, manageable economic analysis.

Unfortunately, there is no general theory that determines such a balance. It depends on the context of the decision (scale and scope) and the questions asked. Questions that an analyst might consider when planning economic research can include: What is the broader purpose, goal, or objective of the analysis? Are there specific costs, benefits, or impacts that may be particularly relevant or substantial? Are there significant nonmarket implications, and if so, what methods should be used to evaluate them? Will the decisions have large distributional impacts? Will the inclusion of uncertainty and risk preferences in the model(s) change the decision, and if so, what areas of uncertainty are most critical? What are the primary elements that need a sensitivity analysis? What level of accuracy is required? What tradeoffs are the policymakers or analysts willing to make between accuracy, study budget, and time required to complete the study? These and other questions, considered in coordination with experts familiar with economic analysis, can help ensure that the chosen analytical frameworks and methods serve their anticipated purpose.

Applying Economics to Decisions in Coastal Ecosystem Management

As implied above, the appropriate economic tools for ocean and coastal management depend on the policy context. This section discusses ways in which economic analysis can be applied to different types of policy considerations in the coastal zone. The case studies in appendix A illustrate the choices and tradeoffs involved in more detail. Because appropriate approaches for economic analysis depend on the specifics of the policies and contexts being considered, the following discussions should be viewed as a broad set of recommendations rather than inflexible prescriptions.

Example 1: Wind Energy in the Coastal Zone—The Case of Cape Wind

Wind is among the more economically viable sources of renewable energy, and the abundant resource of offshore wind in U.S. coastal waters has yet to be tapped. Cape Wind,[1] a proposed installation off the coast of Nantucket, MA, may be the first commercial-scale offshore wind farm in U.S. waters. The contentiousness of this project can be traced in large part to the heterogeneity of expected benefits and costs that would be realized by different groups. Specific interest groups often sponsor economic research to either support or oppose projects with unevenly distributed benefits or costs. In such cases, the interpretation and validity of economic methods must be considered carefully when comparing results, to ensure that the full range of benefits and costs have been estimated appropriately.

The Cape Wind project would include more than 100 wind turbines (each standing 440 feet high, between 4 and 11 miles offshore) sited in the Horseshoe Shoals area near Nantucket, where the water is approximately 50 feet deep. The electricity generated by this offshore wind park would be conveyed to a land-based electricity grid through a network of underwater and underground cables. Part of this planned network lies in Massachusetts waters, while the wind farm itself is in federal waters.[2]

Although the wind farm will be a privately funded business venture, it will occupy publicly owned marine space. Consequently, it requires approvals from various local, state, and federal agencies. Moreover, because this project involves the use of public resources, one of the most relevant economic questions from society's perspective is whether the proposed wind farm is the most beneficial long-term use of these scarce resources. If the answer is no, then society is better off not allocating these resources to a wind farm.

CBA is the best analytical framework to address this and related questions. Although the project will also occupy federal waters, a major portion of its market and nonmarket benefits and costs will likely be borne by residents in the region of the project site, a feature shared by many large infrastructure projects. While a CBA may focus on these regional costs and benefits, a comprehensive analysis is needed to consider the net benefits of the project from the perspective of the entire U.S. public, because the project might also affect ecosystem resources and services in both federal and state waters. Given the substantial heterogeneity of benefits and costs (i.e., there will be winners and losers), analysts might also want to determine the distribution of net benefits across all these groups.

Estimating the full range of benefits and costs via CBA often requires a variety of valuation methods. Given the resources and time required to implement different economic analyses, it can be necessary to limit the scope and the number of analytical methods and address only those benefits or costs likely to be most significant in the specific policy context. For Cape Wind, this entails a number of costs and benefits that are related to market goods, for example, the costs of designing and building the wind farm itself and the value of the electricity it will produce. These benefits and costs are often estimated using traditional market analysis methods (as discussed in chapter 3), and would likely be included in a CBA of a project of this type.

There are also important nonmarket benefits and costs that a reasonably comprehensive CBA should include. For benefits, some consumers might be willing to pay a price premium for renewably generated electricity, reflecting their additional value for "green" energy. The premium could be estimated using a stated preference survey (as discussed in chapter 4). Alternatively, estimates of value might be derived using benefit transfer techniques, based on estimates from prior surveys of consumers' willingness to pay for green electricity or even from markets in which consumers already purchase renewable energy. The usefulness of such market data for economic analysis, however, depends on many factors, including the specific consumer choices available and mechanisms through which consumers purchase renewable energy. The choice of benefit transfer versus case-specific primary research depends on whether decisionmakers have the time and resources to obtain more costly, but more accurate estimates from primary studies or can make do with quicker and less costly approximations of nonmarket value derived through benefit transfer.

There are also a number of potential costs that can require nonmarket valuation techniques to quantify. There is, for example, the possibility of marine habitat loss due to construction and maintenance activities at the project site, as well as mortality or injury of birds (particularly migratory birds) from turbine rotors. In addition, since the turbines will be visible from the shore, people who prefer an unrestricted view of the ocean may be negatively affected by impacts to the seascape. Associated losses in economic value, which represent costs to the public, can be estimated using hedonic property value or stated preference methods, or perhaps benefit transfer if primary data collection is infeasible. A key issue here is accounting for the various types of nonmarket benefits and costs that are measured using various available techniques, to ensure both that the full range of primary benefits and costs are measured and that certain benefits and costs are not double-counted.

Available evidence, although tentative, indicates that wind turbine structures may have mixed effects on recreational and commercial fisheries.[3] Estimating costs related to displacement of fishermen or declines in fishery productivity may also require nonmarket techniques, including ecological productivity models. Accordingly, a full understanding of the long-term ecological impacts of a wind farm may require models of how the wind farm will affect the behavior of marine organisms, such as fish communities, and how people's behavior—and ultimately net economic benefits—will be affected.

There is also likely to be substantial uncertainty concerning both benefits and costs of the proposed wind farm. On the benefit side, this includes uncertainty about the value of the electricity that will be produced, how much will actually be produced, and when the project will be completed. On the cost side, there may be uncertainty regarding the costs of building the wind farm (including the regulatory transactions costs associated with permitting), as well as uncertainty about the effects the wind farm may have on the ecosystem and its services and uses, such as fisheries and recreation. These are just some of the many areas of uncertainty that face policymakers. Since the installation of turbines may result in impacts that will be difficult or impossible to reverse, it may also be appropriate to consider the quasi-option value,[4] in which future research may provide more accurate information about uncertain costs and benefits of the project, thereby providing at least a partial incentive to delay implementation.

In addition, since the Cape Wind project entails large upfront costs but presumably will produce electricity for many years, the choice of an appropriate discount rate may be critical in this case. All these factors suggest that sensitivity analysis (i.e., replicating the analysis under various sets of assumptions to illustrate the range of likely outcomes) is a critical complement to CBA in this case. A sensitivity analysis can indicate whether the model conclusions (e.g., about whether the net benefits are positive or negative) are robust to key assumptions and uncertainties, and the importance of specific assumptions to model outcomes and associated policy guidance.

While a CBA of the Cape Wind project would likely focus on the merits of its proposal in the recommended location, policymakers might also consider how the proposed project fits into the broader mix of coastal ecosystem uses. What other future uses of this area might be impeded or perhaps aided[5] by this installation? It may be useful to identify in advance additional preferred sites for wind farms or other exclusive uses (i.e., those sites for which the expected net benefits are highest) and zone these areas to allow for such uses. This can help ensure that only the best-suited areas are designated for wind energy generation, which may substantially reduce the costs of permitting proposed installations. This, in part, is one of the goals of the recently released (June 2009) draft Massachusetts Ocean Management Plan, which covers 1,500 miles of Massachusetts coastline and 1.6 million acres of subtidal lands under state jurisdiction. Such plans can help establish the range of projects and possibilities considered within an economic analysis, allowing greater attention to those possibilities that are most likely or relevant.

In addition to CBAs, it is common to encounter EIAs for projects like Cape Wind. Estimates of economic impacts often provide a relatively more favorable perspective on development projects and a less favorable perspective on preservation initiatives. One of the reasons for this is that preservation initiatives often generate substantial nonmarket benefits that are not reflected in EIAs, whereas development projects often generate market activities that are reflected in these models. These analyses can shed light on potential effects of projects, such as wind farms on local income, employment, or similar measures of economic activity. As noted in prior chapters, these results are not comparable to economic benefits or costs and should not be added to the outcomes of a CBA. Rather, EIA represents a distinctly different perspective on the potential economic outcomes of the proposed project that, while not directly related to social well-being, may nonetheless be of interest to policymakers. For the Cape Wind project, an EIA would likely focus on economic impacts to the local region or state, in contrast to the national scale at which a CBA might be conducted. (Additional information on Cape Wind, together with details of analyses that have already been conducted, is presented in case study 1 in appendix A.)

Example 2: Beach Nourishment and Offshore Sand Mining

Coastlines evolve over time. Since coastal erosion can be detrimental to man-made structures, such as houses, roads, and harbors built along the coasts, various structural and nonstructural means have been employed to protect shores against the loss of sand. Structural methods (e.g., groins and break-waters) may have limited effectiveness and can displace erosion problems to other areas. Thus, beach nourishment is often recommended instead of, or in conjunction with, engineering solutions. As the name suggests, beach nour-ishment involves replenishing the sand on a beach that is subject to erosion. Despite the perceived benefits of beach nourishment, some challenge the wis-dom of shoreline stabilization projects and recommend shoreline retreat—a planned repositioning of coastal structures away from the shoreline that al-lows natural erosion (and replenishment)—as the best strategy to prevent or mitigate damages caused by coastal erosion. In addition, there is often contro-versy surrounding potential ecological and related economic impacts at sites from which sand is removed or mined.

Winthrop Beach is a popular metropolitan recreation area close to Bos-ton, MA. Over the past 100-plus years, many hard structures have been built in attempts to prevent shore retreat in the area, but the beach remains vulnerable to substantial coastal erosion. The Massachusetts Department of Conservation and Recreation has proposed nourishing 37 acres of Winthrop Beach, using an offshore source of sand. The nourishment project requires about 500,000 cubic yards of sand that would be mined from an offshore site called NOMES I. (See case study 2 in appendix A for additional details.)

As in all cases, the most informative types of economic analysis for Win-throp Beach depend on the policy question(s) at hand. If policymakers de-termine *beforehand* that shoreline stabilization or beach nourishment is to be conducted, then CEA is an appropriate analytical framework to ascertain the most efficient means of obtaining such a predetermined outcome. On the other hand, because the project involves the use of public resources (taxpayer funds, sand deposits from other locations, etc.) and would have other public nonmarket effects, a CBA would provide a more comprehensive perspective on economic benefits and costs.

A CBA in this case would compare the discounted value of the stream of benefits over the life of the project against the discounted stream of costs of the project. These benefits and costs would be referenced against an appropriate status quo, or the outcome with no new policy. In the case of Winthrop Beach, a shoreline retreat alternative might be considered as either the status quo op-tion or one of the considered alternatives—although it might not be feasible for the Winthrop area due to the density of local housing and infrastructure.

With either alternative (renourishment or shoreline retreat), because benefits and costs are meaningful only if measured from a policy baseline (often the status quo in the absence of any policy change), it is important that this baseline be specified clearly.

The nature of the Winthrop Beach nourishment project suggests that there are at least three benefits of potentially significant magnitude. First, residents in the area whose houses are close to the beach might enjoy enhanced protection from storms. Hedonic property value methods or benefit transfer of similar results from other locations could help estimate the influence of greater storm protection on related property values and provide insight into consumer willingness to pay for increased protection. Second, the project might enhance storm protection of public infrastructure and property (such as roads). Such benefits might be quantified by estimating the reduction in risk of damage or loss and the associated market (or nonmarket) value (i.e., the change in the expected value of monetized storm damages, appropriately quantified). Similar benefits might accrue to firms operating in the affected area, whose business properties would be at lower risk of damage. The primary third category of benefits of the project would be the amenity value associated with a wider beach (e.g., for recreation). Nonmarket techniques, such as revealed (e.g., models of recreation demand) or stated preference techniques, could be used to estimate these values. Resulting indirect effects on local tourism-related businesses (e.g., hotels and restaurants), however, should not be counted as an economic benefit of the project; these are secondary effects that should not be included in a CBA, as discussed in chapter 2.

The market costs of beach nourishment projects include the engineering and materials costs of dredging sand from an offshore site (or procuring sand from an inland site) and spreading it on the beach. Since nourished beaches continue to lose sand over time, the costs of periodically replacing sand on the beach should be taken into consideration, if such replacement is included. An earlier CEA suggested that acquiring sand through offshore dredging would be considerably less costly than acquiring sand from terrestrial sources. However, dredging sand from the offshore site might affect commercial fisheries adversely (by harming fish stocks), so the damages suffered by the fisheries sector should be included as project costs. Excavation of sand from the ocean floor may also be detrimental to demersal marine life.[6] Depending on the types of market and nonmarket values associated with these ecological resources, various valuation methods may be appropriate. For example, ecological models might be used to estimate impacts on fishery benefits, whereas stated preference methods might be used to identify related use and nonuse values to the public.

As in many projects in the coastal zone, the outcomes and net benefits of beach nourishment are subject to considerable uncertainty related to weather, erosion rates, human behavior, and other future events. While it would be ideal to quantify these uncertainties (e.g., estimate a probability distribution of the potential net benefits or costs of the project), at a minimum these uncertainties should be acknowledged and an attempt made to explain how they might affect estimated net benefits. This could be accomplished using sensitivity analysis. In addition, it is important to make policymakers aware of potential long-term outcomes of beach nourishment that might influence benefits or costs, in addition to short-term effects. For example, beach nourishment can encourage development in areas prone to storm damage, and it might become increasingly expensive to protect these areas in the future, if climate change causes sea levels to rise or storm activity to increase.

Finally, as with many policy contexts, the primary benefits and costs of beach nourishment are likely to be realized by different user and nonuser groups. For example, primary costs would likely be borne by taxpayers (who would pay for mining the sand and depositing it on the beach). If sand mining reduces the productivity of fisheries or interferes with fishing activities, those costs will be borne by recreational anglers and commercial fishermen. Local residents who benefit from shoreline protection and recreation, visitors who use the nourished beach for recreation, and taxpayers who would be subject to fewer costs for repair and replacement of coastal infrastructure would likely realize the primary benefits. Estimates of net benefits received or lost by different user groups, in addition to total social net-benefit estimates, can often provide policymakers with relevant information for developing policy. However, when measuring net benefits, it is important to avoid double counting, in other words, the temptation to measure secondary effects (e.g., more spending at restaurants and hotels due to increased beach visitation, as noted above). Including secondary effects in CBA will only bias estimates of net benefits and contribute to inappropriate policy guidance.

Example 3: Spatial Controls to Environmental Impacts of Fisheries

North Atlantic right whales are listed as endangered throughout their range. The primary actions recommended in the "Recovery Plan for North Atlantic Right Whales"[7] are to 1) reduce or eliminate injury or mortality caused by ship collision, 2) reduce or eliminate injury and mortality caused by fisheries and fishing gear, 3) protect habitats essential to the survival and recovery of the northern right whale, 4) minimize disturbance by vessels, and 5) maximize efforts to free entangled or stranded right whales. As part of this plan, the National Marine Fisheries Service has designated areas of critical habitat for the western population of the North Atlantic right whale, which include areas of Massachusetts Bay and Cape Cod Bay. Regulations to reduce whale entanglements in these areas when the whales are present were first implemented in 1997 and periodic adjustments have been made since.

Because northern right whales are a federally listed endangered species, there is a fixed and non-negotiable objective to reducing the risk of whale injuries and mortality from fishing gear. In such a setting, policymakers may be interested primarily in determining the cost-effectiveness of alternative means of right whale protection, and they may be interested or required (in a social and environmental impact statement) to provide estimates of the costs and other economic impacts of proposed or existing policies. Accordingly, in this case, a CEA may be a more applicable analytical framework than a full-scale CBA, and an EIA may be useful and possibly required.

The primary cost of closing a fishing area is the reduction in benefits to those who would otherwise have fished in the area. However, the loss in benefits will generally be less than the total producer surplus associated with the excluded fishing activities because in most cases, the closure will redirect some of that activity to other areas (unless there is a simultaneous reduction in total allowable catch or effort). This is particularly true if the restricted area affects only a small part of the overall fishery. Net losses from fishery closures can be estimated by comparing the producer surplus that displaced fishers can expect to make from their next most valuable option, relative to the restricted option. One approach to this analysis would be to simply estimate the producer surplus for each individual fisherman (or use group averages) in the location they had been fishing and subtract from that the projected producer surplus from the fishery where they might be expected to relocate.[8]

Additional costs can be generated by imposing gear restrictions in areas that remain open for fishing. Here again, the appropriate measure of costs is the change in producer surplus, taking into account the change in behavior after the policy is implemented. The costs of requiring gear modifications (such as breakaway devices and floating lines replaced with sink lines[9]) and requiring special rules for deploying lobster pots could be partially measured by quantifying the out-of-pocket cost of modifying the current gear in the fishery. However, this will only be an approximation since the required measures may induce other, less costly responses and because there may be other costs imposed on fishing operations. Less costly responses to gear restrictions might include a reduction of effort in affected areas or diversion of effort to other, unrestricted areas. The mandated use of sink lines also increases ongoing costs of operation and potentially loss of gear because sink lines are damaged by abrasion on the sea bottom and require more frequent replacement. Because these costs are not included in the initial cost of gear modification, estimation of these costs would require additional, more involved analysis.

A comprehensive CEA would also account for potential cost-offsetting benefits. For example, by reducing competition for the local fish stock and space, the exclusion of one group of fishermen from an area is likely to lead to an increase in consumer surplus for recreational anglers who are not excluded or restricted. The exclusion of commercial activities may also draw new anglers to the affected area. If expected changes in the quality of fishing for anglers can be quantified, either stated preference or revealed preference methods could be used to estimate the net benefits to recreational fishers (see chapter 4).

Not surprisingly, many of the effects of area closures and gear restrictions are subject to uncertainty. Hence, as is often the case, sensitivity analysis—or other formal treatment of uncertainty—is generally required to quantify the range of possible outcomes and impacts of uncertainty.

Closing specific areas at specific times or restricting gear use (e.g., not allowing sink gill nets in the critical habitat area during part of the year) is likely to divert fishing effort and commercial landings, such that they shift expenditures and incomes among communities (and potentially states). These measures may also result in overall changes in revenues or expenditures. It may be possible to use behavioral models to predict these changes and to include this information in an input-output model (such as IMPLAN) to determine regional economic impacts. This information may help policymakers prepare for impacts of their policies and understand the distributional effects. For example, policymakers may care about retaining viable fishing communities in specific areas, and the feasibility of such goals can sometimes be informed by EIA. However, as discussed in detail in chapter 2, results of EIA are often misinterpreted by the lay public. For example, lost income for one community or group of fishermen is interpreted as a net economic loss without considering countervailing benefits that may accrue in other areas or to other parties (e.g., those who value increased protection of right whales). Results of these models—like any form of economic analysis—should be interpreted with care.

Conclusion

While economics is not the only perspective that one might take in assessing EBM proposals—many natural and social sciences have valuable insights to offer—economic methods can provide valuable tools for policy analysts. Without input from economists or economic models, managers risk implementing policies that can have undesired, unpopular, or harmful consequences; these may include unforeseen behavioral responses and unexpected reductions of social welfare. Similar consequences can result when economic data are used or interpreted inappropriately, or when only partial analyses are conducted. There is no one-size-fits-all template for economic analyses, but there are correct and incorrect ways to interpret and apply economics. Although the case studies presented above and in the appendix summarize some of the ways that economics could be applied to various policy contexts, the specific types of analysis that are most relevant in any particular case will depend on a variety of factors, including the principal questions of interest to decisionmakers.

This chapter and this book close with a final note emphasizing the need for more truly integrative, user-friendly, and policy-responsive economic analysis of marine ecosystems. Although economics can provide significant insight into ocean and coastal policy, to be most useful, economic guidance needs to be comprehensible to managers, policymakers, and citizens. It should also be cognizant of the broader policy and governance context. Policymakers have neither the time to read academic journal articles nor patience for analysis that does not recognize the realities of the policy context. This book is written in the hope that readers will welcome the advantages that economics offers and that they will take it upon themselves to effectively integrate economic tools into ocean and coastal management. This integration requires policymakers who are willing to consider economic insight and economists who are willing to devote greater attention to policy guidance and the policy process.

Endnotes

1. Cape Wind was first proposed in 2001. As of August 2009, it had completed its state and local permitting process (with all permits and approvals granted in one composite certificate) and is expected to complete the federal permitting process by the end of 2009.
2. Cape Wind (2007).
3. Hagos (2007); Wiersma (2008).
4. Quasi-option value is the value of delaying a decision that is impossible or very costly to reverse to allow time for more information to be gathered, in order to determine which decision will be beneficial. It reflects the value of the additional information that might become available in the future and that might allow an improved decision to be made. The availability of new information is uncertain, however, and is only possible if the irreversible decision is delayed.
5. For example, there might be some complementarity between aquaculture and wind farms in some sites. For example, aquaculture may be able to be sited in the wind farm areas and possibly benefit from its structures for anchoring.
6. The demersal zone is the part of the ocean or water column near, and affected by, the seabed and the benthos.
7. See NMFS (2004, rev.).
8. An alternative approach for estimating costs to fishery participants is a random utility model (RUM) of location choice to estimate the cost of the closure to individual fishers and then aggregate this to all excluded fishers. For example, Curtis and Hicks (2000) and Hicks et al. (2004) used RUMs of location choice in Pacific tuna fisheries and the mid-Atlantic surf clam fishery, respectively, to estimate welfare losses associated with area closures.
9. As the name implies, sink lines or sink ropes are designed to sink to the sea bottom (as opposed to traditional floating ropes), where they pose less danger of entanglement for whales, turtles, and other species. They hold lobster pots or dredges, for example, and can be variously made of denser polyester or even have lead cores.

Four Case Studies from Massachusetts

This appendix deliberately does not contain new analysis of existing proposals, nor does it draw conclusions about the economic desirability of specific projects in Massachusetts waters. Rather, its purpose is to summarize how economics may be brought to bear on the social and economic desirability of the projects highlighted in the case studies, so that more informed choices can be made. These case studies apply various economic models and analytical frameworks to wind energy, sand mining, pollutants in coastal zones, and spatial controls to manage environmental impacts of fishing in Massachusetts.

Case Study 1: Offshore Wind Farms

The exhaustibility of conventional fuels, the pollution caused by nonrenewable energy sources (including greenhouse gases, such as CO_2, that contribute to climate change), and the uncertainties in the prices and the supply of fossil fuels have all emphasized the need to develop renewable energy. Although the initial capital cost of renewable energy sources is often higher than conventional energy technologies, the "fuel" required for such energy generation—for example, wind and solar power—is virtually free. Recognizing the potential benefits of renewable energy, governments in many countries now offer incentives, including tax breaks and subsidies, to spur development of renewable energy sources. Renewable energy production has grown in the past few years, although its growth is uneven across the world.

Economists use the term "negative externality" to denote harmful effects of an activity on individuals whose interests are not given due consideration when deciding how much of the activity should be undertaken. In other words, negative externalities are undesirable side effects of an activity on the welfare of another. In the context of energy generation, negative externalities can include pollution of various types, ecological damage caused by the intake and output of cooling water (from power plants), and many others. For example, left to itself, the management of a power plant would likely not take into account the pollution the plant causes when deciding how much electricity to generate. As a result, to ensure that an appropriate amount of both energy and pollution is "produced," the government often regulates power plant activities, using one of a variety of available management tools. Government support of renewable energy is partly motivated by the avoidance of negative externalities (such as pollution) that are usually associated with more conventional forms of energy. However, as the case of wind energy in general—and offshore wind energy in particular—demonstrates, even renewable energy resources can have negative externalities that policymakers must confront.

Wind energy is among the more economically viable sources of renewable energy. In the United States, wind energy contributed about 0.28% of the total energy requirement of the nation in 2006.[1] In 2005, its share of total electricity generation was about 0.89%, and generation from renewable sources was 8.8%.[2] Historically, wind turbines have often been built on land. However, in some densely populated areas, sufficient land may not be available for large wind parks. In addition, wind speeds may be more favorable for energy generation in the open ocean than on land. In offshore wind facilities, wind turbines are placed in the ocean in relatively shallow waters. The pillar that supports each wind turbine is driven into the sea-floor, with the turbine and the blades mounted well above sea level. Construction of wind parks is currently economically infeasible beyond a certain depth; as a result, offshore wind projects are not built farther than a few miles from the shore, although the technology for deep-water installations is now being developed.

Despite the potential benefits of electricity generation from offshore wind energy, some projects have faced resistance from the local coastal population and some environmental groups. The former express concerns about the impairment of the ocean view (because, in many cases, the wind turbines are visible on the horizon) and associated impacts on coastal property values and tourism. Findings of such adverse effects are not universal, however, and can depend on the location and characteristics of the wind farm, the preferences of residents and tourists, and other factors.[3] There are also concerns about potential effects on commercial and recreational fisheries and boating, and potential navigational hazards, related to the placement of large structures in coastal waters. While many environmental groups support offshore wind-energy proposals, some oppose these projects because they fear damage to marine life from wind turbines and underwater electrical cables, and possible injury to birds from turbine blades.

Harnessing offshore wind energy involves numerous tradeoffs. A critical distinction in analysis and policy design is between those who receive benefits and those who bear costs, and in particular the concentration of some costs with small user groups. While the potential *benefits* of wind energy can be large in aggregate, they are dispersed across the population, with each individual typically receiving a small per capita benefit. The potential negative side effects of such facilities, however, are often concentrated with a relatively small number of individuals who live close to them—each of whom may bear a more significant personal or household cost. Hence, even if wind power generates positive net benefits in the aggregate (which is not certain), it may nonetheless face staunch opposition from local forces. This shows the critical importance that benefit distribution plays in the political feasibility of various types of projects, notwithstanding whether total net benefits are positive or negative.

Cost-Benefit Analysis

Research conducted at actual and potential wind energy facilities worldwide highlights the type of tradeoffs that may be expected with coastal wind facilities in Massachusetts. These tradeoffs may be particularly contentious, given the divergence between those who realize the benefits of wind energy and those who bear the costs. Tradeoffs between environmental benefits, such as reducing use of nonrenewable fuels and mitigating climate change, and costs related to possible damage to local environmental amenities (e.g., obstruction of landscape and ocean views) arise even in the context of land-based wind turbines. Krohn and Damborg (1999), for example, noted that, even though people favor renewable energy and wind energy in general, they may oppose wind power installations at specific sites. They reviewed past public surveys and concluded that people who have lived in areas where wind power is generated tend to favor such sources of electricity. However, people who have never experienced local wind power operations often oppose these projects. Krohn and Damborg (1999) also hypothesized that this happens mainly due to lack of communication between project proponents and the local residents, although other explanations are possible. Scholars have also studied general attitudes toward wind energy in other countries, such as France, Germany, and Sweden.[4] The findings of this research are not unique to wind parks, but the siting of different types of facilities presents similar tradeoffs.

A typical CBA compares the present value of net benefits of alternative projects. For example, a utility company might be interested in adding another 300-MW power plant to the existing installed capacity for electricity generation. Suppose there were three alternative projects under consideration to achieve this goal: a coal-based power plant, a natural gas facility, and an offshore wind farm. A CBA of these alternatives would seek to identify the project with the highest present value of net benefits—an important (although certainly not the only) consideration in choosing among projects. For purposes of this illustration, the focus is on estimating the benefits and costs of the offshore wind energy alternative from a national perspective. Note, however, that a major portion of the nonmarket costs of this project will likely be borne by residents in the immediate vicinity of the project site, a feature shared by many large infrastructure projects.

Benefits of Offshore Wind Energy

If there is no change in the average price of electricity that consumers pay after the offshore wind energy project increases the supply of electricity, then the revenue collected by the generation facility (the product of the market price per unit of electricity and the amount of electrical energy generated) would be a good initial estimate of the project's *gross* market benefits (benefits before subtraction of costs).[5] If, however, the price of electricity declines as a result of the additional supply, consumers would benefit (an increase in consumer surplus), while the suppliers of electricity would lose some revenue as a result of the price change.[6] The gross market benefits of the project would then exceed the revenue earned by the utility by an amount equal to the difference in the benefit and the loss, respectively, faced by the consumer and the producer. A project might also be beneficial because it would provide additional generating capacity for states that have a renewable portfolio standard (RPS)[7] in place.

The project would also provide a new generation source to meet consumers' demand for more environmentally conscious energy alternatives. It is well established that some consumers are willing to pay a premium for "green" products, including electricity generated by renewable means.[8] For these consumers, benefits of wind energy may include an increase in net benefits (i.e., consumer surplus) from energy consumption. While not all consumers will realize such benefits, potential aggregate benefits related to the increase in willingness to pay for renewable energy, compared to conventionally generated energy, can be sizable. For example, Borchers et al. (2007) showed that in a sample of residents of Delaware, the average amount they were willing to pay for a "generic" green energy source was $14.77 per month and $17.00 per month, respectively, when 10% and 25% of respondents' electricity demand was met by renewable energy sources. The study also demonstrated that individuals have preferences for the specific renewable energy source used to generate their electricity; the willingness to pay for electricity generated from solar, wind, farm methane, and biomass energy decreases in this order.

Benefits are also related to the potential reduction in pollution that would be caused by nonrenewable energy generation. The generation of electricity using fossil fuels, such as coal and natural gas, causes environmental pollution, particularly air pollution. By "producing" pollution along with electricity, power plants impose a cost on society. Plant operators do not normally (or readily) take these costs into account and in addition produce more electricity (and more pollution) than a rational society would allow or desire, if it had a say in deciding the quantity of electricity generation. Pollution can be counted as a "cost" in a CBA of electricity generation based on fossil fuels. Alternatively, avoiding pollution can be viewed as a "benefit" in the CBA of offshore wind energy. In either case, the measurement of associated nonmarket benefits would proceed in the same way. There are well-established guidelines for using nonmarket methods to assess economic costs associated with pollution.[9]

The Commonwealth of Massachusetts is one of many states that has adopted an RPS to promote the development of renewable energy resources. In its RPS program, an electricity generation facility receives one renewable energy certificate (REC) when it produces one megawatt hour (MWh) of electrical energy from a renewable source. The RPS requires retail electricity distributors in the Commonwealth to buy sufficient RECs every year to ensure that the proportion of electricity from renewable energy resources to the total amount of electricity that they supply is equal to the target set for that year. For example, the RPS for the year 2007 was 3%. Thus, if a distribution company delivered 1,000,000 MWh of electrical energy to its consumers in 2007, it had to buy at least 30,000 RECs (or 30,000 MWh) that year to comply with the RPS. The RPS was adopted in 2002 and is scheduled to reach a level of 4% in 2009, and then increase by 1% every year after that unless further regulatory changes occur.

With the RPS program, all customers of the utility share the additional cost of generating the target percent of electricity from renewable energy resources; it is not a voluntary option. Wiser (2003), however, created a useful framework for classifying the efforts and incentives to promote renewable energy for electricity generation. In his model, the RPS programs require collective payment by electricity consumers, as described, and include private enterprises as providers of renewably generated electricity to state utilities. Beyond this, consumers who demand more "green" electricity from renewable sources and are willing to pay a premium price (a slightly higher per-unit price) could make voluntary payments to private utilities to obtain these services.

Partly due to the higher costs of electricity generation from renewable sources and partly because environmentally aware consumers are willing to pay more for clean electricity, utility companies in Massachusetts (and other states) have instituted "utility green-pricing programs." National Grid, for example, offers a "GreenUp" program, in which participating consumers can choose between two sources of renewable energy: one that combines wind and small hydro (a 30/70 ratio) for an additional 2 cents per kWh, and another that draws 25% from wind, solar, and biomass and the remaining 75% from low-impact hydro at a price premium of 2.4 cents per kWh. Similarly, NSTAR's "Green" program offers Massachusetts consumers the option of wind-generated energy by paying price premiums that depend on whether they use wind energy for half their total electricity requirement (1.75 cents per kWh) or all of it (3 cents per kWh). Additional electricity generating facilities that use renewable energy resources (such as offshore wind energy) not only help the Commonwealth achieve its RPS targets more easily but also provide more choices to consumers who desire renewable energy sources for their electricity. Of course, an appropriate estimation of benefits would have to account for variations in prices faced by different consumers and associated revenues received by providers. This can be accomplished using standard market tools.

Costs of Offshore Wind Energy

The engineering and labor costs of constructing, maintaining, and eventually decommissioning wind energy facilities are often relatively straightforward to estimate, using standard market cost measures as inputs. In addition to these market costs, wind energy projects can also involve significant nonmarket costs. For example, the environmental impacts associated with offshore wind turbines cannot be valued using market observations because there is no market "price" per unit of the impact. As discussed in chapter 4, there are well-developed mechanisms for measuring such nonmarket effects. Each has its own advantages and disadvantages.

Although offshore wind energy projects are environmentally beneficial in the sense that they do not emit conventional pollutants during their operation, available evidence (although tentative) indicates that wind turbine structures may have mixed effects on recreational and commercial fisheries.[10] Despite the possibility of marine habitat loss from construction and maintenance of the turbines, experience from past offshore wind energy projects suggests that the turbine structures may also provide new habitat (artificial reefs) for certain marine life and thereby enhance recreational fisheries. Commercial fishermen, in turn, may not be able to use certain equipment (e.g., trawler gear) near project sites, which may have direct negative impacts on their net benefits. But if fish populations also improve in such de facto "protected" areas, this would lead to indirect benefits to fishermen from increased fish stocks. The net effect will depend on the balance between these and perhaps other opposing impacts.

Offshore wind turbines will be visible from the shore as long as they are limited to shallower waters by economics and technology. People who want an unblemished view of the ocean from home or beach may lose value because of visible "intrusions" in their seascape. Aesthetic effects may also have direct impacts on other uses, such as recreational boating and fishing, which may become less attractive in the area. These uses can also be negatively affected if the wind farm creates a navigational hazard. Property owners along the coast contend that the value of their property is likely to be affected by the visibility of the turbines on the horizon. However, such effects are not unambiguous. Sterzinger et al. (2003), for example, concluded that wind power projects on land do not adversely affect values of properties in their line of sight. These lost values can be estimated using various nonmarket valuation methodologies, including recreation demand models, hedonic property value models, and stated preference approaches.

It is often thought that local opposition to wind power projects, whether land-based or offshore, is a reflection of the NIMBY (not in my back yard) mindset of local populations. However, Wolsink (2000) argued that the slow development of wind power in Denmark was attributable to institutional factors and not local resistance. Additionally, as van der Horst (2007) argued,

TABLE A1.1   COMMON BENEFITS AND COSTS OF AN OFFSHORE WIND ENERGY PROJECT

Benefit	Who benefits?	How to measure it?
Increased availability of electricity	Consumers and producers of electricity	Estimate the market value of the electricity generated by the project (consumer and producer surplus). Estimates must account for potential changes in market prices as well as quantities.
Increased availability of "green" energy	Consumers and producers of "green" electricity	Measure the willingness to pay expressed by environmentally conscious consumers, using either market methods or stated preference techniques. Producers may benefit if consumer willingness to pay for green energy leads to increased producer surplus; this can be measured using market methods.
Pollution avoided if the alternative is to use fossil fuel–based energy	If CO_2 is avoided, the whole world; for local pollutants, such as NO_x, residents of a small or large region	Determine monetary value of human health effects, other market and nonmarket values associated with pollutants (various appropriate measurement methods), and market and nonmarket benefits and costs associated with global warming, although these will likely be small for any single facility. (Use various appropriate measurement methods.)
Structures in water becoming artificial reefs for marine life, increasing natural productivity	Consumers and producers of goods and services (e.g., fish) whose natural "production" is enhanced; individuals who value other use or nonuse services related to enhancements in marine life	Use ecological productivity methods, stated preference methods, and revealed preference methods.
Cost	Who bears the cost?	How to measure it?
Engineering costs (construction and maintenance)	Project owner, although some costs passed on to consumers	Measure market value or opportunity cost of the required inputs, plus any other associated changes in producer and consumer surplus.

Continued

TABLE A1.1   COMMON BENEFITS AND COSTS OF AN OFFSHORE WIND ENERGY PROJECT *(Cont.)*

Loss of commercial fisheries	Producers and consumers of commercial fish	Evaluate market values (producer and consumer) of the decline in catch or available fishing areas.
Cost	**Who bears the cost?**	**How to measure it?**
Loss of recreational value (fishing, boating, and beach use)	Consumers and providers of affected recreation services	Measure nonmarket values using recreation demand and/or stated preference methods. Losses in producer surplus for commercial recreation providers (e.g., charter boats) may be measured using standard market methods.
Loss of property value	Property owners in the project area	Use hedonic property value methods to estimate property value impacts. (Before the project, one would use data from similar projects. After the project, use data on property values surrounding the project site.)
Negative impact on wildlife and habitats (marine creatures and birds)	Environmentally conscious individuals; individuals using services "produced" by affected ecosystems	Measure with stated preference methods, ecological productivity methods, revealed preference methods (e.g., for effects on marine recreation, such as whale watching).
Loss of net benefits related to limitations on other commercial uses (e.g., marine transportation)	Consumers and producers of related products	Determine market values (producer and consumer) related to affected commercial uses and related products.

assessing the true extent of NIMBY effects can be difficult. Hence, opposition to wind power facilities may be more complex than is often assumed and is likely related to a combination of NIMBY effects and the variety of potential nonmarket costs that may be associated with such facilities.

Alternative Methods of Economic Analysis: CEA and EIA

If the major benefits of a policy cannot be easily monetized, a CEA can be performed instead of a complete CBA. For example, the state government may implement an RPS to maximize the benefits of reduced air pollution, achieve energy independence, or diversify the sources of commercial energy. In this case, a CEA might assess each competing electricity generation project to find the most efficient way of meeting the RPS target.

On the other hand, an EIA of an offshore wind-energy project would include description and estimation of ways the project might affect economic activity indicators for local communities, the state, and the nation. It could predict the number of jobs created in the manufacturing, construction, and maintenance phases of the project; estimated impacts on regional income or output; the tax revenue expected by town, county, and/or state government from energy surcharges; and changes in the tax revenues from possible declines in property values or attraction of new residents due to availability of renewable energy, among other effects of an offshore wind farm. The latter effect (changes in tax revenues due to property value changes or new residents) would require additional models to quantify property value or population changes; such models are not typically included in EIA methods.

The Cape Wind Project

The Cape Wind project proposed for Nantucket Sound would be the first offshore wind energy installation in the United States and has been the subject of vigorous debates. The outcome will likely shape government policy—both in Massachusetts and at the federal level—on offshore wind farms. Discussion of the project details provides insight into the ways in which economic insight can be used in project assessments, and the types of findings that can be generated by different economic approaches.

Before the Cape Wind project gathered momentum, the firm Winergy LLC withdrew its earlier proposal (in July 2003) to build a wind farm in Buzzards Bay in the face of resistance by the local populace. More recently, an offshore wind energy proposal by Patriot Renewables LLC was disallowed by the Massachusetts Environmental Policy Act Office, which found it to be in conflict with the Ocean Sanctuaries Act. At the same time, there was another plan to put 40 wind turbines generating 3.6 MW south of Jones Beach Island in Long Island Sound (which is not addressed here).

The Cape Wind project filed for federal approval with the U.S. Army Corps of Engineers in November 2001. Legislative changes caused by the passage of the 2005 Energy Policy Act transferred the regulatory authority on offshore alternative energy projects from the Army Corps of Engineers to the Minerals Management Service (MMS) of the U.S. Department of the Interior. MMS issued a Draft Environmental Impact Statement (DEIS) for the project in January 2008 that evaluated the following alternative courses of action: 1) no action; 2) alternative energy-generating technologies, including renewable energy; 3) comparison of upland (higher elevation) versus offshore wind energy facilities; and 4) an assessment of submarine and upland cable routes.[11] Meanwhile, the Commonwealth's secretary of environmental affairs issued a certificate on the Final Environmental Impact Report submitted by the promoter of the Cape Wind project. As of May 2009, Cape Wind had completed the state and local permitting processes, with all permits and approvals granted in one composite certificate. The project is expected to complete the federal permitting process during the summer and fall of 2009.

The project as currently envisioned would site 130 wind turbine generators in an area of about 25 square miles of Horseshoe Shoals in Nantucket Sound, where the water depth is about 50 feet. The turbines will be spaced one-third to one-half nautical miles apart. During turbine rotation, the tips of the rotor blades will reach 417 feet to 75 feet above the water at their highest and lowest points, respectively. Each turbine will be mounted on a 16-foot-diameter pillar, driven 80 feet below the seafloor. At its peak, the wind farm should generate about 454 MW of electricity, which will be conveyed to a land-based electricity grid via a network of submarine and underground cables. Part of this network lies within Massachusetts waters, while the wind farm itself is in federal waters.[12]

The Cape Wind proposal has received considerable attention from the general public, policymakers, environmental organizations, the popular press, and the academic world.[13] A number of different economic analyses of the project have been conducted by various groups; these predict both positive and negative outcomes. A CBA by the Beacon Hill Institute[14] concluded that the project would impose net costs on the Massachusetts public: the discounted value of project benefits was estimated to be $735.5 million and project costs to be $947.2 million. The economic benefits considered were associated with reduced consumption of fossil fuels, reduced capital expenditure on other types of electricity generation, and the monetary value of pollutant emissions that would be prevented because of wind power. The costs of the project included construction and maintenance expenses, the costs of assimilating the wind-generated electricity into the grid (wind power may not be available when natural conditions are not favorable), and the nonmarket costs of a wind farm in Nantucket Sound.

Interestingly, the estimate of the nonmarket costs of the project is quite modest ($39.2 million), compared to the estimate of total project costs ($947.2 million). This figure is derived from another report by the Beacon Hill Institute,[15] based on the opinions of residents of Cape Cod and tourists about how much royalty the Cape Wind project should pay for operating the windmills. This approximates what economists call the "willingness to accept compensation" for loss of an environmental amenity.[16] Haughton et al. (2003), also from the Beacon Hill Institute, estimated a loss of about $1.35 billion to property owners because of potential decline in property values; similar results are reported in Haughton et al. (2004). This assessment of the loss of property values was not used in the CBAs reported by Giuffre et al. (2004) and Haughton et al. (2004), possibly because the estimate was based on the *expectations* of homeowners and realtors in the area about the future prices of houses rather than on any *revealed* price changes in a similar market. Giuffre et al. (2004) and Haughton et al. (2004) also predicted that the tourism industry would lose approximately 1,000 jobs on account of the offshore wind energy project.

TABLE A1.2   BENEFITS AND COSTS OF THE CAPE WIND PROJECT

Benefit category	Estimated amount ($millions)*	How was it measured?
Fuel saved	523.3	Projected value of the total fossil fuel saved
Capital costs saved	97.9	Estimated savings in capital because fewer gas-based power plants would be built
Emissions reduced	107.4	Monetary value of the reduction in human mortality and morbidity because of the avoided pollution
Greater energy independence	6.8	Based on the Moore et al. (1997) study that values energy dependence at 8 cents per gallon of imported oil (adjusted to 2004 prices)
Total benefits	*735.5*	
Cost category	Estimated amount ($millions)*	How was it measured?
Capital and operating costs	882.4	Estimated construction and maintenance costs discounted over project's life
Grid integration	25.6	Costs of having a readily available "backup" source to counter unpredictability of wind power; estimate of $0.18/kWh based on an earlier study
Environmental effects	39.2	Willingness to accept compensation on the part of the tourists and homeowners, expressed in a survey, as royalties that ought to be paid by the project promoters for the loss of environmental amenities
Total costs	**947.2**	
Net benefits	**– 211.8**	

Source: Giuffre et al. (2004, *10*, table 1).

* Mean value of the net present value with a discount rate of 10%

An arguably less extensive economic analysis conducted as part of the Final Environmental Impact Statement (EIS) for Cape Wind—in which most nonmarket benefits and costs remain unquantified—reaches other conclusions.[17] This report is not a formal CBA but seeks to provide general insight into a number of areas of economic impact, benefit, and cost. This report concludes, for example, that Cape Wind would have minor impacts on population, economics, fisheries, recreation, tourism, and competing uses of waters and the seabed, among other elements. As a case in point, the EIS concludes that "available information does not support any firm conclusion with respect to the wind facility's effect on property values."[18] This stands in contrast to the estimate by Haughton et al. (2003) that over $1.3 billion in property value would be lost. The divergence between findings of the EIS and the Beacon Hill Institute studies shows the importance of careful attention to the methods used to model economic benefits and costs, as seemingly small changes in assumptions or methods can sometimes lead to large differences in predicted outcomes. It also highlights the importance of sensitivity analysis, in which the impact of assumptions and methods on model results can be examined.

An EIA of the Cape Wind project by Global Insight (2003, rev.) also painted a more positive picture of estimated changes in such economic indicators as number of jobs, economic output, labor, income, and tax revenue during the manufacturing, construction, and operation of the wind farm:

(1) *Manufacturing, assembly, construction, and installation phases*
597–1,013 direct, indirect, and induced full-time jobs created
$85 million–$137 million annual increase in state economic output
$44 million–$71 million annual increase in value added
$32 million–$52 million annual increase in labor income
$4.8 million–$7.8 million increase in personal income tax revenue
$9.2 million–$14.8 million annual increase in property income and
    corporate profits
$1.3 million–$2.1 million increase in corporate income tax revenue
75 more construction jobs in Barnstable County
(2) *Operation phase*
154 new annual permanent employees, beginning in 2007
$22 million increase in annual state economic output
$346,500 annual increase in personal income tax revenue
$113,900 annual increase in corporate income tax revenue
Barnstable and Yarmouth towns initially to receive $62,500 and $217,200,
    respectively, in annual property tax revenues
$25-million annual savings in wholesale power costs, resulting in a
    $5.1 million–$6.1 million increase in state economic output and
    142–215 new permanent employees

This case study does not draw conclusions about the validity or appropriateness of its findings or arguments for Cape Wind but rather highlights a variety of economic analyses of this project that have already been conducted, and that these analyses use methods that differ widely. Findings from these analyses highlight the variations in findings that can be provided by different methods and modeling approaches and suggest the care that must be taken when assessing the specific methods used by any economic analysis. The validity of results for any economic analysis depends on the methods used, and these methods can vary widely across different studies. Such methodological divergences are particularly likely in contentious cases, such as Cape Wind.

For example, this case study shows the stark variations that can occur between the outcomes of CBA and EIA. Here, for example, the CBA of Haughton et al. (2004) suggests negative net benefits of the project, while the EIA of Global Insight (2003, rev.) suggests positive economic impacts. Within this context, it is important to recognize that CBA and EIA are not comparable types of analyses. For example, only the CBA attempts to estimate the net economic benefits of the project. As noted previously, positive economic impacts

TABLE A1.3   COMPARISON OF THE THREE ALTERNATIVE TECHNIQUES OF ECONOMIC ANALYSIS USED FOR EVALUATING OFFSHORE WIND ENERGY PROJECTS

Impact category	CBA	CEA	EIA
Increased availability of electricity	✓	—	*
Increased availability of "green" energy	✓	—	—
Pollution avoided if the alternative is to use fossil fuel–based energy	✓	—	—
Engineering and operating costs (construction and maintenance)			*
Loss of commercial fisheries	✓	***	*
Loss of recreational value (fishing, boating, and beach use)	✓	***	*
Loss of property value	✓	***	—
Positive or negative impact on wildlife (marine creatures and birds)	✓	—	—
Effect on other industries (e.g., marine transportation)	✓	***	*
Efficient achievement of renewable energy goals	✓	✓	—
Employment	**	**	✓
Regional or national economic output	—	—	✓

Note: In the table, a black check mark (✓) indicates that the particular factor is included in an analysis by that method. Asterisks indicate that the factor is sometimes or partially included (see below).

* Can be included only inasmuch as it influences measurable direct and indirect effects on industry revenues and related economic impacts.

** Included only to the extent that direct employment changes generate valid benefits or costs.

*** Most likely would not be included, but could be at least partially incorporated, depending on the scope of costs considered.

estimated by an EIA—even very large ones—do not imply that society's welfare will be improved by a project. As a result, findings such as those described above in which economists predict negative net benefits and positive economic impacts, or vice versa, are not uncommon.

Conclusion

There is a high level of support among the public for greater use of renewable energy resources. European countries have been operating offshore wind turbines for the last few years. Although there is potential to develop offshore wind energy along the U.S. coast, to date there are no completed projects. Of the wind energy projects proposed for U.S. waters, the Cape Wind project in Nantucket Sound is the closest to construction. The illustrated applications of economic analysis to Cape Wind, however, are likely to be similar to those encountered in future offshore wind facility proposals, many of which will have similar types of positive and negative effects.

Economic analyses conducted for the Cape Wind project illustrate different ways in which economic information may be used in an attempt to inform, guide, or influence policy decisions. There are a variety of general conclusions that may be drawn. First, the Cape Wind project exemplifies challenges that can arise when comparing and interpreting findings across different types of economic analysis, as well as the controversy that can arise when economic benefits and costs are split among different groups. Second, the results illustrate a common case in which an EIA projects positive economic impacts for a proposal that, at least according to some analyses, has negative net benefits (i.e., will make society worse off). This provides a concrete illustration of the point made in chapter 2, that EIA is not a substitute for CBA. Third, differing results from prior evaluations of the Cape Wind project's economic outcomes (e.g., possible effects on property values) illustrate the potentially significant influence of methodological choices (i.e., how a study is conducted) on model results. All of these conclusions suggest that economic analyses, whether CBA, CEA, or EIA, should be evaluated closely not only in terms of the final results, but in terms of the methods that are used to generate those results.

Endnotes

1. EIA (2007b).
2. EIA (2007a).
3. See, for example, Giuffre et al. (2004) and Sterzinger et al. (2003).
4. France and Germany (Jobert et al. 2007); Sweden (Soderholm et al. 2007)
5. This is distinct from the concept of net market benefits, which are equal to gross benefits minus costs.
6. This discussion does not address issues related to whether electricity is a regulated or unregulated industry, which can have important implications for the price effects of new generation facilities. For example, regulated utilities often

use average cost pricing, while unregulated utilities would be expected to use marginal cost pricing.

7. A renewable portfolio standard (RPS) is a set of standards and requirements mandated by a state, specifying that a certain percentage of electric utilities' output (power plant capacity and/or generation) come from renewable sources, usually by a given date or increasing annually or every so many years (Pew Center on Global Climate Change 2009).

8. For example, see Borchers et al. (2007) and Rose et al. (2002), among many others.

9. See, for example, U.S. EPA (2000).

10. See Hagos (2007) and Wiersma (2008), for example.

11. MMS (2008).

12. CWA (2007).

13. The academic literature includes studies on various aspects of the Cape Wind project. For example, after interviewing a sample of the local population, Kempton et al. (2005) identified reasons why interviewees either opposed or supported the project. Firestone and Kempton (2007) similarly suggested a list of socioeconomic factors that likely influenced support or opposition to the Cape Wind project. In particular, for the opponents of the project, aesthetic considerations were related to possible damage to wildlife. Firestone and Kempton also argued that the reasons people take particular positions on the project were many times at odds with the conclusions of the environmental impact statement for the project. They also assessed the factors that might make people change their position and suggested that if individuals are given a long-term vision of the future of offshore wind energy, they might support large-scale implementation of this kind of electricity generation across the country. However, this view is not necessarily shared by all researchers.

14. See Giuffre et al. (2004). Similar estimates (i.e., benefits of $744 million and costs of $952 million) are provided the Beacon Hill Institute in Haughton et al. (2004).

15. Haughton et al. (2003, 2004).

16. Willingness to accept compensation is a theoretically well-defined welfare measure that represents the minimum amount of money or other compensation, that an individual (or group) would be willing to accept in order to allow a negative change to occur.

17. U.S. Department of the Interior (2009).

18. Ibid.

Case Study 2: Offshore Sand and Gravel Mining for Beach Nourishment

Coastlines evolve over time, and their erosion is a part of a broader natural process. Sometimes human intrusions, such as navigation channels, intensify rates of erosion. Because coastal erosion can damage man-made structures, such as houses, roads, and harbors built along the coasts, various structural and nonstructural means have been employed to prevent the loss of sand. Structural alternatives (e.g., groins and breakwaters) to mitigate coastal hazards have only limited effectiveness and they often displace the problem to adjoining areas.[1] Because of this, beach nourishment is often preferred or is used in conjunction with hard engineering structures.[2] Beach nourishment is also used to maintain the size and shape of recreational beaches. As the name suggests, beach nourishment involves replenishing the sand after a stretch of the shoreline has eroded. The Massachusetts Coastal Hazards Commission appears to favor these projects. One of its four priority recommendations is to "implement a program of regional sand management through policies, regulations, and activities that promote nourishment as the preferred alternative for coastal hazard protection."[3]

For example, at the time this book was written, the Massachusetts Department of Conservation and Recreation (DCR) was considering nourishment of Winthrop Beach, using an offshore source of sand. This is one of the components of the Winthrop Shores Reservation Restoration Project, itself a part of DCR's "Back to the Beaches" program. The DCR determined that a combination of nonstructural (beach nourishment) and structural (restoration of existing groins) interventions is the best strategy to combat the severe erosion at Winthrop Beach over the last few years.[4] The proposed nourishment project would cover 37 acres of Winthrop Beach, requiring about 500,000 cubic yards of sand mined from a site called NOMES I. This site is located about 8 miles off the Winthrop Beach coast, 80–90 feet below the surface of the ocean. It covers approximately 50 acres of ocean bottom. The beach nourishment component of the project is estimated to cost about $11.5 million. After reviewing the final environmental impact report submitted by DCR in January 2006, the Executive Office of Environmental Affairs allowed the Winthrop project to proceed to permitting by various government agencies.[5] The U.S. Army Corps of Engineers denied the Winthrop Beach renourishment proposal "with prejudice" in June 2008. This decision was appealed, and in October 2008, the chief of engineers determined that the appeal had partial merit and the denial decision was remanded to the North Atlantic Division for further review.[6]

Literature Review

The most obvious benefits of beach nourishment projects are increased storm protection for private and public properties near the shoreline and enhanced opportunities for recreation.[7] Silberman et al. (1992) also found that beaches can have existence value, and individuals who do not intend to use a beach may nonetheless be willing to pay some positive amount to protect it. Beaches may also support wildlife habitat, which may be a source of use and nonuse values. In addition to these sources of benefits and costs, beaches can influence economic impacts. For example, local businesses may experience revenue increases related to tourism and governments may draw revenue from appreciation of beach property values and consequent rise in tax revenue.

Despite these possible benefits, some people challenge the wisdom of large beach nourishment projects. Pilkey and Coburn (2007), for example, argued against beach nourishment on the following grounds:

1) Beach nourishment projects are undertaken to protect the "status quo"—coastal properties and recreation opportunities—which lies in the middle of a dynamic natural system that will be increasingly difficult to protect as climate change induces the sea level to rise.
2) Development should be avoided in areas prone to erosion, and beach nourishment may, in fact, promote further development along the coast.
3) Nourished beaches continue to lose sand, so periodic replenishment of sand is necessary, forcing governments to spend money on such projects at regular intervals.
4) Oceanfront property owners benefit disproportionately from nourishment projects, particularly when funded by the state and federal governments.

As a result of these arguments, Pilkey and Coburn maintained that shoreline retreat—planned repositioning of coastal structures away from the shoreline that allows natural erosion—is the best strategy to mitigate damages caused by coastal erosion.

This last proposition is subject to debate and likely depends on the specific case. Parsons and Powell (2001) compared the present value of the possible loss of land and investments in structures over a 50-year time horizon, if beaches in Delaware were allowed to erode naturally, with the current costs of beach nourishment. They concluded that it is worth protecting the shoreline by refilling beaches with sand from other sources. It is noteworthy that they did not include the amenity value of beaches in their analysis because, as they argued, when beaches erode, such values will be eventually transferred to properties that currently lie inland. Landry et al. (2003), in contrast, concluded that shoreline retreat should be preferred over beach nourishment, if erosion management costs are likely to rise drastically over time.

Neither of these last two studies accounted for the value that people hold for resources damaged in the process of extracting sand for renourishment. This can include damage to commercial fisheries and wildlife habitats by offshore sand-mining projects. Related costs (the loss of value related to ecological damage to sand-mining sites) might reduce the net benefits associated with beach nourishment. Huang et al. (2007) noted that valuation studies of beach erosion-control measures can be grossly overestimated if they do not account for such negative environmental impacts. Hence, a comprehensive economic evaluation of beach nourishment may need to go beyond a comparison of benefits and costs of the nourishment project if, as in Massachusetts, sand from offshore sites is considered. Sand may also be acquired from dredging streams and other inland water bodies for beach nourishment. However, the availability of sand from these two sources has not kept up with demand, and interest in obtaining sand offshore has swelled (ACRE 2000).

Cost-Benefit Analysis

The first step in a CBA of any proposed project is to identify alternative ways of achieving the desired objectives. The techniques of CBA are then applied to all candidate alternatives to find the alternative with the highest expected net benefits. While policymakers can then implement this alternative if desired, other non-economic factors may influence the choice of a different alternative with lower net benefits but persuasive mitigating advantages.

For a sound CBA, one also needs to ascertain the life of the project over which the costs and the benefits will be distributed because projects deliver a stream of benefits through time that must be compared to the stream of costs. These benefit and cost streams should be discounted to present value terms, as described in chapter 2.

Benefits

The final environmental impact report prepared for the Winthrop Shores Reservation Restoration Program discusses four main elements or sources of potential benefit (in order of priority):

1) improved shore protection at Winthrop Beach,
2) storm drainage improvements at Winthrop Beach,
3) revitalization of beach and amenities at the Winthrop and Short Beaches, and
4) reconstruction of Winthrop Shore Drive.[8]

Beach nourishment with sand from offshore sources is critical only for shore protection and improved recreation. Hence, the economic analysis outlined here focuses on these two benefits and the various costs of depositing sand on the beach.

Analysis of the Winthrop Beach nourishment project suggests that there are at least three possible benefits. First, residents of the area whose houses are within a short distance of the beach will enjoy increased storm protection. Only one road separates approximately 100 homes from the existing seawall, and about 4,500 people live close to Winthrop Beach. The monetary value of the benefits of beach nourishment that accrue to these people can be estimated by determining its effect on the value of their homes. A hedonic study of home values could estimate this value, assuming it can differentiate the additional value associated with the protection of the beach.

One might also seek to approximate these lost benefits using damage or defensive cost methods, although these will not, in general, provide well-defined measures of economic benefit or cost. This might be done by estimating the change in probability and monetary value of storm damage or destruction with and without the beach nourishment. For example, if engineers calculate that the probability of complete destruction of a home is reduced by 10% on an ongoing basis with beach nourishment, this might suggest that the benefit to a home owner is 10% of the value of the home. Similarly, one might consider how much repair costs from storm damage (short of complete destruction) would be reduced by the project. Benefits of property protection might also be estimated by comparing insurance costs for similar homes with and without the natural storm protection afforded by a beach. Again, however, these measures are only approximations based on damage or defensive costs and should not be confused with well-defined benefit measures. At best, they will usually provide only upper or lower bounds on true benefits.

Second, the project will enhance storm protection of existing public properties (such as roads) in the area. Under a set of strict assumptions, the benefits of this protection might be approximated by projecting reductions in future repair costs to public infrastructure that would result from the beach nourishment project.[9] One could then calculate the present value of the stream of benefits over the life of the project. The Army Corps of Engineers estimated the storm damage to public infrastructure in the area (including shore-protection structures and roads) to be over $900,000 in 1991 and 1992. During these two storm seasons, estimated damage to properties along the beach was $250,000. Expenditures in these two years may not be representative of average annual damages in future years, however. In addition, it is important to quantify the marginal change in expected damages or repair costs associated with the beach nourishment project since some storm damage will occur even if the project is undertaken. Finally, as discussed in chapter 4, it is important to recognize that data on avoided damage and defensive costs alone will rarely provide accurate and comprehensive insight into benefits realized through the storm protection services of beach nourishment. For example, there is often a loss of public benefits due to the loss of interim use of storm-damaged infrastructure, prior to repairs. Prevention of such benefit losses through beach nourishment is not captured by the public cost of infrastructure repair.

The third category of benefits of the Winthrop project is the amenity value associated with a broader beach. Because Winthrop is an urban (local) beach, it may not receive many visitors from outside the immediate community. This may make a recreation demand model difficult to estimate (as travel costs might be trivial for most visitors). Instead, a stated preference technique, such as a choice experiment survey of beach visitors, could be used to estimate willingness to pay for preservation or enhancement of the beach. Since Winthrop Beach has been degraded for some time and it may not attract as many visitors at present, it may also be important to consider willingness to pay of potential as well as existing beach users. It may also be possible to use benefit transfer to quantify benefits if estimated recreation benefits from another similar beach are available.

Costs

A CBA in this case would compare the discounted value of the stream of benefits over the life of the project against the discounted stream of costs of the project. The market costs of beach nourishment projects include the costs of engineering and materials to dredge sand from an offshore site (or from an inland site) and spread it on the beach. Since nourished beaches erode over time, the costs of periodically replacing sand on the beach should also be taken into consideration. Dredging sand from offshore may affect commercial fisheries adversely, and these damages should also be included as project costs. Excavation of sand from the ocean floor may also harm marine life. Various market and nonmarket methods can measure associated costs, depending on the species involved. For example, stated preference methods may be used to estimate public values associated with affected flora and fauna, whereas market analysis might be used to quantify any possible effect on net benefits in the commercial fishery (e.g., due to reduced harvests in affected areas).

According to the project documents, potential sources of sand for the project include a land-based deposit (delivered either by a hopper dredge or an oceangoing barge) or the offshore NOMES I site. The total engineering, construction, and monitoring costs for the offshore sand source (the alternative preferred by the promoter) is estimated at $11.15 million. The cost of acquiring sand from upland sites was considerably higher, ranging from $30.5 million to $36 million. This does not include the cost of sourcing future sand to maintain the nourished beach with intermittent additions of sand. Beach nourishment serves as a "sacrificial rather than fixed barrier"[10] and periodic replenishment of sand is therefore necessary to sustain project benefits. The project promoter anticipates that "the gravel/sand mixture to nourish Winthrop beach will exceed design expectations, allowing small scale renourishment maintenance programs to use upland borrow sources."[11]

With respect to the losses to commercial fisheries and damage to marine habitat caused by sand mining, the offshore sand site lies within a known habitat for cod, lobster, and winter flounder.[12] The potential damage to fisheries has been estimated by DCR at $0.1 million–$0.5 million, depending on assumptions of recovery time that vary from 3 to 10 years.[13] These are likely overestimates because they are based on forgone revenues, assuming all marketable fish on the site are caught and that there are no reductions in harvest costs associated with reduced catch.[14]

Sand mining can also cause environmental damage in addition to lost fishery profits. Efforts to systematically document the possible environmental impacts of offshore sand mining in Massachusetts Bay date back to 1972, when the New England Offshore Mining Environmental Study (NOMES) was jointly initiated by the National Oceanic and Atmospheric Administration (NOAA) and the Commonwealth of Massachusetts. Although this study was abandoned before the experimental excavation of the seafloor could begin, a few sites in the bay were identified as having large usable deposits of sand, including the NOMES I site, proposed for the Winthrop project. The NRC (1995) found that lasting transformations in the physical characteristics of the dredged sites have been systematically documented only for a few sites, and they show decline in the average grain size and slow rates of refilling at the excavated pits. The biological impacts at a sand-mining site may occur indirectly through physical changes caused by dredging or more directly through the removal of benthic organisms and environment along with the sand. Recovery of benthic species differs in their response to the dredging operations.[15] Stated preference methods would likely be required to determine the public's willingness to pay to avoid environmental damage from offshore sand mining.

The benefits and costs of the project (over the relevant time scale), once measured for each time period, must then be discounted to account for the fact that some benefits and costs will occur in the future. Particular attention must be paid to maintenance costs because they are likely to be significant and recur frequently. Renourishment may be required every 2 to 3 years, for example. If the life of the project is assumed to be 10 years, this means that renourishment expenses in years 3, 5, and 7 should be forecasted and discounted. Other costs and benefits may also have to be discounted. For example, the value of the beach to the recreational users is typically estimated on an annual basis and must be aggregated over the project life after proper discounting. As always, this will require that analysts choose a discount rate for the analysis, although sensitivity analysis may be used to assess the impact of varying discount rates on projected benefits and costs.

Other issues that should be addressed in a CBA include the potential uncertainty in project outcomes and associated costs and benefits. There are several sources of uncertainty in the prediction of benefits and costs of beach nourishment projects. For example, project benefits are likely to be affected by uncertain variables, such as rates of beach erosion after nourishment, intensity of storms, and costs of future renourishment. Again, sensitivity analysis should be used to illustrate the range of possible outcomes and net benefits associated with these and other major areas of uncertainty.

TABLE A2.1   COMMON BENEFITS AND COSTS OF AN OFFSHORE SAND-MINING PROJECT

Benefit	Who benefits?	How to measure it?
Storm protection	Property owners and taxpayers (the effective owners of public infrastructure)	Hedonic property value studies of coastal home prices (with different levels of storm protection), comparison of insurance costs, historical costs or repairs from storm damage
Amenity values of improved beach	Waterfront home owners and beach visitors	Recreation demand models, stated preference methods, benefit transfer, hedonic property value analysis
Value of wildlife and habitat on nourished beaches (e.g., piping plover nesting grounds)	Members of the public with use or nonuse values for wildlife and/or habitat	Various methods, depending on source of value, including stated preference methods in particular
Cost	**Who bears the cost?**	**How to measure it?**
Engineering and materials costs	State and federal taxpayers	Market value of the required inputs and labor
Damage to commercial fisheries	Producers and consumers of commercial fish	Market value of the decline in catch minus associated harvest costs, consumer surplus from demand analysis
Impact on marine wildlife in sand-mining areas	Members of the public with use or nonuse values for marine wildlife and/or habitat	Various methods, depending on source of value, including stated preference methods in particular

Other Economic Analysis: CEA and EIA

While a full-scale CBA compares the benefits of beach nourishment against project costs, a decision may be made to proceed with beach nourishment without a full quantitative assessment of benefits and costs (perhaps because there are insufficient resources or time for evaluating benefits). In this case, a CEA may still be useful if there are different options available for beach nourishment. For example, one might wish to compare the costs of beach nourishment using terrestrial versus offshore sand mining from one or more alternative sites. The analysis for the Winthrop project undertook a limited CEA by comparing costs of alternative upland sources for sand. As noted above, a full accounting of costs may not be limited to the monetary engineering costs of the alternatives. The value of damages to marine habitat and fisheries should also be considered as costs.

An EIA may also provide useful information to decisionmakers, although its information is not comparable to a CBA or CEA. An EIA of an offshore sand-mining project (and the associated beach nourishment project) would compile information on the impact of the project on various economic and/ or fiscal indicators. For example, the EIA might quantify the employment generated by the sand mining and the beach restoration projects, the impact on the tax revenue on the towns (from protection of valuable properties), changes in the region's economic output, and perhaps the loss in revenues and employment associated with loss of fishing opportunities due to damage from sand mining.

Conclusion

Beach nourishment projects are expensive and require careful planning. Benefits related to property protection and amenity values may be substantial—but their costs may also be substantial. Beach nourishment may encourage development in areas prone to storm damage, and it may become increasingly expensive to protect these areas in the future if the sea level rises or storms

TABLE A2.2   COMPARISON OF ISSUES ADDRESSED BY THREE ALTERNATIVE TECHNIQUES OF ECONOMIC ANALYSIS USED FOR EVALUATING OFFSHORE SAND- AND GRAVEL-MINING PROJECTS

Factor	CBA	CEA	EIA
Improved beach access, visitation, and economic value	✓	—	—
Change in housing values	✓	—	—
Engineering costs and related expenditures	✓	✓	**
Benefits or costs related to habitat, marine/terrestrial species, and ecosystem services	✓	✓	—
Loss in fishing profits	✓	✓	***
Loss in fishing revenues	—	—	***
Changes in employment	✓*	✓*	✓
Changes in regional or national economic output	—	—	✓

Note: In the table, a black check mark (✓) indicates that the particular factor is included in an analysis by that method. Aseterisks indicate that the factor is sometimes or partially included (see below).

* Only to the extent that direct employment changes generate valid benefits or costs.

** Only inasmuch as expenditures for these costs affect regional economic impacts.

***Most EIAs would *not* include fishing revenue losses or profit changes, as this requires the use of additional bioeconomic models to estimate effects on fish harvest and fishing cost. However, in theory, the loss of fishing revenues could be included and profits could in some cases be approximated by an EIA.

increase. As a result, it is crucial to take a long-term perspective with a beach nourishment project. Planning for shoreline retreat (i.e., the status quo) as an alternative should be seriously considered.

The benefits of beach nourishment may accrue to a fairly narrow group of property owners, but the costs may be spread widely. This is, in many ways, the opposite of wind farms (discussed in case study 1), in which benefits are distributed widely and costs are concentrated. The majority of construction costs for beach nourishment, for example, will fall on local, state, and/or federal taxpayers, each of whom will pay a small amount. Environmental costs associated with offshore sand mining may affect the commercial fishing industry, as well as the broader public that consumes commercial fish or that values affected marine habitat and marine species. While it is generally not the place of the economic analyst to make judgments on how benefits and costs *should be* distributed, clarifying the expected distribution of costs and benefits may be important to policymakers and stakeholders.

Endnotes

1. CHC (2007).
2. With shorelines, soft engineering uses ecological means (creating marshes, allowing natural erosion, planting vegetation) to reduce erosion and stabilize shorelines, while improving habitat and aesthetics, usually at lower cost. Hard engineering generally means countering natural processes with man-made structures of concrete, iron (steel), imported boulders, landfill, etc.
3. CHC (2007), Recommendation No. 22.
4. DCR (2005).
5. EOEA (2006).
6. Official letter from James Hannon, acting chief of operations (civil works), U.S. Army Corps of Engineers, to Ian Bowles, secretary of Massachusetts Office of Environmental Affairs, October 1, 2008, www.oceanscience.net/Winthrop_Appeal/Appeal_Decision_Remand.pdf.
7. Several empirical studies lend support to these arguments; see, for example, Bell and Leeworthy (1990); Pompe and Rinehart (1995); and Lew and Larson (2005).
8. DCR (2005).
9. These assumptions include that repairs are automatically implemented by the government, that no interim losses are incurred by society prior to the repairs, and that no additional benefits or costs are realized as a result of rebuilding.
10. NRC (1995, *2*).
11. DCR (2005, *ES-14*).
12. EOEA (2006).
13. DCR (2005).
14. The short-run damages that should be considered as costs in a CBA are the losses in producer surplus (revenues minus harvest costs) and consumer surplus.
15. See discussions of effects on benthic organisms by NRC (1995) and Byrnes et al. (2004).

Case Study 3: Impacts of Pollutants in the Coastal Zone

Coastal watersheds offer many beneficial goods and services, such as transportation, waste dilution and assimilation, food, energy, and opportunities for recreation. Natural causes and human activities discharge pollutants into the coastal seas through surface water, groundwater, and the atmosphere.[1] These pollutants can have many detrimental effects on coastal habitats and for people who derive resources and services from the sea. Coastal areas all over the world are more densely populated than inland regions, further exacerbating the problem, and the Commonwealth of Massachusetts is no exception. Population pressure and the associated development and waste generation are added stressors on the ecosystems along the coast of the Commonwealth.

Two designated areas that are important for the Commonwealth's residents—the Massachusetts Bays Program and the Buzzards Bay Program—are part of the National Estuary Program of the U.S. Environmental Protection Agency (U.S. EPA). In a recently released report, the U.S. EPA identified the following environmental concerns for Massachusetts bays: "increasing storm water runoff, sewage-related pollution, and the effects of human development on fragile coastal habitats. . . . [Some parts of the Massachusetts bays are also] affected by toxic contamination problems, including elevated levels of PAHs [polycyclic aromatic hydrocarbons], copper, arsenic, lead, cadmium, mercury, chromium, nickel, zinc, PCBs [polychlorinated biphenyls], and pesticides."[2] Similarly, the Buzzards Bay National Estuary has recorded "toxic contamination of the ecosystem, closures of shellfish beds due to bacterial contamination, nonpoint source pollution, habitat loss, and nitrogen loading and resulting coastal eutrophication" in recent years.[3] Table A3.1 shows the condition of these two national estuaries based on four indices of environmental quality.

Water pollution originates from both point and nonpoint sources. With point sources, the contaminants can be attributed to one particular source (e.g., effluents flowing from an industrial plant). Because the origin of the problem can be more easily identified and monitored, pollution from point sources is easier to manage. For example, sewage water discharged into the coastal sea caused the quality of water in Boston Harbor to deteriorate. An improved wastewater treatment facility and a 10-mile marine outfall (a pipeline or tunnel that discharges municipal or industrial wastes farther into the sea) were built to improve the quality of water. The outfall conveys the effluent (which now passes through the water treatment facility) deeper into the ocean for more effective dilution and dispersal.

It is more difficult to identify causal relationships when pollution stems from nonpoint sources. For example, fertilizer added to farmland, along with rain water or snowmelt, washes into the nearest water body, and as a result the quality of water may decline. However, it is difficult to hold any particular farm responsible for this phenomenon. In urban areas, oil from automobiles leaks

TABLE A3.1   ENVIRONMENTAL CONDITION OF TWO MASSACHUSETTS ESTUARIES

Index	Massachusetts Bay	Buzzards Bay
Water quality index	Good	Good
Sediment quality index	Poor	Fair
Benthic index	Poor	Good to Fair
Fish tissue contaminants index	Fair	Poor
Overall	Fair	Fair

Source: U.S. EPA (2007).

onto pavements and washes off with rain and snow into nearby streams. Here again, the contamination of water in the stream cannot be ascribed to any one car. The very nature of nonpoint pollution makes regulation more difficult. It is not easy, for example, to implement economic incentives (e.g., effluent fees) that effectively control pollution from nonpoint sources.[4]

According to the U.S. EPA (1996), "nonpoint source pollution remains the nation's largest source of water quality problems."[5] Its list of nonpoint source pollutants includes chemicals originating from agricultural practices (e.g., fertilizers and pesticides); oil and other toxic chemicals from urban areas; sediment from construction sites, agricultural and forest lands, and channel erosion; pathogens and nutrients from livestock, pet wastes, and faulty septic systems; deposits of certain air pollutants; and sediment churned up by engineering works (e.g., dredging channels) in bodies of water.

Observed impacts of nonpoint source pollutants include loss of recreational opportunities (e.g., beach closures), loss of habitat, contamination of drinking water, and fish kills. Often, excessive levels of nutrients, such as nitrogen and phosphorus, can lead to eutrophication—the substantial growth of some plants and organisms, particularly algae, in the water with an associated decline in the dissolved oxygen levels. This phenomenon has the potential to cause significant changes to aquatic ecosystems.

The Massachusetts Office of Coastal Zone Management and the Department of Environmental Protection jointly administer the Coastal Nonpoint Pollution Control Program in the state. The program provides grants to municipalities to reduce nonpoint source pollution from storm water flowing from their jurisdiction. It also funds the development of documents, model regulations, and management practices that can be replicated in other situations.[6]

Literature Review

Analyses of nonpoint source pollution in U.S. rivers and coastal waters often revolve around the control of nutrients released from agricultural operations, especially in the Midwest, in order to ensure the maintenance of water quality in freshwater aquatic systems. Stokes and Tozer (2002) showed that a cost-effective way to control the phosphorus output of large dairy farms is to modify the cattle feed. Ribaudo et al. (2001) compared the costs of controlling nitrogen loading by limiting application of fertilizers by farmers and filtering the nutrients in restored wetlands. They found that the two strategies are cost-effective for different ranges of the abatement target. Wu et al. (2003) showed that, when paid to do so, farmers will often adopt farm-management practices (such as conservation tillage and crop rotations) that reduce nitrogen loading in the Mississippi River. However, they do not implement these practices on a large-enough proportion of their lands for the policy to be effective. Johansson (2004) suggested that policies for reducing phosphorus contamination from farms can be better targeted by accounting for the differences in the productivity and nutrient potential of the individual farms. Gibbs (2002) showed that the decline in water clarity (resulting from eutrophication) in a New Hampshire lake reduced the property values in the area.

There have been a number of studies of coastal nonpoint source pollution in other areas, including the Baltic Sea. Drainage systems in Sweden, Finland, Russia, Estonia, Latvia, Lithuania, and Poland empty into the Baltic Sea, which has limited access to the open seas. For many years, the influx of nitrogen and phosphorus into the Baltic Sea has been a concern. Turner (1999a) found that a majority of these countries would derive net economic benefits if the nitrogen and phosphorus flows were reduced to about 50% of the current level. Markowska and Zylicz (1999) proposed that the bordering countries share the costs of a cleanup effort that is based on the abatement costs for the countries involved and the willingness to pay for lower nutrient influx. Gren (2001) arrived at an intuitively straightforward result that the total net benefits derived by the countries would be higher if they acted together rather than alone. Elofsson (2003) showed that if the uncertainty in the level of nutrient loading corresponding to the abatement effort is ignored, total abatement costs may be underestimated. Hokby and Soderqvist (2003) concluded that people in Sweden are likely to think that lower eutrophication of the Baltic Sea is a necessity (rather than a luxury) and that richer people are willing to pay more to reduce eutrophication.

Cost-Benefit Example for a Water Infiltration Structure

Cost-benefit analysis can be used to evaluate a project that seeks to reduce the discharge of pathogens and other nonpoint source pollutants into coastal waters. Often storm water runoff contains nonpoint source pollutants, such as suspended solids and fecal coliform bacteria. These pollutants have been responsible for the closure of shellfish beds and public beaches in Massachusetts. One possible remedy is to build infiltration structures designed to hold and treat storm water runoff, especially the first half inch or so of the precipitation. Infiltration structures are built just before the points where the storm water is released into the ocean.

Massachusetts has undertaken projects with this objective in the past. For example, the towns of Wareham and Tisbury used Section 319 funds (U.S. EPA grant funds) to build infiltration structures to reduce bacterial and other pollutants in the storm water flowing from their towns into the adjacent water bodies.[7] In these two cases, the structures were successful in removing not only the fecal coliform bacteria from storm water but also other nonpoint source pollutants, such as petroleum oil, grease, hydrocarbons, zinc, barium, chromium, and lead. Consequently, shellfish beds near the towns' shores are now open longer each year, and it is only after heavy rains that a bed closure is imposed.

Consider, for example, a town project to build an infiltration structure to remove bacterial contamination and other nonpoint source pollutants from storm water. Estimating the construction and maintenance (over the expected lifetime) costs of the infiltration structures is relatively straightforward, but valuing the benefits may not be. Two potential benefits of this project are that shellfish beds would remain open for harvesting for a greater proportion of the year and beaches with public access would be closed less often. In addition, there may be other benefits associated with improved water quality and associated ecosystem health.

Shellfish beds are important to the local fishermen and the revenue losses incurred can be estimated by combining the information on the number of days the beds were closed, the average landings per day, and the average annual price of the shellfish. This, of course, assumes that these harvests are forever lost. If shellfish that are not harvested during closed periods are harvested later, then these benefits will at least partially offset losses during closures. The DMF (2005) described the procedure for estimating compensation due to Massachusetts fishermen following the 2005 red tide phenomenon—a toxic algal bloom caused by *Alexandrium fundyense*—that forced the closure of most shellfish beds in Massachusetts. It is important to remember that a CBA should not consider the reduction in the gross value of landings but rather the reduction in producer surplus and consumer surplus associated with these landings. Benefits may also accrue to recreational harvesters of shellfish. Nonmarket valuation techniques, such as recreation demand methods, might be used to determine these values.

The other benefits of having the infiltration structures in place are improved beach conditions and fewer beach closures. The associated benefit to recreational users is the change in total value that visitors place on the beach associated with both better water quality and more access, compared to the status quo. Other recreational users, such as bird-watchers, may also value the improved ecosystem health associated with improved water quality. As explained in previous chapters, recreation demand methods can be used to estimate associated nonmarket values. Stated preference survey methods could also be applied to measure a broad range of use and nonuse values, including recreational and nonrecreational benefits. Unlike estimates from revealed

TABLE A3.2   COMMON BENEFITS AND COSTS OF A WATER INFILTRATION PROJECT

Benefit	Who benefits?	How to measure it?
Shell fish beds are closed less often	Recreational and commercial fishermen, and consumers of commercial shellfish	Estimate producer and consumer surplus associated with commercial harvest using market analysis; estimate willingness to pay of recreational users with recreation demand models
Beaches are closed less often, and beach quality improves	Recreational users	Recreation demand methods, and stated preference survey methods
Condition of ecosystem improves and ecosystem services increase	Fishers, recreational and other users of ecosystem services, and the broader population	Ecological and economic production methods; recreation demand methods; stated preference methods for both users and non-users
Cost	Who bears the cost?	How to measure it?
Engineering costs (construction and maintenance)	Municipal or state tax payers	Market value of the required inputs

preference methods (e.g., recreation demand), stated preference estimates could capture benefit realized by other groups who do not necessarily use the coast but value preservation of the ecosystem.

CBA can also be used to assess the benefits and costs associated with other point source and nonpoint source pollutants that find their way into coastal waters. The analysis of the costs of controlling pollutants in runoff water that can cause eutrophication is more complicated than the solutions by the towns of Wareham and Tisbury, which illustrated pathogen control. Collective action by many farmers—especially those near the coastline—may be necessary to control the amount of pollution entering coastal waters. This requires designing regulation and incentive schemes for the farmers. Also, there may be tradeoffs involved if the use of fertilizers is curtailed (e.g., related to reductions in crop yields).

Alternative Methods of Economic Analysis: CEA and EIA

In some instances, public authorities may choose not to balance benefits and costs to determine management actions but may instead decide that beaches should be kept open a certain minimum number of days during the year. In such cases, CEA may be used to determine the most efficient means to achieve such goals. An appropriate cost-effectiveness indicator, for example, might be the ratio of the cost of measures needed to keep the beach open and the

TABLE A3.3   COMPARISON OF CBA, CEA, AND EIA FOR EVALUATING WATER INFILTRATION PROJECTS

Impact category	CBA	CEA	EIA
Value of the avoided loss of commercial fish catches	✓	—	—
Value of the avoided loss to recreational fishermen	✓	—	—
Value of improved beach access	✓	—	—
Value associated with improved ecosystem health	✓	—	—
Cost of building and operating infiltration structures (interpreted as project expenditures within an EIA)	✓	✓	✓
Changes in employment	*	*	✓
Regional or national economic output	—	—	✓

Note: In the table, a black check mark (✓) indicates that the particular factor is included in an analysis by that method. Asterisks indicate that the factor is sometimes or partially included (see below).
* Only to the extent that direct employment changes generate valid benefits or costs.

number of days the beach would remain open with that alternative. Various alternative means of reducing the pollution, necessary to keep beaches open more often, could be compared on this basis. These might include alternative designs or locations for infiltration structures or other means of reducing pollution, such as investments in wetland restoration. An EIA analysis, in contrast, would likely focus on the impact of proposed projects on employment and income in the construction, fisheries, and tourism sectors, especially in regions near the project site. Effects on the state's economic output and tax revenues could also be estimated. Naturally, there is no *a priori* reason that CBA and EIA could not both be conducted for such a project, as each provides unique information for project evaluation.

Conclusion

As with all other policies related to use of coastal resources, economic analysis can help inform decisions about the control of water pollutants. CBA can be used to analyze simpler projects, such as pathogen control, or more complex situations, such as control of nutrients flowing into the coastal seas. In many instances, the costs of the pollution control measures can be calculated fairly easily, but the primary benefits of these measures will be improvements to ecosystem services that require nonmarket valuation methods for appropriate monetization.

Table A3.3 offers examples of the categories that are commonly counted and not counted using CBA, CEA, and EIA in evaluating the aforementioned water infiltration project. Keep in mind that there are a number of caveats, and that the inclusion of an element in any type of analysis will often depend on the details and comprehensiveness of the studies involved. (See chapter 2 for a more in-depth discussion of the tradeoffs involved with the different approaches.)

Endnotes

1. Jickells (1998).
2. U.S. EPA (2007, 76). Also, exposure to PAHs can occur from breathing air contaminated by wild fires or coal tar, eating grilled foods, or smoking.
3. Ibid., 87.
4. Interestingly, the distinction between point and nonpoint sources is becoming less relevant over time as the ability to track and monitor flows of nutrients improves. Nonetheless, the distinction is important when developing policy solutions.
5. U.S. EPA (1996, 1).
6. Under Section 319 of the Clean Water Act, the federal government (through the U.S. EPA) sponsors projects for reducing nonpoint source pollution in coastal waters of states like Massachusetts.
7. U.S. EPA (2002b).

Case Study 4: Spatial Controls to Address Environmental Impacts of Fishing

Fishing can result in environmental impacts, such as habitat damage and marine mammal entanglements. Closing certain areas of the sea at certain times (time-area closures) and restricting specific types of gear in certain areas (spatial gear restrictions) can help mitigate these environmental impacts when they are place- and time-specific (see chapter 7). Closures and gear restrictions may provide benefits to resource users, such as recreational fishers not excluded from the area; resources uses, such as viewing marine life, that are nonextractive; and to nonusers, such as those who wish to protect animals and habitat valued by the public at large. However, closures generally represent a cost to users who are excluded. These costs and benefits must be compared to determine whether the overall net benefits of the policy are positive.

This case study looks at how an economist might evaluate the net benefits of spatial fishery management measures, such as area closures and gear restrictions. It focuses on an example of seasonal closures and gear restrictions implemented in Cape Cod Bay to protect endangered North Atlantic right whales to illustrate ways in which an evaluation of those measures might be undertaken.

Reducing Interactions between Right Whales and Fixed Fishing Gear

North Atlantic right whales are the rarest of all large whale species and among the rarest of all marine mammal species, with a total population size around 300 in the North Atlantic. The population is estimated to have been over 1,000 individuals in the 1600s and may have dropped below 100 animals before international protections came into effect in 1935.[1] They are listed as endangered throughout their range. It is unclear whether the population has remained stable, is undergoing slight growth, or is in decline. However, a recent model predicts that, under current conditions, the population will be extinct in less than 200 years.[2] Injury and mortality of the northern right whales are believed to be caused by two primary sources: ship strikes and entanglements in trap and gill net fishing gear. Disease and predation by killer whales or large sharks may also contribute to mortality.

The primary actions recommended in the "NOAA Recovery Plan for Endangered North Atlantic Right Whales (rev. 2005)" intend to reduce or eliminate injury or mortality caused by ship collision, reduce or eliminate injury and mortality caused by fisheries and fishing gear, protect habitats essential to the survival and recovery of the northern right whale, minimize effects of vessel disturbance, and maximize efforts to free entangled or stranded northern right whales. Federal and Massachusetts state laws prohibit approaching a right whale closer than 500 yards, unless permitted by the National Marine Fisheries Service (NMFS) or one of the limited exemptions applies. As part of this plan, NMFS designated areas of critical habitat for the western population

FIGURE A4.1   NORTH ATLANTIC RIGHT WHALE (*EUBALAENA GLACIALIS*), CAPE COD BAY CRITICAL HABITAT AREA (50 CFR 226.203)

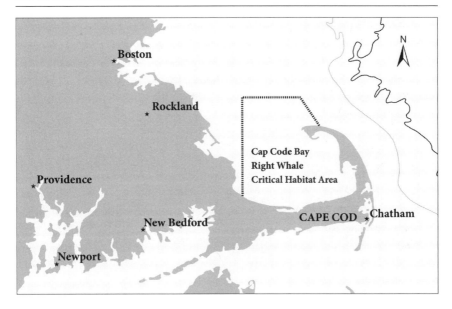

in the North Atlantic, which includes areas of Massachusetts Bay and Cape Cod Bay. It first implemented regulations intended to reduce whale entanglements in these areas during the times the whales are present in 1997 and periodic adjustments have been made since.

Cost-Benefit Analysis

This case study considers how to evaluate the benefits and costs of specific fishing restrictions and gear requirements in Cape Cod Bay. In particular, use of gill nets is prohibited in Cape Cod Bay between January 1 and May 15. In addition, certain modifications to the way lobster pots are deployed are in effect during this period to reduce the number of vertical lines in the water and to ensure that pots that do become entangled break away. Lobster pots and gill nets are also prohibited from using floating lines.

The benefits of these policies result from a reduction in the risks of whale entanglements in fishing gear and consequent injuries or death. The main costs of these measures are loss of earnings or increases in costs for fishermen who must comply with the new rules. As discussed in chapter 2, these costs and benefits should be quantified and compared to determine whether the regulations provide a net benefit to society. Since the fishing restrictions are likely to remain in place for some time and the benefits of whale protection are ongoing (rather than a one-off benefit), the stream of costs and benefits over time must be considered and properly discounted and their present values compared.

Costs of Fishing Restrictions in Cape Cod Bay

The primary cost of closing an area to fishermen is the reduction in benefits to those who would have fished in the area had it been open. However, the loss in benefits will generally be less than the total producer surplus[3] associated with the excluded fishing activities because, in most cases, the closure will redirect some fishing activity to other places, unless there is a simultaneous reduction in total allowable catch or effort. This is particularly true if the restricted area affects only a small part of the overall area of the fishery. Restrictions on fishing location choices or practices can be expected to reduce the profitability of fishermen initially, but the net losses will depend on the value of the alternatives still available. There is a substantial and growing literature on modeling location choice and entry-exit decisions in commercial fisheries.[4] These modeling techniques, which mostly utilize discrete choice random utility models (RUMs)—discussed in chapter 3—can be used to predict where effort will be displaced, which may be useful in modeling expected impacts on catches and costs.

Net losses from fishery closures can be estimated by comparing the producer surplus or profits that that displaced fishers can expect to make from their next most valuable option, relative to the restricted option. One approach to this analysis would be to simply estimate the producer surplus for each individual fisherman (or group averages) in the location they had been fishing and subtract from that the projected producer surplus in the fishery to which they are expected to relocate. An alternative approach is to use a RUM of location choice itself to estimate the cost of the closure to individual fishermen and then aggregate these for all excluded fishermen.[5] With this approach, the RUM model is used to estimate how much the expected profit in the next best alternative areas would have to increase in order to induce fishermen to choose it over the location being closed. This provides an estimate of the opportunity cost to fishermen of switching to those areas, which can be interpreted as a loss in welfare.

The costs of gear modifications (e.g., breakaway devices and sinking lines instead of floating lines) and special restrictions for deploying lobster pots could be partially measured by quantifying the out-of-pocket cost of gear modifications. However, this will only be an estimate, and probably on the high side, since these measures may induce other responses that are less costly, such as reducing effort and catch in the area or diverting it to other areas. Again, the appropriate measure of costs is the change in producer surplus, taking into account the change in behavior after the policy is implemented. The requirement for sinking lines also increases ongoing costs of operation and potential loss of gear because sinking lines are abraded by dragging along the sea bottom and need more frequent replacement.

Another consideration to include in a CBA of area closures or gear restrictions is the potential increase in management and enforcements costs for both management agencies and fishing vessels. For example, seasonal area closures might be enforced with electronic vessel monitoring systems (VMS). This may be less expensive than on-the-water monitoring by enforcement personnel or on-vessel observers, but requires additional expenditures in government infrastructure, personnel, fishing equipment, and VMS operation costs. Enforcement of gear requirements, such as use of sinking ropes, may require on-the-water monitoring.

Benefits of Fishing Restrictions in Cape Cod Bay

Area closures and spatial gear restrictions designed to protect right whales may provide a variety of benefits, including both use and nonuse values. One use benefit of the policies might be better whale watching, if the measures increase the presence of whales in the area. These values accrue to individuals who are expected to engage in whale watching. They can be measured with a recreation demand model, based on observations of whale-watching activity in areas where whale watching varies, or with a stated preference study that evaluates how users would respond to and value expected improvements in whale watching in Cape Cod Bay.

While the measures in question exclude some fishermen, they may improve fishing for those who are not excluded (e.g., recreational anglers who are allowed to continue fishing in an area closed to gillnetting). By reducing competition for the local fish stock and space, the exclusion of one group of fishermen from an area could increase consumer surplus for recreational anglers who fished there before the new restriction and may draw fishermen from other areas. If the expected changes in the quality of fishing for anglers can be identified, either stated preference (e.g., contingent valuation or contingent choice models) or revealed preference methods (e.g., travel cost models or RUMs applied to observed choices in response to these types of changes in fishing quality) could be used to estimate the net benefits to recreational fishers.

Nonuse values affected by these policies are primarily existence and bequest values associated with reducing the risk of extinction of the whales. People may also simply value saving individual whales from entanglement, and they may value increases in the whale population independent of the risks of extinction. These benefits potentially accrue to the global population, although a CBA would likely be confined to the benefits of U.S. residents. Since both use and nonuse values are of interest, it may be preferable to use a survey to estimate total economic value, which would require some type of stated preference methods. Separate valuations of use and nonuse values may lead to double counting and should be avoided or done with care.

It may be difficult to value the benefits of the measures in Cape Cod Bay in isolation, partly because they are part of a larger package of measures intended to preserve the species and because the marginal impact on mortality of these particular measures is highly uncertain and has not been quantified. Nevertheless, it is instructive to consider how the value of these measures could be correctly measured. One alternative is to design a survey to specifically measure the willingness to pay of the U.S. public for these particular measures in Cape Cod Bay. Alternatively, one could use a stated choice method that allows the valuation of several alternatives within the same survey. Respondents could be asked about their preferences across two or more alternatives, possibly including the status quo or a no-action alternative. For example, the respondents might choose between sets of discrete packages of measures with different probabilities of avoiding extinction of the species and different associated costs.[6] With such a study, an analyst might be able to map out a benefit function associated with different risk levels of extinction.

The NMFS commissioned an initial inquiry into a nonmarket valuation study of the economic benefits of right whale protection in the northwest Atlantic that has recommend proceeding in roughly this fashion,[7] but a full valuation study has not yet been undertaken. If it were feasible to estimate how much the Cape Cod Bay measures reduced the risk of extinction, then the value of this risk reduction could be quantified, using the benefit function derived from the stated preference model.

The challenges of estimating the change in risk should not be underestimated, and the change is likely to be highly uncertain. A recent report by the Government Accounting Office (2007) states the following:

> [T]here is general agreement among scientists, conservationists, federal and state regulators, and industry groups that requiring the use of sinking groundlines [sinking lines] will reduce risks to whales. However, uncertainties remain regarding how many fewer serious injuries and mortalities will occur. NMFS was unable to quantify how much the risk of whale entanglement will be reduced by sinking groundlines because researchers cannot quantify the extent to which each component of fishing gear poses a risk to whales.[8]

Nevertheless, this information would define the approach required to measure the net benefits associated with the Cape Cod Bay measures.

Cost-Effectiveness Analysis

The fishing restrictions in Cape Cod Bay are expected to help reduce whale mortality, but there may be a variety of measures that can be implemented there or in other locations to provide similar levels of mortality reduction. These could be fishery-related restrictions in other areas, as well as measures intended to reduce mortality from ship strikes. If the objective of regulators

TABLE A4.1 PRIMARY BENEFITS AND COSTS OF SEASONAL FISHERY CLOSURES AND GEAR
RESTRICTIONS IN CAPE COD BAY

Benefit	Who benefits?	How to measure it?
Improved whale watching	Whale viewers	Recreation demand methods and stated preference survey methods
Improved recreational fishing	Recreational fishers	Recreation demand methods and stated preference survey methods
Reduced risk of whale entanglements, injury, or death	Public at large	Stated preference methods
Cost	Who bears the cost?	How to measure it?
Seasonal closings for gill net fishermen	Gill net fishermen	Estimate change in producer surplus with random utility model of location choice
New gear requirement for lobstermen	Lobstermen	Estimate change in producer surplus with use of new gear
More enforcement costs	Taxpayers and fishermen	Estimate cost of enforcement measures and equipment

is to achieve a given level of mortality reduction, a CEA to evaluate the net costs of the Cape Cod Bay fishing restrictions should be considered to determine whether the same reduction in mortality could be achieved at lower cost some other way. Costs associated with alternative fishing restrictions in other areas could be estimated with the methods discussed above. Evaluating costs of measures to reduce ship strikes requires a quite different measurement approach.[9] The difficulty noted in assessing the mortality reductions that will be achieved by specific fishery and shipping regulations may make a CEA unfeasible or at least highly uncertain.

Economic Impact Analysis

Time-area closures and gear restrictions in specific areas and seasons are likely to divert fishing effort and (potentially) commercial landings that may shift expenditures and incomes among fishing communities (and even states). These measures may also result in overall changes in revenues or expenditures. It may be possible to use behavioral models to predict these changes, and this information could be fed into an input-output model (such as IMPLAN) to determine regional economic impacts. This information may be useful to policymakers to understand the impacts and distributional effects of policies. However (as discussed in depth in chapter 2), EIA can be misleading. Impacts should not be confused with net benefits, and an impact analysis should not be substituted for a CBA.

TABLE A4.2   COMPARISON OF CBA, CEA, AND EIA FOR EVALUATING SPATIAL GEAR RESTRICTIONS

Impact category	CBA	CEA	EIA
Loss in producer surplus to displaced gill net fishermen	✓	✓	—
Loss in producer surplus associated with meeting new gear requirements for lobstering	✓	✓	—
Value of improved whale watching	✓	—	—
Value of improved recreational fishing	✓	—	*
Value of reduced risk of whale deaths from entanglements	✓	—	—
Increased revenues from sale of new fishing gear	—	—	✓
Increase in hotel revenues associated with more whale-watching tourism	—	—	✓
Changes in employment	*	*	✓
Regional or national economic output	—	—	✓

Note: In the table, a black check mark (✓) indicates that the particular factor is included in an analysis by that method. Asterisks indicate that the factor is sometimes or partially included (see below).

* Only to the extent that direct employment changes generate valid benefits or costs.

As noted above, the fishery restrictions in Cape Cod Bay may result in some loss of revenues to fishermen and could result in reduced effort that, in turn, could reduce employment and expenditures on various inputs, such as fuel, ice, and maintenance services. It may also increase economic activity by requiring fishermen to make new and more frequent expenditures on gear (e.g., sinking rope, break-away gear, etc.). However, these expenditures represent costs rather than generation of new value, except to the extent that they create nonmarket value by reducing whale mortality. This is an example of why EIA may be misleading and should not be confused with an analysis of the net economic value of the measures.

Conclusion

Time-area closures and spatial gear restrictions can be useful in reducing conflicts between different user groups and in mitigating environmental impacts of fishing. In some instances, these measures may increase the net benefits derived from the fisheries by separating incompatible activities. However, poorly designed measures may do the opposite. Identifying and quantifying the benefits and costs of management measures and policies (relative to the status quo or alternative measures) will facilitate design of management measures that increase overall benefits and avoid unintended consequences.

Even when total net benefits are increased, these types of measures will create winners and losers. Equity considerations are likely to be important to policymakers, and the most economically efficient solutions will not necessarily be the preferred ones. Nevertheless, good information on benefits and costs can help counteract political pressure to take action that is not in the interest of the public. The examples of fishery conflicts in Cape Cod Bay illustrate the need to consider the impacts of mitigation measures beyond the area of specific interest. Many fisheries prosecuted in state waters are part of larger fisheries that extend into federal waters or waters of other states. An appropriate economic analysis requires understanding the connections between areas directly affected by an area closure or gear restriction and the surrounding areas to which effort may be displaced.

Table A4.2 shows examples of the categories that are counted and not counted using CBA, CEA, and EIA in the evaluation example.

Endnotes

1. NMFS (2007).
2. NMFS (2006a).
3. This is an economic measure of the difference between the amount that producers (of a good) receive and the minimum amount that they would be willing to accept for the good (generally the costs of production). It is similar to profit, but accounting for profit can differ, depending on how costs are included.
4. See, for example, Bockstael and Opaluch (1983), Curtis and Hicks (2000), Dupont (1993), Eales and Wilen (1986), Hicks et al. (2004), Holland and Sutinen (1999; 2000), Mistiaen and Strand (2000), and Smith and Wilen (2003).
5. For example, Curtis and Hicks (2000) and Hicks et al. (2004) used RUMs of location choice in Pacific tuna fisheries and the mid-Atlantic surf clam fishery, respectively, to estimate welfare losses associated with area closures.
6. This might involve asking each respondent to approve or disapprove of several individual packages or choose between or rank sets of measures.
7. Chapman and Bishop (2005).
8. Government Accounting Office (2007, *15*).
9. Methodologies and cost estimates are discussed in the NMFS draft environmental impact statement on a whale ship strike reductions strategy (NMFS 2006b).

A Mathematical Example of Quasi-Option Value

This appendix derives a simple, stylized example of quasi-option value associated with a question on whether to develop an area today or in the future, adapted from Gollier and Treich (2003).

The example requires the following assumptions: 1) the economy consists of risk-neutral agents; 2) net benefits of developing area C are unclear because there is uncertainty about the benefits of preservation that would be lost; 3) there are one-time costs associated with developing area C; 4) there are two periods, today and the future (which means next year and all subsequent years combined); and 5) the discount factor, which equals one over one plus the discount rate, and is equal to d, where d is between zero and one. Given the scientific uncertainty regarding the benefits of developing area C, the benefits per period are equal to B.

Following Gollier and Treich (2003), it is assumed that there are two competing theories about the future benefits associated with development. Specifically, benefits could be either aB or $(1 + a)B$, where a is between zero and 1. In other words, there are two states of the world in period 2, one characterized by high development benefits $(1 + a)B$ and one characterized by low development benefits aB. The probability that benefits will be high is p and the probability that benefits will be low is $(1 - p)$.

The expected net present value (NPV) from developing the area immediately is, therefore, equal to

$$NPV^1 = \frac{(1-p)aB + p(1+a)B}{1-d} - C = \frac{(p+a)B}{1-d} - C$$

where the expected benefits, $(p + a)B$, are discounted to reflect the reduced present value of benefits or costs realized in future time periods. So far, this example does not allow for future learning, which is the source of quasi-option value. In this case, if the expected flow of benefits $((p + a)B/1 - d)$ is greater than the fixed one-time cost of developing area C, then the optimal decision would be to develop the area. That is, if NPV^1 is positive, then one would choose to develop.

How might this decision change if the possibility of learning before the next decision period (period 2) is incorporated, and thereby allow for quasi-option value? If this possibility is introduced, another decision rule could be to wait until the second period and to develop area C only if development benefits turn out to be high, $(1 + a)B$. To make the analysis interesting, add the additional assumption that the development is socially beneficial (i.e., net benefits are positive) only if high benefits are realized. That is, if it is discovered in the future that the development benefits are only aB, then the optimal decision would be to leave the area undeveloped.[1] Because of this assumption, one can simplify the decision in period 2, where now the decision rule only considers the net present value from developing the area, conditional on high benefits being realized. The expected net NPV of this strategy is equal to

$$NPV^2 = 0 + p\left(\frac{(1+a)B}{1-d} - C\right)d,$$

where zero is the return from not developing in the first period. Given the assumptions, including a risk-neutral society, if the expected net present value of decision strategy 2, NPV^2, is greater than the expected net present value from rule one, NPV^1, the decision is to delay development until period 2.

What are the costs and benefits of delaying? If the area is not developed in the first period and it turns out the benefits were $(1 + a)B$ rather than aB, then the decisionmakers would lose out on the returns that would have been gained from earlier development (i.e., in period 1). On the other hand, it could be that the decision was to develop, the returns were low, and the project should never have been implemented in the first place (i.e., it would have failed a cost-benefit test). The benefit of waiting, therefore, is the ability to abandon the project if the value of development turns out to be low. The difference between expected payoffs, $NPV^2 - NPV^1$, is the quasi-option value of delaying the investment in the project, which is positive or zero. The decision, therefore, depends on the economic benefits, probabilities, discount factor, and one-time cost. These variables will most likely be determined by economic-ecological relationships in EBM frameworks and/or in stated preference methods discussed in chapter 4.

Endnote

1. This is mathematically equivalent to saying that $\dfrac{aB}{1-d} < C < \dfrac{(1+a)B}{1-d}$.

References

Abdalla, C.W., B.A. Roach, and D.J. Epp. 1992. Valuing Environmental Quality Changes Using Averting Expenditures: An Application to Groundwater Contamination. *Land Economics* 68(2): 63–69.

ACRE (Applied Coastal Research and Engineering). 2000. Assessing Potential Environmental Impacts of Offshore Sand and Gravel Mining. Draft report prepared for the Commonwealth of Massachusetts by ACRE, May 2000.

Adamowicz, W.L., P. Boxall, M. Williams, and J. Louviere. 1998. Stated Preference Approaches for Measuring Passive Use Values: Choice Experiments and Contingent Valuation. *American Journal of Agricultural Economics* 80(1): 64–75.

Adamowicz, W.L., and T. Graham-Tomasi. 1991. Revealed Preference Tests of Non-market Goods Valuation Methods. *Journal of Environmental Economics and Management* 20: 29–45.

Adamowicz, W.L., J. Louviere, and M. Williams. 1994. Combining Revealed and Stated Preference Methods for Valuing Environmental Amenities. *Journal of Environmental Economics and Management* 26: 271–92.

Adamowicz, W., J. Swait, P. Boxall, J. Louviere, and M. Williams. 1997. Perceptions versus Objective Measures of Environmental Quality in Combined Revealed and Stated Preference Methods of Environmental Valuation. *Journal of Environmental Economics and Management* 32: 64–84.

Adamowicz, W.L. 1994. Habit Formation and Variety Seeking in a Discrete Choice Model of Recreation Demand. *Journal of Agricultural and Resource Economics* 19(1): 19–31.

Ames, R.T., G.H. Williams, and S.M. Fitzgerald. 2005. Using Digital Video Monitoring Systems in Fisheries: Application for Monitoring Compliance of Seabird Avoidance Devices and Seabird Mortality in Pacific Halibut Longline Fisheries. NOAA Technical Memo NMFS-AFSC-152. Washington, DC: U.S. Department of Commerce.

Armsworth, P., G.C. Daily, P. Kareiva, and J.N. Sanchirico 2006. Land Market Feedbacks Can Undermine Biodiversity Conservation. *Proceedings of the National Academies of Sciences (PNAS)*, 103(14)5403-5408.

Arrow, K., and A. Fisher. 1974. Environmental Preservation, Uncertainty, and Irreversibility. *Quarterly Journal of Economics* 98: 85–106.

Arrow, K., and L. Hurwicz. 1972. An Optimality Criterion for Decision-Making under Ignorance. In *Uncertainty and Expectations in Economics*, edited by C.F. Carter and J.L. Ford. Oxford: Basil Blackwell.

Arrow, K., R. Solow, E. Leamer, P. Portney, R. Rander, and H. Schuman. 1993. Report of the NOAA Panel on Contingent Valuation. *Federal Register* 58 (January): 4602–14.

Barbier, E.B. 1994. Valuing Environmental Functions: Tropical Wetlands. *Land Economics* 70(2): 155–74.

―――. 2000. Valuing the Environment as Input: Review of Applications to Mangrove-Fishery Linkages. *Ecological Economics* 35(1): 47–61.

Barbier, E.B. and I. Strand.1998. Valuing Mangrove-Fishery Linkages: A Case Study of Campeche, Mexico. *Environmental and Resource Economics* 12(2):151-66.

Barbier, E.B., I. Strand, and S. Sathirathai 2002.*Environmental and Resource Economics* 21(4)343-67.

Bateman, I.J., R.T. Carson, B. Day, M. Hanemann, N. Hanley, T. Hett, M. Jones-Lee, G. Loomes, S. Mourato, E. Ozdemiroglu, D.W. Pearce, R. Sugden, and J. Swanson. 2002. *Economic Valuation with Stated Preference Surveys: A Manual.* Northampton, MA: Edward Elgar.

Bell, F., and V. Leeworthy. 1990. Recreational Demand by Tourists for Saltwater Beach Days. *Journal of Environmental Economics and Management* 18: 189–205.

Bennett, J., and R. Blamey, eds. 2001. *The Choice Modeling Approach to Environmental Valuation.* Northampton, MA: Edward Elgar.

Berger, J.O. 1985. *Statistical Decision Theory and Bayesian Analysis.* New York: Springer-Verlag.

Bergstrom, J.C., and P. De Civita. 1999. Status of Benefits Transfer in the United States and Canada: A Review. *Canadian Journal of Agricultural Economics* 47(1): 79–87.

Bergstrom, J.C., J.H. Dorfman, and J.B. Loomis. 2004. Estuary Management and Recreational Fishing Benefits. *Coastal Management* 32: 417–32.

Bergstrom, J.C., J.R. Stoll, J.P. Titre, and V.L. Wright. 1990. Economic Value of Wetlands-Based Recreation. *Ecological Economics* 2(2): 129–47.

Bergstrom, J.C., and L.O. Taylor. 2006. Using Meta-analysis for Benefits Transfer: Theory and Practice. *Ecological Economics* 60(2): 351–60.

Berrens, R., D. Brookshire, M. McKee, and C. Schmidt. 1998. Implementing the Safe Minimum Standard. *Land Economics* 74: 147–61.

Bishop, R. 1978. Endangered Species and Uncertainty: The Economics of a Safe Minimum Standard. *American Journal of Agricultural Economics* 60: 10–18.

―――. 1979. Endangered Species, Irreversibility, and Uncertainty: A Reply. *American Journal of Agricultural Economics* 61(2): 376–79.

Blamey, R.K., J.W. Bennett, and M.D. Morrison. 1999. Yea-Saying in Contingent Valuation Surveys. *Land Economics* 75(1): 126–41.

Boardman, A.E., D.H. Greenberg, A.R. Vining, and D.L. Weimer. 2001. *Cost-Benefit Analysis: Concepts and Practice.* 2nd ed. Upper Saddle River, NJ: Prentice Hall.

―――. 2006. *Cost-Benefit Analysis: Concepts and Practice.* 3rd ed. Upper Saddle River, NJ: Prentice Hall.

Boardman et al. (1996)

Bockstael, N.E., A.M. Freeman III, R.J. Kopp, P.R. Portney, and V.K. Smith. 2000. On Measuring Economic Values for Nature. *Environmental Science and Technology* 34(8): 1384–89.

Bockstael, N., W.M. Hanemann, and C.L. Kling. 1987. Estimating the Value of Water Quality Improvements in a Recreational Demand Framework. *Water Resources Research* 23(5): 951–60.

Bockstael, N., K.E. McConnell, and I.E. Strand. 1989. A Random Utility Model for Sportfishing: Some Preliminary Results for Florida. *Marine Resource Economics* 6: 245–60.

Bockstael, N.E., and J.J. Opaluch. 1983. Discrete Modeling of Supply Responses under Uncertainty: The Case of the Fishery. *Journal of Environmental Economics and Management* 10: 125–37.

Borchers, A.M., J.M. Duke, and G.R. Parsons. 2007. Does Willingness to Pay for Green Energy Differ by Source? *Energy Policy* 35: 3327–34.

Boyd, J., J.N. Sanchirico, and L. Shabman. 2004. Habitat Benefit Assessment and Decisionmaking: A Report to the National Marine Fisheries Service. RFF Discussion Paper 04-09. Washington, DC: Resources for the Future. www.rff.org/RFF/Documents/RFF-DP-04-09.pdf. Accessed August 2009.

Boyle, K.J., P.J. Poor, and L.O. Taylor. 1999. Estimating the Demand for Protecting Freshwater Lakes from Eutrophication. *American Journal of Agricultural Economics* 81(5): 1118–22.

Brodziak, J., and M. Traver. 2006, rev. Haddock: Distribution, Biology, and Management. In Status of Fishery Resources off the Northeastern U.S. NEFSC/NOAA website. www.nefsc.noaa.gov/sos/spsyn/pg/haddock/. Accessed August 2009.

Brog, W., A.H. Meyberg, and P.R. Stoperher, eds. 1981. *New Horizons in Travel Behavior*. Lexington, MA: D.C. Heath.

Brouwer, R., and I.J. Bateman. 2005. Benefits Transfer of Willingness to Pay Estimates and Functions for Health-Risk Reductions: A Cross-Country Study. *Journal of Health Economics* 24(3): 591–611.

Brown, G., and J. Roughgarden. 1997. A Metapopulation Model with Private Property and a Common Pool. *Ecological Economics* 22(1): 65–71.

Brown, M.T., and R.A. Herendeen. 1996. Embodied Energy Analysis and EMERGY Analysis: A Comparative View. *Ecological Economics* 19: 218–35.

Byrnes, M., R.M. Hammer, T.D. Thibaut, and D.B. Snyder. 2004. Physical and Biological Effects of Sand Mining Offshore Alabama, U.S.A. *Journal of Coastal Research* 20(1): 6–24.

Camerer, C. 2000. Prospect Theory in the Wild: Evidence from the Field. In *Choices, Values, and Frames*, edited by D. Khaneman and A. Tversky. Cambridge: Cambridge University Press: New York: Russell Sage Foundation, 288–300.

Capewind.org. 2007. Frequently Asked Questions about Cape Wind. www.capewind.org/downloads/faqs4.pdf. Accessed August 2009.

Carson, R.T., and T. Groves. 2007. Incentive and Informational Properties of Preference Questions. *Environmental and Resource Economics* 37: 181–210.

Carson, R.T., M.W. Hanemann, and R.C. Mitchell. 1986. The Use of Simulated Political Markets to Value Public Goods. Working Paper. San Diego, CA: University of California–San Diego, Department of Economics.

Champ, P.A., and R.C. Bishop. 2001. Donation Payment Mechanisms and Contingent Valuation: An Empirical Study of Hypothetical Bias. *Environmental and Resource Economics* 19(4): 383–402.

Champ, P.A., K.J. Boyle, and T.C. Brown, eds. 2003. *A Primer on Non-Market Valuation*. Dordrecht, The Netherlands: Kluwer Academic Publishers.

Chapman, D.J., and R.J. Bishop. 2005. Study of the Economic Benefits of Right Whale Protection in the Northwest Atlantic: Phase 1, Year 1 Report. Prepared for National Oceanic and Atmospheric Administration, National Marine Fisheries Service, Woods Hole, MA, USA.

CHC (Coastal Hazards Commission). 2007. Preparing for the Storm: Recommendations for Management of Risk from Coastal Hazards in Massachusetts, Recommendation No. 2. In Final Report of the Coastal Hazards Commission, Commonwealth of Massachusetts, USA, May 2007. www.mass.gov/czm/chc/recommendations/final_recommendations.htm. Accessed August 2009.

Chichilnisky, G. and G.M. Heal, 1993, Global Environmental Risks. Journal of Economic Perspectives. 7(9):65-86.

Chilton, S.M., and W.G. Hutchinson. 1999. Do Focus Groups Contribute Anything to the Contingent Valuation Process? *Journal of Economic Psychology* 20: 465–83.

Ciriacy-Wantrup, S.V. 1952. *Resource Conservation: Economics and Policies.* Berkeley and Los Angeles, CA: University of California.

Ciriacy-Wantrup, S.V., and W.E. Phillips. 1970. Conservation of the California Tule Elk: A Socioeconomic Study of a Survival Problem. *Biological Conservation* 3(1): 23–32.

Conrad, J. 1980. Quasi-option Value and the Expected Value of Information. *Quarterly Journal of Economics* 94(2): 813–20.

Cooke, R. 1991. *Experts in Uncertainty: Opinion and Subjective Probability in Science.* New York and Oxford: Oxford University Press, 319.

Costanza, R., R. d'Argec, R. Groot, S. Farber, M. Grasso, B. Hannon, K. Limburg, S. Naeem, R.V. O'Neill, J. Paruelo, R.G. Raskin, P. Sutton, and M. van den Belt. 1997. The Value of the World's Ecosystem Services and Natural Capital. *Nature* 387 (May): 253–60.

Costello, C., S.D. Gaines, and J. Lyman. 2008. Can Catch Shares Prevent Fisheries Collapses? *Science* 321: 1678–81.

Crome F.H.J., M.R. Thomas, and L.A. Moore. 1996. A Novel Bayesian Approach to Assess the Impacts of Rain Forest Logging. *Ecological Applications* 6: 1104–23.

Crompton, J.L. 1995. Economic Impact Analysis of Sports Facilities and Events: Eleven Sources of Misapplication. *Journal of Sport Management* 9(1): 14–35.

Cropper, M.L., and A.M. Freeman. 1991. Environmental Health Effects. In *Measuring the Demand for Environmental Quality,* edited by J.B. Braden and C.D. Kolstad. Amsterdam: Elsevier Science Publishers, 165–211.

Crowder, L.B., G. Osherenco, O.R. Young, S. Airame, E.A. Norse, and N. Baron. 2006. Resolving Mismatches in U.S. Ocean Governance. *Science* 313: 617–18.

Curtis, R., and R. Hicks. 2000. The Cost of Sea Turtle Preservation: The Case of Hawaii's Pelagic Longliners. *American Journal of Agricultural Economics* 82(5): 1191–98.

CWA. 2007.

DCR (Massachusetts Department of Conservation and Recreation). 2005. Winthrop Shores Reservation Restoration Program: Final Environmental Impact Report. EOEA, No. 10113. Boston: DCR.

Desvousges, W.H., and V.K. Smith. 1988. Focus Groups and Risk Communication: The "Science" of Listening to Data. *Risk Analysis* 8(4): 479–84.

Desvousges, W.H., V.K. Smith, D.H. Brown, and D.K. Pate. 1984. *The Role of Focus Groups in Designing a Contingent Valuation Survey to Measure the Benefits of Hazardous Waste Management Regulations.* Research Triangle Park, NC: Research Triangle Institute.

Dillman, D.A. 2000. *Mail and Internet Surveys: The Tailored Design Method.* New York: John Wiley and Sons.

DMF (Massachusetts Division of Marine Fisheries). 2005. Red Tide Disaster Relief. See www.mass.gov/dfwele/dmf/spotlight/red_tide_relief.htm and www.mass.gov/dfwele/dmf/programsandprojects/pspmoni.htm#shelsani. Doremus, H. 2007. Precaution, Science, and Learning while Doing in Natural Resource Management. *Washington Law Review* 82(3): 547–80.

Dupont, D.P. 1993. Price Uncertainty, Expectations Formation, and Fishers' Location Choices. *Marine Resource Economics* (8): 219–47.

Eales, J., and J.E. Wilen. 1986. An Examination of Fishing Location Choice in the Pink Shrimp Fishery. *Marine Resource Economics* 2(4): 331–51.

Edwards, S.F. 1987. *An Introduction to Coastal Zone Economics*. New York: Taylor and Francis.

———. 1990. An Economics Guide to Allocation of Fish Stocks between Commercial and Recreational Fisheries. NOAA Technical Report NMFS 94. Washington, DC: U.S. Department of Commerce.

———. 1991. A Critique of Three "Economics" Arguments Commonly Used to Influence Fishery Allocations. *North American Journal of Fisheries Management* 11: 121–30.

———. 2007. Ocean Zoning, First Possession, and Coasean Contracts. *Marine Policy* 32(1): 46–54.

Ehrlich, P., and A. Ehrlich. 1997. *Betrayal of Science and Reason*. Washington, DC: Island Press.

EIA (Energy Information Administration, U.S. Department of Energy). 2007a. Online document. Renewable Energy Annual 2005. U.S. Department of Energy, July 2007. www. tonto.eia.doe.gov/ftproot/renewables/060305.pdf. Accessed August 2009.

———. 2007b. Energy Consumption and Electricity Preliminary 2006 Statistics. U.S. Department of Energy, August 2007. www.eia.doe.gov/cneaf/solar.renewables/page/prelim_trends/rea_prereport.html. Accessed August 2009.

Ellsberg, D. 1961. Risk, Ambiguity, and the Savage Axioms. *Quarterly Journal of Economics* 75: 643–69.

Elofsson, K. 2003. Cost-Effective Reductions of Stochastic Agricultural Loads to the Baltic Sea. *Ecological Economics* 47(1): 13–31.

Englin, J., and R. Mendelsohn. 1991. A Hedonic Travel Cost Analysis for Valuation of Multiple Components of Site Quality. *Journal of Environmental Economics and Management* 21: 275–90.

Epstein, L. 1980. Decision Making and the Temporal Resolution of Uncertainty. *International Economic Review* 21: 264–83.

Feather, P.M., D. Hellerstein, and T. Tomasi. 1995. A Discrete-Count Model of Recreational Demand. *Journal of Environmental Economics and Management* 29: 214–27.

Firestone, J. and W. Kempton. 2007. Public Opinion about Large Offshore Wind Power: Underlying Factors *Energy Policy* 35(3): 1584-1598.

Freeman, A.M. 2003. *The Measurement of Environmental and Natural Resource Values: Theory and Methods*. 2nd ed. Washington, DC: Resources for the Future.

French, D., and H. Shuttenberg. 1998. Estimated Food Web and Habitat Values for Habitats in the Peconic Estuary System. Report submitted to Economic Analysis Inc., Peacedale, RI.

Freixas, X. and Laffont, J.-J. (1984). On the irreversibility effect, in M. Boyer and R. Kihlstrom (eds), *Bayesian Models in Economic Theory*, NHPC, pp. 105–114.

Garrod, G., and K.G. Willis. 1999. *Economic Valuation of the Environment: Methods and Case Studies*. Cheltenham, UK: Edward Elgar.

Gibbs J.P., 2002. A Hedonic Analysis of the Effects of Lake Water Clarity on New Hampshire Lakefront Properties. *Agricultural and Resource Economics Review* 31(1): 39–46.

Giuffre, D., J. Haughton, and D.G. Tuerck. 2004. Free But Costly: An Economic Analysis of a Wind Farm in Nantucket Sound. Boston, MA: Beacon Hill Institute at Suffolk University.

Glass, G.V. 1976. Primary, Secondary, and Meta-analysis of Research. *Educational Researcher* 5(10): 3–8.

Global Insight. 2003, rev. Impact Analysis of the Cape Wind Offshore Renewable Energy Project on Local, State, and Regional Economies. Report prepared for Cape

Wind Associates, revised September 23, 2003. www.mms.gov/offshore/PDFs/CW-Files/68.pdf. Accessed August 2009.

Gollier, C., B. Jullien, and N. Treich. 2000. Scientific Progress and Irreversibility: An Economic Interpretation of the "Precautionary Principle." *Journal of Public Economics* 75: 229–53.

Gollier, C., and N. Treich. 2003. Decision-Making under Scientific Uncertainty: The Economics of the Precautionary Principle. *Journal of Risk and Uncertainty* 27(1): 177–203.

Gordon, H.S. 1954. The Economic Theory of a Common Property Resource: The Fishery. *Journal of Political Economy* 62(2): 124–42.

Goulder, L., and R. Stavins. 2002. Discounting: An Eye on the Future. *Nature* 419: 673–74. doi: 10.1038/419673a.

Government Accounting Office (GAO). 2007. Improved Economic Analysis and Evaluation Strategies Needed for Proposed Changes to Atlantic Large Whale Protection Plan. Washington, DC: GAO.

Graham-Tomasi, T. 1995. Quasi-option Value. In *Handbook of Environmental Economics*, edited by D.W. Bromley. Oxford, UK: Blackwell.

Greene, W.H. 2000. Simultaneous Equations Models. In *Econometric Analysis*. 4th ed. Upper Saddle River, NJ: Prentice Hall.

———. 2003. *Econometric Analysis*. 5th ed. Upper Saddle River, NJ: Prentice Hall.

Gregory, R., S. Lichtenstein, and P. Slovic. 1993. Valuing Environmental Resources: A Constructive Approach. *Journal of Risk and Uncertainty* 7: 177–97.

Gren, I. 2001. International versus National Actions against Nitrogen Pollution of the Baltic Sea. *Environmental and Resource Economics* 20(1): 41–59.

Griffiths, C., and W. Wheeler. 2005. Benefit-Cost Analysis of Regulations Affecting Surface Water Quality in the United States. In *Cost-Benefit Analysis and Water Resources Management*, edited by R. Brouwer and D. Pearce. Cheltenham, UK: Edward Elgar.

Grumbine, R.E. 1994. What Is EM? *Conservation Biology* 8(1): 27–38.

Haab, T.C., and R.L. Hicks, 1997. Accounting for Choice Set Endogeneity in Random Utility Models of Recreation Demand. *Journal of Environmental Economics and Management* 34(2): 127–47.

Haab, T.C., and K.E. McConnell. 2002. *Valuing Environmental and Natural Resources: The Econometrics of Non-Market Valuation*. Cheltenham, UK: Edward Elgar.

Hagos, K.W. 2007. Impact of Offshore Wind Energy on Marine Fisheries in Rhode Island. White Paper for Integrated Coastal Science. Coastal Institute IGERT Project, EVS 614, University of Rhode Island, Kingston, July 28, 2007.

Hahn, R.W., and R.N. Stavins. 1992. Economic Incentives for Environmental Protection: Integrating Theory and Practice. *American Economic Review* 82: 464–68.

Hammond, T.R., and J.R. Ellis 2002. A Meta-Assessment for Elasmobranches Based on Dietary Data and Bayesian Networks. *Ecological Indicators* 1: 197–211.

Hanemann, M.W. 1984. Welfare Evaluations in Contingent Valuation Experiments with Discrete Responses. *American Journal of Agricultural Economics* 66(3): 332–41.

———. 1994. Valuing the Environment through Contingent Valuation. *Journal of Environmental Perspectives* 8(4): 19–43.

Hanley, N., S. Colombo, D. Tinch, A. Black, and A. Aftab. 2006a. Estimating the Benefits of Water Quality Improvements under the Water Framework Directive: Are Benefits Transferable? *European Review of Agricultural Economics* 33(3): 391–413.

Hanley, N., R.E. Wright, and B. Alvarez-Farizo. 2006b. Estimating the Economic Value of Improvements in River Ecology Using Choice Experiments: An Application to the Water Framework Directive. *Journal of Environmental Management* 78(2): 183–93.

Hau, J.L., and B.R. Bakshi. 2004. Promise and Problems of Emergy Analysis. *Ecological Modelling* 178 (1–2): 215–25.

Haughton J., D. Giuffre, and J. Barrett. 2003. Blowing in the Wind: Offshore Wind and the Cape Cod Economy. Boston, MA: Beacon Hill Institute at Suffolk University.

Haughton J., D. Giuffre, J. Barrett, and D.G. Tuerck. 2004. An Economic Analysis of a Wind Farm in Nantucket Sound. Boston, MA: Beacon Hill Institute at Suffolk University.

Henry, C. 1974. Option Values in the Economics of Irreplaceable Assets. *Review of Economic Studies* 41: 89–104.

Hensher, D., and V. Le Plastrier. 1985. Towards a Dynamic Discrete-Choice Model of Household Automobile Fleet Size and Composition. *Transport Research* 19(6): 481–95.

Hensher, D.A., and P.R. Stopher, eds. 1979. *Behavioral Travel Modeling*. London: Croom Helm.

Herrera, G.E. 2006. The Benefits of Spatial Regulation in a Multispecies Fishery. *Marine Resource Economics* 21(1): 249–61.

Herriges, J.A., and C.L. Kling. 1999. *Valuing Recreation and the Environment*. Cheltenham, UK: Edward Elgar.

Hicks, R., D. Holland, J.E. Kirkley, and I. Strand. 2001. Economic Impacts and Protecting Essential Fish Habitat, Amendment 13 to the Summer Flounder, Scup, and Black Sea Bass Fishery Management Plan. Prepared for the Mid-Atlantic Fishery Management Council, Dover, DE.

Hicks, R., J. Kirkley, and I. Strand. 2004. Short-Run Welfare Losses from Essential Fish Habitat Designations for the Surf Clam and Ocean Quahog Fisheries. *Marine Resource Economics* 19(1): 113–30.

Hoeting, J.A., D. Madigan, A. Raferty, and C. Volinsky. 1999. Bayesian Model Averaging: A Tutorial. *Statistical Science* 14(4): 382–417.

Hokby, S., and T. Soderqvist. 2003. Elasticities of Demand and Willingness to Pay for Environmental Services in Sweden. *Environmental and Resource Economics* 26(3): 361–83.

Holland, D.S. 2000. A Bioeconomic Model of Marine Sanctuaries on Georges Bank. *Canadian Journal of Fisheries and Aquatic Sciences* 57: 1307–19.

———. 2004. Spatial Fishery Rights and Marine Zoning: A Discussion with Reference to Management of Marine Resources in New England. *Marine Resource Economics* 19(1): 21–40.

———. 2007. Managing Environmental Impacts of Fishing: Input Controls versus Outcome Oriented Approaches. *International Journal of Global Environmental Issues* 7(2–3): 255–72.

Holland, D.S., and K.E. Schnier. 2006. Individual Habitat Quotas for Fisheries 2006. *Journal of Environmental Economics and Management* 51(1): 72–92.

Holland, D.S., and J.G. Sutinen. 1999. An Empirical Model of Fleet Dynamics in New England Trawl Fisheries. *Canadian Journal of Fisheries and Aquatic Sciences* 56: 253–64.

———. 2000. Location Choice in New England Trawl Fisheries: Old Habits Die Hard. *Land Economics* 76(1): 133–49.

Hotelling, H. 1949. An Economic Study of the Monetary Evaluation of Recreation in the National Parks. Washington, DC: US National Park Service.

Huang, J., T. Haab, and J., Whitehead. 1997. Willingness to Pay for Quality Improvements: Should Revealed and Stated Preference Data Be Combined? *Journal of Environmental Economics and Management* 34: 240–55.

Huang, J., P.J. Poor, and M.Q. Zhao. 2007. Economic Valuation of Beach Erosion Control. *Marine Resource Economics* 22(3): 221–38.

Hushak, L.J. 1987. Use of Input-Output Analysis in Fisheries Assessment. *Transactions of the American Fisheries Society* 116: 441–49.

Irwin, E.G. 2002. The Effects of Open Space on Residential Property Values. *Land Economics* 78(4): 465–80.

Jaffe, A.B., R.G. Newell, and R.N. Stavins. 2002. Environmental Policy and Technological Change. *Environmental and Resource Economics* 22: 41–69.

Jaffe, J., and R. Stavins. 2004. The Value of Formal Quantitative Assessment of Uncertainty in Regulatory Analysis. Washington, DC: AEI-Brookings Joint Center for Regulatory Studies. Accessed August 2009.

Jiang, Y., S.K. Swallow, and M. McGonagle. 2005. Context-Sensitive Benefit Transfer Using Stated Choice Models: Specification and Convergent Validity for Policy Analysis. *Environmental and Resource Economics* 31(4): 477–99.

Jickells, T.D. 1998. Nutrient Biogeochemistry of the Coastal Zone. *Science* 281: 217–22.

Jin, D., and P. Hoagland. 1998. Economic Activity Associated with the Northeast Shelf Large Marine Ecosystem: Application of an Input-Output Approach. Woods Hole, MA: Marine Policy Center, Woods Hole Oceanographic Institution.

Jobert A., P. Laborgne, and S. Mimler. 2007. Local Acceptance of Wind Energy: Factors of Success Identified in French and German Case Studies. *Energy Policy* 35: 2751–60.

Johannesson, M. 1997. Some Further Experimental Results on Hypothetical versus Real Willingness to Pay. *Applied Economics Letters* 4: 535–36.

Johansson, R.C., P.H. Gowda, D.J. Mulla, and B.J. Dalzell. 2004. Meta-modelling Phosphorus Best Management Practices for Policy Use: A Frontier Approach. *Agricultural Economics* 30(1): 63–74.

Johnston, R.J., M.H. Ranson, E.Y. Besedin, and E.C. Helm. 2006. What Determines Willingness to Pay per Fish? A Meta-Analysis of Recreational Fishing Values. *Marine Resource Economics* 21(1): 1-32.

Johnston, R.J. 2006. Is Hypothetical Bias Universal? Validating Contingent Valuation Responses Using a Binding Public Referendum. *Journal of Environmental Economics and Management* 52(1): 469–81.

———. 2007. Choice Experiments, Site Similarity, and Benefits Transfer. *Environmental and Resource Economics* 38(3): 331–51.

Johnston, R.J., and E.Y. Besedin. 2009. Estimating Willingness to Pay for Aquatic Resource Improvements Using Benefits Transfer. In *Environmental Economics for Watershed Restoration*, edited by H.W. Thurston, M.T. Heberling, and A. Schrecongost. Boca Raton, FL: CRC Press.

Johnston, R.J., E.Y. Besedin, R. Iovanna, C. Miller, R. Wardwell, and M. Ranson. 2005a. Systematic Variation in Willingness to Pay for Aquatic Resource Improvements and Implications for Benefit Transfer: A Meta-Analysis. *Canadian Journal of Agricultural Economics* 53(2–3): 221–48.

Johnston, R.J., J.J. Opaluch, M.J. Mazzotta, and G. Magnusson. 2005b. Who Are Resource Nonusers and What Can They Tell Us about Nonuse Values? Decomposing User and Nonuser Willingness to Pay for Coastal Wetland Restoration. *Water Resources Research* 41(7). doi:10.1029/2004WR003766.

Johnston, R.J., T.A. Grigalunas, J.J. Opaluch, J. Diamantedes, and M. Mazzotta. 2002b. Valuing Estuarine Resource Services Using Economic and Ecological Models: The Peconic Estuary System Study. *Coastal Management* 30(1): 47–66.

Johnston, R.J., G. Magnusson, M. Mazzotta, and J.J. Opaluch. 2002a. Combining Economic and Ecological Indicators to Prioritize Salt Marsh Restoration Actions. *American Journal of Agricultural Economics* 84(5): 1362–70.

Johnston, R.J., J.J. Opaluch, T.A. Grigalunas, and M.J. Mazzotta. 2001. Estimating Amenity Benefits of Coastal Farmland. *Growth and Change* 32(Summer): 305–325.

Johnston, R.J., and R.S. Rosenberger. 2009. Methods, Trends, and Controversies in Contemporary Benefit Transfer. *Journal of Economic Surveys* (forthcoming).

Johnston, R.J., and J.G. Sutinen. 1996. Uncertain Biomass Shift and Collapse: Implications for Harvest Policy in the Fishery. *Land Economics* 72(4): 500–18.

———. 1999. Appropriate and Inappropriate Economic Analysis for Allocation Decisions: The Case of Alaska Halibut. Research paper prepared for the Halibut Coalition, Juneau, AK.

Johnston, R.J., J.G. Sutinen, and H. Upton. 2003. A Note on Economics and Fish Habitat Conservation: The Appropriate Use of Economic Tools for Policy Analysis. Kingston, RI: University of Rhode Island, Department of Environmental and Natural Resource Economics.

Johnston, R.J., T.F. Weaver, L.A. Smith, and S.K. Swallow. 1995. Contingent Valuation Focus Groups: Insights from Ethnographic Interview Techniques. *Agricultural and Resource Economics Review* 24(1): 56–69.

Judge, G.G., R.C. Hill, W.E. Griffiths, H. Lutkepohl, and T. Lee. 1988. *Introduction to the Theory and Practice of Econometrics.* 2nd ed. New York: John Wiley and Sons.

Just, R.E., D.L. Hueth, and A. Schmitz. 2004. *The Welfare Economics of Public Policy: A Practical Approach to Project and Policy Evaluation.* Cheltenham, UK: Edward Elgar.

Kahneman, D., and A. Tversky. 1979. Prospect Theory: An Analysis of Decision under Risk. *Econometrica* 47(2): 264–91.

Kaplowitz, M.D., F. Lupi, and J.P. Hoehn. 2004. Multiple Methods for Developing and Evaluating a Stated-Choice Questionnaire to Value Wetlands. In *Methods for Testing and Evaluating Survey Questionnaires*, edited by S. Presser, J.M. Rothget, M.P. Coupter, J.T. Lesser, E. Martin, J. Martin, and E. Singer. New York: John Wiley and Sons.

Kempton, W., J. Firestone, J. Lilley, T. Rouleau, and P. Whitaker. 2005. The Offshore Wind Power Debate: Views from Cape Cod. *Coastal Management* 33(2): 119–49.

Kim, T.Y., S. Kwak, and S. Yoo. 1998. Applying Multi-attribute Utility Theory to Decision Making in Environmental Planning: A Case Study of the Electric Utility in Korea. *Journal of Environmental Planning and Management* 41(5): 597–609.

Kling, C. 1997. The Gains from Combining Travel Cost and Contingent Valuation Data to Value Nonmarket Goods. *Land Economics* 73(3): 428–39.

Knight, F. (1921): *Risk, Uncertainty and Profit*, Houghton, Mifflin, Boston.

Kopp, R.J., and V.K. Smith. 1993. *Valuing Natural Assets: The Economics of Natural Resource Damage Assessment.* Washington, DC: Resources for the Future.

Krohn, S., and S. Damborg. 1999. On Public Attitudes towards Wind Power. *Renewable Energy* 16: 954–60.

Lamont, A. 2006. Policy Characterization of Ecosystem Management. *Environmental Monitoring and Assessment* 113(1): 5–18.

Landry, C.E., A.G. Keeler, and W. Kriesel. 2003. An Economic Evaluation of Beach Erosion Management Alternatives. *Marine Resource Economics* 18: 105–27.

Layman, R.C., J.R. Boyce, and K.R. Criddle. 1996. Economic Valuation of the Chinook Salmon Sport Fishery of the Gulkana River, Alaska, under Current and Alternate Management Plans. *Land Economics* 72(1): 113–28.

Leggett, C.G., and N.E. Bockstael. 2000. Evidence of the Effects of Water Quality on Residential Land Prices. *Journal of Environmental Economics and Management* 39(2): 121–44.

Lew, D.K., and D.M. Larson. 2005. Valuing Recreation and Amenities at San Diego County Beaches. *Coastal Management* 33(1): 71–86.

Lipton, D.W., and K.F. Wellman.1995. *Economic Valuation of Natural Resources: A Handbook for Coastal Policy Makers.* Decision Analysis Series, No. 5. Silver Spring, MD: NOAA Coastal Ocean Office, U.S. Department of Commerce.

List, J.A., and C. Gallet. 2001. What Experimental Protocols Influence Disparities between Actual and Hypothetical Stated Values? *Environmental and Resource Economics* 20(3): 241–54.

Little, J.A., and R. Berrens. 2004. Explaining Disparities between Actual and Hypothetical Stated Values: Further Investigation Using Meta-analysis. *Economics Bulletin* 3(1): 1–13.

Louviere, J.J., D.A. Hensher, and J.D. Swait. 2000. *Stated Preference Methods: Analysis and Application.* Cambridge: Cambridge University Press.

Machina, M. 1987. Choice under Uncertainty: Problems Solved and Unsolved. *Journal of Economic Perspectives* 1(1): 121–54.

Machina, M., and D. Schmeidler. 1992. A More Robust Definition of Subjective Probability. *Econometrica* 60(4): 745–80.

Maddala, G.S. 1983. *Limited Dependent and Qualitative Variables in Econometrics.* Cambridge, UK: Cambridge University Press.

Maler, K.G., and A. Fisher. 2005. Environment, Uncertainty, and Option Values. In *Handbook of Environmental Economics*, vol. 2, edited by K.G. Maler and J.R. Vincent. Amsterdam: Elsevier.

Marcot, B.G., R.S. Holthausen, M.G. Raphael, M.M. Rowland, and M.J. Wisdom. 2001. Using Bayesian Belief Networks to Evaluate Fish and Wildlife Population Viability under Land Management Alternatives from an Environmental Impact Statement. *Forestry Ecology and Management* 153(1–3): 29–42.doi:10.1016/S0378-1127(01)00452-2.

Markowska, A., and T. Zylicz. 1999. Costing an International Public Good: The Case of the Baltic Sea. *Ecological Economics* 30(2): 301–16.

Maskin, E. 1979. Decision-Making under Ignorance with Implications for Social Choice. *Theory and Decision* 11: 319–37.

Massachusetts Ocean Partnership. www.massoceanpartnership.org.whoweare.html. Accessed August 2009.

Massachusetts Office of Coastal Zone Management. 2005. Massachusetts Aquaculture White Paper. Boston, MA.http://www.mass.gov/czm/wptoc.htm.

McConnell, K.E. 1987. The Damages to Recreational Activities from PCBs in the New Bedford Harbor. Unpublished report.

McConnell, K.E., I. Strand, and L. Blake-Hedges. 1995. Random Utility Models of Recreational Fishing: Catching Fish Using a Poisson Process. *Marine Resource Economics* 10: 247–61.

McFadden, D. 1999. Rationality for Economists? *Journal of Risk and Uncertainty* 19: 73–105.

McGonagle, M.P., and S.K. Swallow. 2005. Open Space and Public Access: A Contingent Choice Application to Coastal Preservation. *Land Economics* 81(4): 477–95.

McLeod, K.L., J. Lubchenco, S.R. Palumbi, and A.A. Rosenberg. 2005. Scientific Consensus Statement on Marine Ecosystem-Based Management. Signed by 221 academic scientists and policy experts with relevant expertise and published by Communication Partnership for Science and the Sea. www.compassonline.org/pdf_files/ EBM_Consensus_Statement_v12.pdf. Accessed August 2009.

Millennium Ecosystem Assessment (MEA). 2003. *Ecosystems and Human Well-Being: A Framework for Assessment*. Washington, DC: Island Press.

Milon, J.W. 1988. A Nested Demand Shares Model of Artificial Marine Habitat Choice by Sport Anglers. *Marine Resource Economics* 5: 191–213.

Mistiaen, J., and I. Strand. 2000. Location Choice of Commercial Fishermen with Heterogeneous Risk Preferences. *American J. Agricultural Economics* 82(5): 1184–90.

Mitchell, R.C., and R.T. Carson. 1989. *Using Surveys to Value Public Goods: The Contingent Valuation Method*. Washington DC: Resources for the Future.

MMS (Minerals Management Service, U.S. Department of the Interior). 2008. Cape Wind Energy Project: Final Environmental Impact Statement. OCS Publication No. 2008-040. Herndon, VA: MMS, U.S. Department of the Interior.

Moore J., C. Behrens, and J. Blodgett. 1997. "Oil Imports: An Overview and Update of Economic and Security Effects." CRS Report for Congress. Washington, DC: Congressional Research Service, Environment and Natural Resources Policy Division. www.ncseonline.org/nle/crsreports/energy/eng-53.cfm?&CFID=12745071& CFTOKEN=232889. Accessed August 2009.

Morrison, M., and J. Bennett. 2004. Valuing New South Wales Rivers for Use in Benefit Transfer. *Australian Journal of Agricultural and Resource Economics* 48(4): 591–611.

Morrison, M., J. Bennett, R. Blamey, and J. Louviere. 2002. Choice Modeling and Tests of Benefit Transfer. *American Journal of Agricultural Economics* 84(1): 161–70.

Morrison, M., and O. Bergland. 2006. Prospects for the Use of Choice Modeling for Benefit Transfer. *Ecological Economics* 60(2): 420–28.

Murawski, S.A. 2007. Ten Myths Concerning Ecosystem Approaches to Marine Resource Management. *Marine Policy* 31(5): 681–90.

Murphy, J.J., P.G. Allen, T.H. Stevens, and D. Weatherhead. 2005. A Meta-Analysis of Hypothetical Bias in Stated Preference Valuation. *Environmental and Resource Economics* 30(3): 313–25.

Nelson, J.P., and P.E. Kennedy, 2009. The Use (and Abuse) of Meta-Analysis in Environmental and Resource Economics: An Assessment. *Environmental and Resource Economics* 42(3): 345–77.

Nixon, S.W. 1982. Nutrient Dynamics, Primary Production, and Fisheries Yields of Lagoons. *Oceanologica Acta*. 4: 357–72.

NMFS, National Marine Fisheries, Office of Protected Resources. 2004, rev. Recovery Plan for the North Atlantic Right Whale (*Eubalaena glacialis*) Revision.www.nmfs. noaa.gov/pr/pdfs/recovery/whale_right_northatlantic.pdf.

———. 2006a. Environmental Impact Statement to Implement the Operational Measures of the North Atlantic Right Whale Ship Strike Reduction Strategy. Draft Environmental Impact Statement. National Marine Fisheries Service, NOAA, Silver Spring, MD, July 2006. www.nmfs.noaa.gov/pr/pdfs/shipstrike/deis.pdf. Accessed August 2009.

―――. 2006b. National Review of the Status of the Right Whales in the North Atlantic and North Pacific Oceans. National Marine Fisheries Service, NOAA, Silver Spring, MD, December 2006.

―――. 2007. Northern Right Whale (*Eubalaena glacialis*): Western Atlantic Stock. National Marine Fisheries Service, NOAA, Silver Spring, MD, March 2007.www. nefsc.noaa.gov/publications/tm/tm201/6-14.pdf. Accessed August 2009.

Norse, E.A. 2005. Ending the Range Wars on the Last Frontier: Zoning the Sea. In *Marine Conservation Biology: The Science of Maintaining the Sea's Biodiversity*, edited by E.A. Norse and L.B. Crowder. Washington, DC: Island Press, 422–43.

NRC (National Research Council), Committee on Beach Nourishment and Protection. 1995. *Beach Nourishment and Protection*. Washington, DC: National Academy Press.

―――. 2001. *Assessing the TMDL Approach to Water Quality Management*. Washington, DC: National Academy Press.

―――. 2004. *Valuing Ecosystem Services: Toward Better Environmental Decision-Making*. Washington, DC: National Academy Press.

Odum, H.T., 1988. Self-Organization, Transformity, and Information. *Science* 242(4882): 1132–39.

Okmyung et al. 2005.

Opaluch, J.J., T.A. Grigalunas, M. Mazzotta, R.J. Johnston, and J. Diamantedes. 1999. Recreational and Resource Economic Values for the Peconic Estuary. Report prepared for the Peconic Estuary Program. Peace Dale, RI: Economic Analysis Inc.

Opaluch, J.J., S.K. Swallow, T. Weaver, C.W. Wessells, and D. Wichelns. 1993. Evaluating Impacts from Noxious Facilities: Including Public Preferences in Current Siting Mechanisms. *Journal of Environmental Economics and Management* 24(1): 41–59.

Orme-Zavaleta, J., and W.R. Munns Jr. 2007. Integrating Human and Ecological Risk Assessment: Application to the Cyanobacterial Harmful Algal Bloom Problem. In Cyanobacterial Harmful Algal Blooms: State of the Science and Research Needs, edited by H.K. Hudnell. *Advances in Experimental Medicine and Biology* 619: 855–871.

Parsons, G.R., and M. Needelman. 1992. Site Aggregation in a Random Utility Model of Recreation. *Land Economics* 68(4): 418–33.

Parsons, G.R., and M. Powell. 2001. Measuring the Cost of Beach Retreat. *Coastal Management* 29(2): 91–103.

Pearce, D. 1998. Auditing the Earth. *Environment* 40(2): 23–8.

Pew Center on Global Climate Change. 2009. Renewable and Alternative Energy Portfolio Standards. Updated July 2009. www.pewclimate.org/what_s_being_done/in_the_states/rps.cfm. Accessed August 2009.

Pigou, A.C. 1920. *The Economics of Welfare*. London: Macmillan.

Pilkey, O.H., and A. Coburn. 2007. Beach Nourishment: A Guide for Local Government Officials, Professional Dialogue. Beach Nourishment: Is It Worth the Cost? Perspective. www.csc.noaa.gov/beachnourishment/html/human/dialog/series1a. htm. Accessed August 2009.

Pimentel, D., C. Wilson, C. McCullum, R. Huang, P. Dwen, J. Flack, Q. Tran, T. Saltman, and B. Cliff. 1997. Economic and Environmental Benefits of Biodiversity. *BioScience* 47(11): 747–57.

Pompe, J.J., and J.R. Rinehart. 1995. The Value of Beach Nourishment to Property Owners: Storm Damage Reduction Benefits. *Review of Regional Studies* 25(3): 271–85.

Portney, P. 1992. Trouble in Happyville. *Journal of Policy Analysis and Management* 11(1): 131–32.

Powe, N.A. 2007. *Redesigning Environmental Valuation: Mixing Methods within Stated Preference Techniques*. Cheltenham, UK: Edward Elgar.

Rabin, M. 2000. Risk Aversion and Expected-Utility Theory: A Calibration Theorem. *Econometrica* 68: 1281–92.

Ready, R., and R.C. Bishop. 1991. Endangered Species and the Safe Minimum Standard. *American Journal of Agricultural Economics* 72(2): 309–12.

Reckhow, K.H. 2003. Bayesian Approaches in Ecological Analysis and Modeling. In *The Role of Models in Ecosystem Science*, edited by C.D. Canham, J.J. Cole, and W.K. Lauenroth. Princeton, NJ: Princeton University Press.

Ribaudo, M.O., R. Heimlich, R .Claassen, and M. Peters. 2001. Least-Cost Management of Nonpoint Source Pollution: Source Reduction versus Interception Strategies for Controlling Nitrogen Loss in the Mississippi Basin. *Ecological Economics* 37(2): 183–97.

Roberts, L.A., and J.A. Leitch. 1997. Economic Valuation of Some Wetland Outputs of Mud Lake, Minnesota-South Dakota. Agricultural Economics Report No. 381. Fargo, ND: North Dakota State University, Department of Agricultural Economics, North Dakota Agricultural Experiment Station.

Rose, S.K., J. Clark, G.L. Poe, D. Rondeau, and W.D. Schulze. 2002. The Private Provision of Public Goods: Tests of a Provision Point Mechanism for Funding Green Power Programs. *Resource and Energy Economics*, 24(1–2): 131–55.

Rosenberger, R.S., and R.J. Johnston. 2009. Selection Effects in Meta-Analysis and Benefit Transfer: Avoiding Unintended Consequences. *Land Economics* 85(3): 410–28.

Rosenberger, R.S., and J.B. Loomis. 2003. Benefit Transfer. In *A Primer on Non-Market Valuation*, edited by P.A. Champ, K.J. Boyle, and T.C. Brown. Dordrecht, The Netherlands: Kluwer Academic Publishers, 445–482.

Rosenberger, R.S., and T.D. Stanley. 2006. Measurement, Generalization, and Publication: Sources of Error in Benefit Transfers and Their Management. *Ecological Economics* 60(2): 372–78.

Sanchirico, J.N. 2003. Managing Marine Capture Fisheries with Incentive Based Price Instruments. *Public Finance Management* 3(1): 67–93.

Sanchirico, J.N., and P. Mumby. 2007. Economics, Habitats, and Biological Populations: Finding the Right Value. *Resources* 165 (Spring 2007): 11–13.

Sanchirico, J.N., and J.E. Wilen. 2005. Optimal Spatial Management of Renewable Resources: Matching Policy Scope to Ecosystem Scale. *Journal of Environmental Economics and Management* 50(1): 23–46.

Sassone, P.G., and W.A. Schaffer. 1978. *Cost Benefit Analysis: A Handbook*. New York: Academic Press.

Savage, L.J. 1972. *The Foundations of Statistics*. 2nd ed. rev. New York: Dover Publications.

Schkade, D.A., and J.W. Payne. 1994. How People Respond to Contingent Valuation Questions: A Verbal Protocol Analysis of Willingness to Pay for an Environmental Regulation. *Journal of Environmental Economics and Management* 26: 88–109.

Silberman, J., D.A. Gerlowski, and N.A. Williams. 1992. Estimating Existence Value for Users and Nonusers of New Jersey Beaches. *Land Economics* 68(2): 225–36.

Sinden, J.A. 1988. Empirical Tests of Hypothetical Bias in Consumers' Surplus Surveys. *Australian Journal of Agricultural Economics* 32(2–3): 98–112.

Smith, M., and J. Wilen. 2003. Economic Impacts of Marine Reserves: The Importance of Spatial Behavior. *Journal of Environmental Economics and Management* 46(2): 183–206.

Smith, R.W., J.M.Conrad, and D.A. Storey. 1978. An Economic Valuation of Recreational Clamming in Massachusetts. *Massachusetts Agricultural Experiment Station Research Bulletin* 654 (April 1978).

Smith, V.K., and J.V. Krutilla. 1979. Endangered Species, Irreversibility, and Uncertainty: A Comment. *American Journal of Agricultural Economics* 61(2): 371–75.

Smith, V.K., and S.K. Pattanayak. 2002. Is Meta-Analysis a Noah's Ark for Non-Market Valuation? *Environmental and Resource Economics* 22(1–2): 271–96.

Smith, V.K., G. van Houtven, and S.K. Pattanayak. 2002. Benefit Transfer via Preference Calibration: "Prudential Algebra" for Policy. *Land Economics* 78(1): 132–52.

Soderholm, P., K. Ek and M. Pettersson. 2007. Wind Power Development in Sweden: Global Policies and Local Obstacles. *Renewable and Sustainable Energy Reviews* 11(3): 365–400.

Steinback, S.R. 1999. Regional Economic Impact Assessments of Recreational Fisheries: An Application of the IMPLAN Modeling System to Marine Party and Charter Boat Fishing in Maine. *North American Journal of Fisheries Management* 19(3): 724–36.

Sterzinger G., F. Beck, and D. Kostiuk. 2003. The Effect of Wind Development on Local Property Values. A report by the Renewable Energy Policy Project, Washington, DC, May 2003.

Stevens, T. 2005. Can Stated Preference Valuations Help Improve Environmental Decision Making? *Choices* 20(3): 189–94.

Stokes, J.R., and P.R. Tozer. 2002. Cost Minimization and Managing Soil Nutrient Loading: Conflict or Compromise? *Canadian Journal of Agricultural Economics* 50(2): 151–69.

Stopher, P.R., and A.H. Meyberg. 1975. *Urban Transportation: Modeling and Planning.* Lexington, MA, USA: DC Heath.

Sutinen, J.G., and R.J. Johnston 2001. A Note on Economic Benefits and Economic Impacts: The Use and Abuse of Economic Analysis for Fisheries Management. Kingston, RI: University of Rhode Island, Department of Environmental and Natural Resource Economics.

Swallow, S.K. 1996. Economic Issues in Ecosystem Management: An Introduction and Overview. *Agricultural and Resource Economics Review* 25(2): 83–100.

Swallow, S.K.; J.J. Opaluch, T.F. Weaver. 1992.Siting Noxious Facilities: An Approach That Integrates Technical, Economic, and Political Considerations. *Land Economics* 68(3)283-301.

Turner, R.K. 1999a. Managing Nutrient Fluxes and Pollution in the Baltic: An Interdisciplinary Simulation Study. *Ecological Economics* 30(2): 333–52.

———. 1999b. The Place of Economic Values in Environmental Valuation. In *Valuing Environmental Preferences: Theory and Practice of the Contingent Valuation Method in the US, EU, and Developing Countries*, edited by I.J. Bateman and K.G. Willis. Oxford: Oxford University Press.

U.S. Commission on Ocean Policy. 2004. An Ocean Blueprint for the 21st Century: Final Report of the U.S. Commission on Ocean Policy. U.S. Commission on Ocean Policy, Washington, DC.

U.S. Department of the Interior, Minerals Management Service. 2009. *Cape Wind Energy Project: Final Environmental Impact Statement.* OCS Publication 2008-040. Washington, DC.U.S. EPA (Environmental Protection Agency). 1996. Nonpoint Source Pollution: The Nation's Largest Water Quality Problem. Pointer No. 1.

EPA841-F-96-004A. www.epa.gov/owow/nps/facts/point1.htm. Accessed August 2009.

———. 2000. Guidelines for Preparing Economic Analyses. USEPA 240-R-00-003. Washington, DC: U.S. EPA, Office of the Administrator.

———. 2002a. A Framework for the Economic Assessment of Ecological Benefits. Prepared for Ecological Benefit Assessment Workgroup, Social Sciences Discussion Group Science Policy Council, U.S. Environmental Protection Agency, Washington, DC.

———. 2002b. Section 319: Success Stories. Vol. 3, The Successful Implementation of the Clean Water Act's Section 319 Nonpoint Source Pollution Program. EPA 841-S-01-001. Washington, DC: U.S. EPA.

———. 2007. National Estuary Program Coastal Condition Report. EPA-842/B-06/001. Washington, DC: U.S. EPA.

van der Horst, D. 2007. NIMBY or Not? Exploring the Relevance of Location and the Politics of Voiced Opinions in Renewable Energy Siting Controversies. *Energy Policy* 35(5): 2705–14.

Viscusi, W.K. 1993. The Value of Risks to Life and Health. *Journal of Economic Literature* 31(4): 1912–46.

Vossler, C.A., and J. Kerkvliet. 2003. A Criterion Validity Test of the Contingent Valuation Method: Comparing Hypothetical and Actual Voting Behavior for a Public Referendum. *Journal of Environmental Economics and Management* 45(3): 631–49.

Walters, C.J. 1986. *Adaptive Management of Renewable Resources*. New York: McGraw-Hill.

Whitehead, J.C. 1993. Total Economic Values for Coastal and Marine Wildlife: Specification, Validity, and Valuation Issues. *Marine Resource Economics* 8(2): 119–32.

Wiersma, J. 2008. An Economic Analysis of Mobile Gear Fishing within the Proposed Wind Energy Generation Facility Site on Horseshoe Shoal in Nantucket Sound. Kingston, RI: University of Rhode Island, Department of Environmental and Natural Resource Economics.

Wilen, J.E. 2004. Spatial Management of Fisheries. *Marine Resource Economics* 19(1): 7–20.

Wilen, J.E., M. Smith, D. Lockwood, and L. Botsford. 2002. Avoiding Surprises: Incorporating Fisherman Behavior into Management Models. *Bulletin of Marine Science* 70(2): 553–75.

Wilson, M.A., and J.P. Hoehn. 2006. Valuing Environmental Goods and Services Using Benefit Transfer: The State of the Art and Science. Special issue, *Ecological Economics* 60(2): 355–62.

Wiser, R. 2003. Using Contingent Valuation to Explore Willingness to Pay for Renewable Energy: A Comparison of Collective and Voluntary Payment Vehicles. LBNL-53239. Washington, DC: Lawrence Berkeley National Laboratory.

Wolsink, M. 2000. Wind Power and the NIMBY Myth: Institutional Capacity and the Limited Significance of Public Support. *Renewable Energy* 21(1): 49–64.

World Resources Institute. 2003. Millennium Ecosystem Assessment: Ecosystems and Human Well-Being—A Framework for Assessment. Washington, DC: WRI.

Wu, J., R.M. Adams, C.L. Kling, and K. Tanaka. 2003. Assessing the Costs and Environmental Consequences of Agricultural Land Use Changes: A Site-Specific, Policy-Scale Modeling Approach. Staff General Research Papers. Ames: Iowa State University, Department of Economics.

Index